SIGNS ON THE EARTH

Also by Richard Leviton

Seven Steps to Better Vision

The Imagination of Pentecost: Rudolf Steiner and Contemporary Spirituality

Brain Builders! A Lifelong Guide to Sharper Thinking, Better Memory, and an Age-Proof Mind

Weddings by Design: A Guide to Non-Traditional Ceremonies

Looking for Arthur: A Once and Future Travelogue

Physician: Medicine and the Unsuspected Battle for Human Freedom

The Healthy Living Space: 70 Practical Ways to Detoxify the Body and Home

What's Beyond That Star: A Chronicle of Geomythic Adventure

The Galaxy on Earth: A Traveler's Guide to the Planet's Visionary Geography

The Emerald Modem: A User's Guide to Earth's Interactive Energy Body

SIGNS
ON THE
EARTH

*Deciphering the Message
of Virgin Mary Apparitions,
UFO Encounters, and
Crop Circles*

RICHARD LEVITON

HAMPTON ROADS
PUBLISHING COMPANY, INC.

for the evolving human spirit

Cover design by Steve Amarillo
Cover images: Virgin Mary, Sand dune © 2005 Photos.com/Jupiter Images;
Crop Circle © 2005 Digital Vision, Ltd.

Hampton Roads Publishing Company, Inc.
1125 Stoney Ridge Road
Charlottesville, VA 22902

434-296-2772
fax: 434-296-5096
e-mail: hrpc@hrpub.com
www.hrpub.com

If you are unable to order this book from your local
bookseller, you may order directly from the publisher.
Call 1-800-766-8009, toll-free.

Library of Congress Cataloging-in-Publication Data

Leviton, Richard.
  Signs on the earth : deciphering the message of Virgin Mary apparitions,
UFO encounters, and crop circles / Richard Leviton.
     p. cm.
  Summary: "An examination of reports from around the world involving
Virgin Mary apparitions, UFO sightings, and crop circle formations. Focusing his
study on a few global "hot spots," Leviton explains why these events happen,
how the phenomena are connected, and, how they relate to the future of the
Earth"--Provided by publisher.
  Includes bibliographical references and index.
  ISBN 1-57174-246-8 (alk. paper)
  1. Mary, Blessed Virgin, Saint--Apparitions and miracles. 2. Unidentified
flying objects. 3. Crop circles. I. Title.
  BT650.L48 2005
  001.94--dc22

                                    2004028513

                    ISBN 1-57174-246-8
                    10 9 8 7 6 5 4 3 2 1
           Printed on acid-free paper in Canada

For Judith Lewis

Table of Contents

Part II. Cloud of Smoke: UFO and ET Visitations— An Irruption of the Galaxy into the World around Us

Part III. A Pillar of Fire: Crop Circles— A Language of Light in Albion's Golden Band

And in the last days it shall be, God declares, that I will pour out my Spirit upon all flesh. . . . And I will show wonders in the heaven above, and signs on the Earth beneath, blood and fire, and vapor of smoke . . . before the day of the Lord comes, the great and manifest day.

—*Acts of the Apostles, 2:17–20*

Signs on the Earth–Apocalypse or a Planet Being Reborn?

Astonishing things are happening on our Earth. Apparitions of the Virgin Mary are appearing at numerous sites. Evidence of ships and intelligences from elsewhere in the galaxy proliferates across the planet, as do reports of sightings, encounters, and abductions. And enigmatic, beautiful glyphs appear instantaneously in waving grain fields as if stamped from light patterns.

They are signs on the Earth all, but who is making these signs for us? And are they signs of the last days (the End Time, apocalypse, the end of the world), heralds of the arrival of that "great and manifest day" when "the Lord comes"? Or do they signify a new level of benign communication from on high?

My operating assumption is that these three types of signs on the Earth are purposeful and are put before us globally as part of an extraplanetary plan. Another assumption I work with is that a fruitful way to figure out why they are appearing is to look at them collectively, as a three-part message from on high. A third assumption is that God, the spiritual worlds, and higher beings periodically intervene benevolently in human affairs to catalyze something.

I propose that the three different signs on the Earth represent a benevolent, purposeful spiritual intervention in human affairs and our evolutionary agenda.

The signs fill some people with wonder, others with fear. They inspire most authorities, whether theological or governmental, to downplay, deny, ignore, distort, or suppress the fact that these signs are even appearing. Most of the Virgin Mary apparitions go unvalidated by the Vatican or are denied outright or ridiculed. UFO (unidentified flying object) phenomena are routinely denied, ignored, or explained away, or are the subject of disinformation intended to convince the public they were "seeing things," not seeing ETs (extraterrestrials). As for crop circles, they are too palpable, too vivid, too publicly *dramatic* to make people disbelieve their own senses or the photographs, so the strategy is to shift the attention to hoaxes: they are fakes, human-made.

These paranormal phenomena wouldn't be so difficult to understand or accommodate if we hadn't painted ourselves into such a constricted corner with our metaphysically parochial consensus reality. Such phenomena cannot exist because our theories of reality allow no room for such outlandish, freakish things. Culturally, we are conditioned to fragment ourselves: What we see or experience is on one hand; on the other is the truth, reality, the official view.

Ironically, or perhaps, appropriately, since our authorities will not validate the anomalies, each person has to forge a new consensus reality, as if only for oneself at first and based on experience not dogma, that *does* accommodate these phenomena. We seem to be heading toward a planet of a consensus reality of one multiplied by billions. One day, the consensus will flip and the majority of humans worldwide will suddenly realize reality has changed.

Counterpointing this forging of a new consensus reality one person at a time is a frantic effort by governmental and theological authorities to control it. Let's keep the reality dogma constant at all costs, their efforts seem to say. The Vatican says only those Marian apparitions they deem real are real. Nearly all governments flatly deny validity to UFO sightings or ET encounters. The English authorities, who are running point on crop circles, the majority of which occur in England, are conditioning us to regard crop circles as clever hoaxes.

One way or another, the controlling authorities are trying to make these three astonishing signs on the Earth unreal, contrived, hallucinatory, and, ideally, nonexistent. They never happened. You must have imagined it.

So we in the early years of the twenty-first century live amidst this dialectic, this constant tug-of-war between experience and dogma, personal truth and consensus reality. It happened, it didn't happen. It's real, it's not real. The Virgin Mary blessed this hillside. No, she didn't; it wasn't her, or anyone. I saw aliens, there are no aliens. I was abducted by Grays; no, you dreamed it. ETs made the crop circles; no, people made them with boards.

Underlying this struggle for the truth behind events is the growing panic. Are these signs on the Earth—real or unreal, actual or rumored—signs of the big day? We fear it as the biblically foretold Judgment Day or we anticipate it as the end of the Mayan calendar in December 2012. Either way, the world will end, right?[1]

Right—It Will Be the End of the World as We Know It

Except the planet, and we ourselves as humans, will live on. The key bit of this well-exercised prediction is *as we know it*. We will know it differently, freshly, anew—as if, I hope, we've never seen it before in our lives. The planet and its spirit, called Gaia in the classical Greek tradition, say to us: You don't know me. You barely see me. It's time to know who I am, where I came from, and why, and what's next for *us*.

Here is a recent clairvoyant impression of the Earth: I see the planet pockmarked with meteor hits, forming craters and crowns, like stop-action milk-drop photos, like the ancient boils that once formed on the Earth before they matured into geomantic nodes and sacred sites. These are not literally meteor strikes, but something erupting from within the Earth's subtle body in response to human agitation on its surface.

They seem black on the inside. The human war agitation is precipitating, coinciding with, and even supporting the Earth's own process of transformation, like a girl into a teenager, with that embarrassing, almost chaotic plasticity of flesh and personality. The war agitation is allowing the Earth to reveal a layer of its own hidden truth having to do with its origin, alien involvement, operations, and destiny, all of which are potentially very shocking to consensus reality and far more potent than the seemingly powerful forces at play on its surface.

These outwardly forming "meteor" hits and their contents have been in the dark for a long time, but now they're coming into the daylight of collective human awareness. Earth is about to divulge a big secret, almost vomiting it forth, throwing off the millennial layers of lies and obscurations, to show us her cosmic life, her ontological reality, in spite of what we think it is, or don't.

She's doing this through three great signs on the Earth:

1. *Marian apparitions.* The Earth is the soil for Christ consciousness, that is, for independent expanded human cognition, knowing, and self-validated certainty, throwing off all dogmas.

2. *UFOs-ETs.* Our galactic origins, genetic profile, composition, and agenda, and its ramifications for our spacetime experience.

3. *Crop circles.* A new symbol language of light, a fourth-dimensional alphabet imprinted in living grain, the once and future energy-consciousness, light-form codings for a new planetary reality.

I'll explain all this as we move along.

Perhaps the biblical prophet quoted in the Acts of the Apostles foresaw Marian apparitions, crop circles, and UFO phenomena, respectively, as the evidence of "blood and fire, and vapor of smoke," or perhaps not. Perhaps a grim, cataclysmic destructive scenario was more what he had in mind. It doesn't matter. I propose an informal, nontheological interpretation of that prophecy along these lines of the three signs on the Earth because it fits the data and is a convenient frame for seeing the startling, world-changing events in our time.

Ultimately, and even in the short term, the prognosis looks good, much better than one would analytically conclude from the appearance of things. The war agitation is forcing the Earth's shadow—and humanity's—to come to the surface for a moment of awful recognition, but beneath that is the truth revelation, a deific one: God and the spiritual and extraterrestrial hierarchy created me and still look after me, the planet says.

How do these three signs correlate with the prophetic requirement of "blood and fire, and vapor of smoke"? Perhaps I am simplistic here, but I see the Marian apparitions as associated with the "blood" in the sense that they potentially change our self-definition and self/not-self discernments at a molecular, immunological level, which of course is mediated through the blood.

Fire and crop circles? I explain later in the book how the grain glyphs seem to be created as if stamped by complex light patterns—organized cosmic fire, if you will, which seems to burn or brand itself gently onto the living grain.

The UFO and "vapor of smoke" connection is easy. The approach of ET vessels is commonly associated with massive, fast-forming cloud structures believed to cloak them from visibility. There is also the obvious smoke-and-mirrors aspect by which governmental authorities try to cloud our minds about the truth of extraterrestrial visitations to Earth and ET encounters with humans.

The most general statement I can make about the purpose of this book is this: I offer insights on the *meaning* of the three signs on the Earth. What is the *message* of the fact that they are occurring—what is their meta-message? I am not concerned with proving that they are actually happening. I take that for granted. My focus is on *why* they are happening and what they are *telling* us.

How to Research the Signs on the Earth—Psychics Welcome

One of the great and unremitting anxieties enveloping the phenomena of UFOs and ETs primarily, and to a lesser extent, Marian apparitions and crop circles, is the matter of physical proof. This is epistemology—how do we know, how *can* we know, that these are signs of authentic celestial communications?

For decades, the quest in UFOlogy has been to produce professionally validated, certified, and skeptic-proof photographic evidence of ships or aliens. The intensity of this quest has been proportional to the weight of skepticism and ridicule heaped on UFO experiencers by those disbelieving in the phenomena.

With Marian apparitions, photographic or even physical proof of any kind is highly unlikely, so the burden of proof has fallen into the area of theological exactitude or rather, conformity. All attention goes to the few who have seen the Virgin Mary at various locations and to what they report she said. The better it accords with published dogma, the more likely it was a real apparition, so the church authorities think. When the theological aspect is not central, then the religious authorities, both at the Vatican and in most cases the local priests, tend to dismiss the reports, suggesting the witnesses were hallucinating, lying, or subject to demonic misdirection.

With crop circles, the physical proof that there are crop circles—the photographic evidence of patterns in living grain—is irrefutable, so the skeptical emphasis shifts to the identity of the pattern makers. Complicated theories that have been developed to account for these patterns include meteorological factors, plasma vortices, and human hoaxing.

The frenetic search for physical, unarguable proof dissolves when you use clairvoyance as a research tool. In fact, it may be that the signs on the Earth are meant to provoke this epistemological response: Since each sign has many nonphysical or multidimensional aspects, clairvoyance may be the only reliable way to uncover what these signs are about, and perhaps to *see more* of each one.

All three signs may be researched clairvoyantly, and this is the primary method I've used in this book. Aliens and UFO-sighting hotspots may be examined clairvoyantly, free of the physical anxiety of abduction or the high strangeness one gets in the field. Marian apparitions lend themselves perfectly to this style of investigation because, after all—and ironically—hardly anybody actually sees the Virgin's apparitions. With crop circles, there is surely more than meets the physical eye. As marvelous as the variety of whorled patterns are, what we see physically is but the footprint of a multidimensional light frequency template.

Importantly, clairvoyant research is corroborable by peers. A group of six clairvoyants, all looking at the same topic, person, or place, will not produce identical reports and impressions, but the overlaps and consistencies will be high. What will vary will be the decoding software: the metaphors, analogies, and interpretations used to translate a subtle reality into our familiar physical one.

As part of the research for this book, I worked with a few clairvoyant colleagues in "reading" selected topics, specifically, ETs from particular stars, selected UFO hotspots, and crop circles around Wiltshire, England. I also researched these clairvoyantly on my own, and drew on preexisting collegial relationships with an angelic family called the Ofanim, with whom I have collaborated in geomantic studies for over 20 years.

In these studies, I sought the correlations between physical sacred sites and a variety of numinous, psychically accessible inner features. The outer physical aspects (stones, hills, sacred mountains, pyramids) act as doorways into an adjacent realm that I call Earth's visionary geography.

Specifically, I present fresh psychic impressions of 12 major Marian apparition sites, nine UFO hotspots (areas with high frequency and intensity of phenomena, including sightings), and the world's crop circle hotspot, Wiltshire, England, centered on Avebury and Stonehenge. Throughout, I emphasize the correlation between the signs on the Earth (celestial input) and geomantic aspects. My starting premise is that the phenomena as reported are real but require clairvoyant investigation to get a clearer sense as to what they actually are.

As I suggested, one of the intents of the signs on the Earth is to encourage us to investigate them clairvoyantly. Maybe there never will be irrefutable physical proof because this is impossible given the extradimensional nature of the three signs. The only true proof will be corroborable psychic validation, and, again, maybe that's the whole point—to shift our epistemological demands from sense-based to clairvoyance-based.

Anticipating, if not forecasting, this change, Austrian clairvoyant Rudolf Steiner, back in the early decades of the twentieth century, prophesied that humans would gain an etheric clairvoyance, enabling them to see into the spiritual worlds. He said that faculties acquired in the twentieth century through initiation will become universal human faculties; in short, lots of people would gradually become psychic.

Steiner did not specifically reference Marian apparitions, UFOs, or crop circles, of course, but his foresight was right on target. He said that this new clairvoyant faculty would "consist in men [he meant both genders] being able to see in their environment something of the etheric world which hitherto they have not been able to see . . . and also to perceive the *connection* [emphasis added] between deeper happenings in the etheric world."[2]

Perceiving the connection between these "deeper happenings in the etheric world"—that is, between our three signs on the Earth—is a prime focus of this book. Where Steiner says "etheric world," we can reasonably substitute the Earth's visionary geography and its multidimensional array. This is the planet's vast assortment of holy sites that give us access into spiritual realms of perception and experience. I give a brief survey of this subject—I call it "Earth's big secret"—and its relevance to the three signs in chapter 1.

Not only will humans increasingly gain a natural clairvoyance as the twentieth century proceeds, Steiner said, but the keystone of this trend will be "a supersensible event [that] will come to pass in the human supersensible body when man as if through a natural occurrence, will find the risen Christ."[3]

Bear in mind, Steiner was writing this as an esoteric Christian; he had devoted his life and psychic inquiries into penetrating the truth of the Christ Event, as he called it, on Earth. He was not a doctrinaire Christian as such. My approach and use of his language where appropriate are similarly founded in this nondoctrinaire approach.

This blossoming of clairvoyance will be much like the epiphany experienced by the arch skeptic, materialist, and naysayer Saul, who on his solitary way to Damascus was electrified by a spontaneous vision of the risen Christ. So affected was he by this clairvoyant vision that he converted to the new faith of Christ and became Paul. However, the goal here is not to convert people to Christianity, but to enable individuals to attain the same degree of cosmic cognition that is Christ.

We might equate Christ cognition with cosmic consciousness to get an idea of the scale of this knowing that is offered to every human just for being alive. The goal is not dogma, but emulation, and not, as Christianity grimly emphasizes, the crucifixion aspect, but transfiguration and ascension—the risen Christ, which means each of us potentially *rising* to that same level of expanded cognition. Let's construe "risen" here as *risen* into a natural etheric clairvoyance, *risen* into the Earth's subtle body and all the multidimensional activities in it, *risen* into our own independent knowing without dogma, control, or punishment.

I bring this up because one of the conclusions I offer in this book is that the three signs on the Earth are correlated with this spiritual agenda as if by planning of a higher agency. I contend (see chapters 2 and 3) that the intent of the Marian apparitions is largely to get this cognitive ascension started. It may seem that the appearances and blessings of the Virgin Mary at various locales are to reinstill faith in Catholic dogma, but that may well be only the outer aspect. They are catalysts for us to get started on the Christed Initiation in the Buddha Body, a new way (and a new name, courtesy of the angelic kingdom) by which we as individual humans can start ascending into a dogma-free Christ consciousness.

The Marian apparitions consistently happen at places that have unsuspected preexisting geomantic features. The discovery of this is akin to Steiner's statement that we will begin to see in our environment "something of the etheric world which hitherto [we] have not been able to see." I describe in chapter 1 what these geomantic, or Earth-energy, features are, but the essential point here is that the Marian apparitions add something to the system (a blessing of higher consciousness, if you will) just by happening there.

The Earth (and humanity) is being *enriched* in celestial consciousness at a growing variety of geomantically prepared locales by the Marian apparitions. The elegance of the arrangement is that each Marian apparition site has a different combination of geomantic features, so that globally the Earth gets blessed and enriched with the Marian energy through different filters. See table 2-1 for a preview of this spiritually delicious smorgasbord.

In chapter 2, I look behind the scenes at many of the world-famous Marian apparition sites, such as Lourdes, Fatima, Knock,

Walsingham, Tepeyac Hill, and Medjugorje, to examine the preexisting geomantic features present and see how the Marian infusion affected them (and still does) for our spiritual benefit. I also show why these various sites were well suited for grounding the Marian energy.

Of further significance is the fact that the Marian apparitions are returning the Christ to the physical planet and are returning us in our bodies to that same earthy realm. You could say the Marian apparitions are making the Word flesh: We go to a sacred site in our physical body and tune into the Christ. Surely that is a refreshing and regrounding of the original pure Christ impulse.

While I do not wish to offend religious sensibilities, I have found it is easier to psychically comprehend the full scope of the Marian apparitions by steering clear for the most part of orthodox theological interpretations and even, to an extent, the comments she is reported to have made through her visionaries. Steering clear, or perhaps, it's more apt to say *looking through* to the next layer.

I propose that the Virgin Mary as an apparitional being is any one of four female spiritual beings called Ray Masters—and sometimes the four at once—with a long history of benevolent involvement on Earth from long before the Christian era. These Ray Masters are based in the constellation Ursa Major (the Great Bear whose tail is the well-known Big Dipper), though it would be highly inaccurate to call the Ray Masters extraterrestrials or aliens. They have been known in other ancient cultures, such as the Hindu in India, as gods, or *rishis*.

The ultimate identity of the "Mary" behind the Marian apparitions is secondary to the purpose of these continual manifestations of the Virgin. I propose that it is a kind of planetary preparation to create favorable conditions, not for the second coming of the Christ but for the birth of the Christ Child in each of us as a scaffolding for Christ consciousness. It's easier to get a sense of the intent of the Marian apparitions when you look at the phenomena globally, at *all* of them, regardless whether they've been officially validated by the Vatican or not.

On a practical note, I provide some guidelines for an "Imitation of the Christ" on a global geomantic scale. This may sound presumptuous, but the angelic realm is eager for us to get going on assimilating the essential energies of the Christ Event of two thousand years ago. Again, this is different from Christianity as usual. In many respects, it has nothing to do with Christianity as we know it. But the Earth is equipped with geomantic features that enable each of us to undergo a five-stage geomantic initiation into the Christ mysteries. Think of the Marian apparitions perhaps as an intriguing inducement.

Why undergo this initiation? Because it can help us to get into the flow of events already under way, typified by the three signs on the Earth, and particularly heralded by the Marian apparitions. Getting into the flow of major psychic changes happening to our home planet is surely better than resisting them. It could make the difference between fearing that the world is going to end and rejoicing that it is ending, in that the old, tired ways of knowing—faith rather than experience and direct knowing—are ending.

The birth of the Christ Child in each of us allows us to rise out of the morass of physicality, materialism, sense-based consensus reality, and the entrenched atheism that infects us all. This atheism makes us limit spiritual possibilities to a monolithic dualism, God and humankind, Heaven and Earth, good and evil, black and white, with no possibility of a richly diversified middle ground. Mary comes to facilitate the birth of the Christ Child in each of us, and with this, our ascension into a richer cognitive field, sometimes called the fourth dimension, in which all events in time fill space around us *now* like a tableau of past, present, and future.

In chapter 3, I suggest a correlation between Christ consciousness and the spacetime fabric. Just as the Virgin Mary may have antecedents or a broader resume not catalogued by Christianity, I've found it illuminating to look for evidence of the Christ in other cultural guises such as Vishnu (Hindu), Horus (Egyptian), Dionysius (Greek), Balder (Norse), and Logos (Gnostic). One of the insights I draw from this is that consistently this Son of God pervades and holds together all space and time as a unifying consciousness, an ultimate glue. The Christ is the rationality of the cosmos, the universal reason that permeates all creation, which includes the stars, planets, constellations, and all life.

Here's the payoff: When you birth the Christ Child and become the risen Christ yourself, you ascend into the next dimension, the fourth or time tableau, and you share in that distributed awareness of the cosmos that is the Christ. Among the elementary things you become aware of is the vast diversity of created intelligent life, the beings living on other planets in various states of physicality and at varying levels of awareness and sophistication. In other language, your awareness of what is real and part of creation automatically starts to include what we popularly call extraterrestrials or aliens.

It's all there—the multiple dimensions, the parallel and alternate realities, and the high strangeness of experiencing matter, identity, space, and time *differently.* Embedded like luminous marbles in the cross-woven fabric of spacetime are fabulous, fantastic, scary, ambivalent, or benevolent worlds, many of whose residents, aware of the possibility of our upgraded cognition, come to Earth.

In chapter 1, I outline how the Earth's etheric environment, to use Steiner's phrase, is the bedrock or foundation out of which the planet's vast array of sacred and holy sites emerge like flowers in rich soil. This bedrock has an overall design: It is an experiential hologram of the galaxy and spiritual worlds—which means whatever is real *up there* is also real *down here.* So if cognition risen into the fourth dimension affords us a highly expanded view of what's going on in the galaxy (the array of sentient life forms and their activities), then we are likely, if not invited, to see the same here on Earth in human bodies.

One of the benefits of the fact of alien-human encounters is to see this.

Appropriately, UFO literature by witnesses is rich with statements about the surreal atmosphere and quasi-physical conditions experienced. Time flows differently, mind and matter seem to interpenetrate each other, UFOs exhibit seemingly impossible physical behaviors and qualities. The nature of human identity, consciousness, memory, experience are all rearranged *there,* in the highly fluidic, ever-shifting fourth dimension, our next cognitive home.

When we investigate any of these three signs on the Earth, or even better, when we experience them, we're sticking our head up into the fourth dimension (4D). Until we get some orientation, its all-at-once quality, its paradoxes, its defeat of our sense of linearity, can be bewildering, ungrounding. Follow the Marian apparition, the UFO, or crop circle back to its source, and you're speeding into and through this new, cognitively perilous realm.

Later we start to realize that all the attempts to explain away the signs, to deny them, pretend they don't exist, or to give them mundane materialistic causes are but intense resistance to this shifting of our consensus reality into 4D.

So the burgeoning of UFO-ET phenomena on Earth and in human experience testifies to our imminent ascension into a fourth-dimensional perspective. In fact, without a 4D view, we fail to understand what this sign on the Earth is about and means. See table 5-1 for a preview of some of the geomantic features found at selected UFO hotspots.

At the same time, the increasing frequency and intensity of UFO phenomena—the sightings, abductions, missing time, real dreams, enforced amnesia, screen memories, alien past lives, the hyperreality of it all—may be an advance validation of our imminent cognitive upgrade: We're almost there, so here's a little taste of the next level of intelligent life in the galaxy and its spacetime flavor. It's exciting, ambivalent, scary, highly strange, confusing, revelatory.

Coincident with our discovering the Earth's subtle realm (which I later define as visionary geography) and its baffling 4D aspects, we start to find the same terrain in ourselves—our own auric visionary geography. Auric refers to the seven layers, sheaths, or energy fields that surround each of us like a series of diaphanous colored eggs. These are complex information storage fields, and are the "planetary orbits" of our seven chakras, or subtle energy-consciousness centers arrayed from the perineum to the top of the head. Then there is the astral body, a kind of extensible starry, light-filled, nonmaterial duplicate of oneself.

I say this is our personal visionary geography because it is our dream space, and knowing this helps us understand some of the deep anomalies produced by UFO-ET experiences. Clinical hypnosis has proven very effective in recent decades in helping individuals recall deeply buried memories of ET encounters and resolve traumas, even physical symptoms, associated with them. Often abductees or experiencers shelved their anomalous encounters as dreams—what they remembered made it seem like a dream, or *only* a dream.

Often, a person has a bizarre or enigmatic dream fragment. Usually, they do not pursue it, but nor do they entirely forget it. In many cases, though, people do not remember even this. "Generally the patients were surprised, even shocked, to find that they had had close encounters," comments one seasoned UFO recall hypnotherapist.[4]

Here's the interesting part: Metaphysical authorities tell us that when you die, you recall all the events that happened to you during your waking hours by reviewing the memories stored in your etheric body. Then you recall all the events that happened to you while you were unconscious to daytime activities (in dreaming, for example) by viewing them in your astral body. There you find surprising, shocking, unbelievable, amazing content, things you never knew you did, but did do in the dream state. When you're dead, you debrief your two bodies and observe the fabulous, horrible, and mundane things you did alive.

Recall of alien encounters or abductions by clinical hypnotherapy, arguably, is much like this postdeath astral body viewing and recall, except now we are one step ahead of the game in doing a little of the astral body review while still alive. Certainly, this is enough to get the startling *taste* of this level of unsuspected, unremembered yet executed experience. You did it, though you forgot it. So this cognitive upgrade is in keeping with the 4D reality of the UFO phenomena. The UFO-ET field of experience starts to entrain us to this more complex reality field.

It encourages us to download the higher consciousness experiences we've had in our etheric and astral bodies into daytime, physical reality. It's a way of knitting together two otherwise experientially separate realms.

In chapters 4 and 5, I review the complex nature of UFO-ET encounters. There is no simple black-and-white statement to be made: Some aliens, such as the Grays, are essentially hostile to human free will and well-being and seem to be the agents behind the majority of forcible abductions and reputed human-alien genetic breeding and hybridization programs. Other ETs, such as Pleiadians, and intelligences from Sirius, Canopus, and the constellations Orion, Cygnus, Cepheus, and Ursa Major, seem to be benevolent sponsors of human evolution.

Some, like the Pleiadians, seem to have fairly regular interaction with humans, while others are more circumspect in their activities and presence. Still other species are comparatively arcane or unusual to human experience: I report briefly on the appearances and activities of 15 different alien species mandated by higher spiritual authorities to be here on Earth to fulfill tasks for us.

For example: the *White Wheels*—aliens that resemble white wagon wheels with an eye for a hub—wheel around the sky at all angles, rotating rapidly like little whirlwinds. In this way, they help clear the air element of obstructions and toxicity. They were created by another alien race called the *Artilarians*. These came in motherships long ago and their form is like that of the classic Vikings.

I also report psychic impressions of the legitimate functions and tasks in the life of the planet and humanity of intelligences from eight star systems. These include celestial beings from the stars Arcturus, Sirius, Canopus, and the Pleiades, and the constellations Cygnus, Cepheus, Orion, and Ursa Major. This is not an exhaustive list, of course; virtually all the major stars and constellations are intimately involved with human and planetary life, and have been since the inception of both. Just to consider the resume of activities and responsibilities of these eight should be sufficient to expand radically our sense of the ET reality.

To focus our attention, or anxiety, on the possibly hostile intrusions of but one family of aliens, the Grays, is to miss the greater phenomena and reality. Our body and all its subtle aspects, and the planet with it, teem with alien life.

As with the Marian apparitions, my prime interest is the *where*. Why do these phenomena happen precisely where they do? Is the reason geomantic, to do with Earth's etheric body?

Abductions do not seem to be site-specific or relegated to hotspots, but specific to the individuals in question. Wherever they are, that's where the abductions take place, even from a person's bedroom or backyard. These events seem related to specific preexisting relationships people have with the Grays. UFO hotspots—that is, places of heightened, frequent *sightings* over a period of time—are clearly geomantically referenced. Such areas have many high-energy geomantic aspects already embedded in their locales and these seem to draw UFO activity, mainly sightings, as pollen draws bees.

I suggest some geomantic answers as to why certain areas seem to be UFO hotspots, such as Topanga Canyon near Los Angeles, the Hudson River Valley near New York City, and the San Luis Valley in southwestern Colorado. I give psychic impressions of five other locales, some well known for UFO activities, such as Hessdalen in Norway, and some just well known for high strangeness, such as Mount Shasta in California. Not only are there solid geomantic reasons for heightened UFO activity in these areas, but a surprising amount of the evident UFO activity is secondary to the real events. It's like seeing a crowd rushing down a street toward some as yet unknown event. It's easy to mistake the frenetic, dashing crowd for the main event, the flurry of UFO sightings for the real event. Mostly, the UFOs are not the central event.

Much of the UFO activity in certain areas that we can detect is evidence of certain classes or families of ETs buzzing a restricted site where more secret, deeply embedded ET activity is under way. What you can see at such places, such as orbs of colored light, ships, sounds, and the other phenomena, is not the full picture. In Topanga Canyon, the Hudson River Valley, and the San Luis Valley, you have to think bigger scale, in terms of projects that the spirit of our planet—popularly called Gaia—has under way. What is the spirit of our planet up to?

In some locales, including these three, the Earth is voluntarily being used as a womb to gestate new alien life for both our planet and elsewhere in the galaxy. These are sanctioned, mandated cosmic breeding experiments of a level far beyond cloning or genetic engineering as we know it or even imagine it. Here the true ET activity, underneath all the surface flurry and confusion, is that portions of the planet are being used, under contract, as cosmic wombs, and some of the resulting progeny may never even live here.

Here again, following the flurry of UFO phenomena into their hotspots and through this into the Earth reveals yet more startling secrets about its hidden galactic life. An amusing aspect of this is that to some extent the Grays and other ETs with ships—the ones that get the most public attention and have entered popular iconography—are not even invited. Not allowed in, they buzz around it like frustrated paparazzi trying to get a glimpse of the famous star.

With chapter 6, we move into the third sign on the Earth, crop circles. Here my focus is not so much on specific locales where crop circles occur, but on one small area that is home to the majority of the world's crop circle activity. This is the English county of Wiltshire in south-central Britain, about 75 miles west of London. The bulk of the planet's crop circles appear here for an excellent reason: Geomantically, this area is Earth's umbilicus to the galaxy. In this context, the crop circles are a cosmic rash appearing around the belly button of the Earth. This area (specifically the 28.5-acre stone circle called Avebury) is also a hologram of the center of our galaxy and its astrophysically inferred black hole.

The Ofanim refer to this small section of the British landscape as "the golden band within Albion." This is a complex issue, but in simple terms, from their perspective the cosmic soul of the Earth is an anthropomorphic figure they call Albion. The golden band is like a golden box or rectangle at his belly. Inside the box occur most of the world's crop circles, but that's only the start of things.

Here are a few of the conclusions you'll find in chapter 6: Crop circles are interdimensional messages using a language of light, communication from the next dimension humans are to experience. The images must be seen in at least the fourth dimension to get any sense of their full reality. They represent a serial revelation of the fundamental design principles, codings, grammar, and syntax used to make our physical reality, both body and planet—the original toolbox. They are an alphabet of forms, symbols, images, and shapes; once they were withheld from us, but now, the full deck of playing cards is laid out before us.

As with the other two signs on the Earth, the crop circles must be seen collectively, as a total, though slightly encrypted, singular message to us from the cosmos and its higher forms of consciousness.

What's the message? It's more like a payoff for our decoding efforts. As you'll see in chapter 6, if you find the key to open the lock of this golden band of crop circles within Albion, you get a big surprise.

The whole planet, all of humanity, does. Out tumbles a cornucopia of secrets, mysteries, and revelations. The Wiltshire crop circle zone will release its Mystery revelation like a rush of spores to seed the Earth and human awareness with this next dimensional consciousness.

Finally, in chapter 7, I put the signs together as a three-step process designed by spiritual intelligences overseeing human advancement to help us get our heads above the clouds. What clouds? The obscuring mists of three-dimensional, physical reality, our normal consensus reality about everything. Our consensus that reality is only what we can physically see and prove to exist by the evidence of our senses. Busted! The three signs on the Earth, if they do nothing else, intend to bust that misconception of reality and our prospects.

The Marian apparitions raise our perceptions to the threshold of the spiritual worlds, or 4D, the fourth dimension. They incite us to birth a new level of consciousness within us, what we could call the Christ Child, or the Higher Self incarnating as a divine child within. The alien encounters and UFO phenomena demonstrate the unexpected richness of the 4D reality, showing that our planet, ourselves, and the galaxy, and even beyond, teem with intelligent, interconnected, continuously interacting life. Crop circles school us in a new language of light, a higher form of conscious communication with this galactic life, be it aliens or angels, gods or advanced beings in marvelous ships.

So, in brief, what does this book conclude about the three signs?

First, they are real events happening on the surface of the planet.

Second, they are extraplanetary in origin and emanate from a subtler dimension than our physical reality and matter as we know it.

Third, they are purposeful, mandated, and executed with intent to inform us of something.

Fourth, we need to look beyond dogma, belief, tradition, official views, and consensus reality to see them freshly, and be surprised.

Fifth, their appearance is largely site-specific, which means *where* they happen is meaningful and beneficial in terms of the planet's overall geomantic nature.

Sixth, when you understand the geomantic aspects of the

"where," then the purpose and message of the signs are easier to decode.

Seventh, the Earth's sacred sites are being used as a cosmic message board for our edification.

Eighth, the signs can best be understood when seen clairvoyantly rather than through reason or analysis.

Ninth, the signs can best be appreciated when considered collectively, as one message in three parts.

Tenth, the signs as a group are seeking to school human attention and consciousness in a three-part initiation experience.

Eleventh, the signs are intended to help us expand our cognition into the fourth dimension where events in time are spread out across space.

Twelfth, this initiation into the fourth dimension also involves developing Christ consciousness, or the ability to look through and understand all of spacetime.

Thirteenth, the signs collectively intend humanity to master the language of light, as specifically evidenced and encoded within the vast array of crop circle designs.

As for the "day of the Lord" that will come, as the Acts of the Apostle seer foresaw, perhaps that will surprise us too. We expect judgment and punishment. Maybe instead that "great and manifest" day will herald unceasing revelation and epiphany, and the Kingdom of God spread out all around us to see, and we shall be *able to see it*. Perhaps that is what the three signs portend.

1 | *The Earth's Big Secret—Our Planet's Visionary Geography as a Cosmic Message Board*

To make sense of these three signs on the Earth, maybe we need a deeper understanding of the Earth itself. Maybe we need a new view of our planet. Perhaps the signs have as much to do with the Earth's own life as with ours.

Here is a vision of the Earth as seen from a distance: Picture the Earth as the lovely blue-white planet in perfect equipoise in the midst of vast cosmic space. We've all seen the NASA photographs, so this image should come easily to mind. Now picture a single, vast motherly face wrapped benevolently around the globe, just one face, yet somehow wherever you look, there are the face, the eyes, the compassion. There is a susurrus of wings, behind the eyes and around the cheeks.

A third component, a layer between the face and the planet, is like an onion with nine layers, each enveloping the planet. Yet it is

1

also a geometric space, filled with complex shapes edged in light, filled with colors, structures—temples, perhaps—mythical beasts and animals, angels, spirits, stars.

You're looking at a celestial being, possibly a magnificent angel, whose pale rose-tinted form envelops the planet as if it were her body. It is not your typical angel, standing erect, humanlike, with fanning wings, diaphanous form. This one is planet-shaped, and she has nine layers. It's like looking psychically at a person, seeing the layers of their aura like onion folds, each layer filled, even packed, with things—pictures, lights, spirits, toxicity, pain.

Wherever you are on the planet, you are walking through her, in a lovely rosy mist of her soul wrapped around the physical orb we call Earth. She is a very tolerant mother, patient, indulgent, yet sensing the need to become firm. Everything that has ever happened on Earth is in her fields, in one of the nine layers. They comprise a vast library; memory banks recording wars, violence, nastiness, destruction, love, good deeds, epiphanies.

All of humanity's history was a blank slate, since we arrived on this fresh, virginal planet, when its landscape angel, whom we know somewhat uncertainly as Gaia, primed by the Supreme Being for the task. It has been written upon—stained even—and the layers teem with the phantasmagoria of our doings over the eons. It's all there as a vast time tableau, a time-lapse photo archive where past is livingly present. And it is not just *our* past presented timelessly as the contents of the vast now of the present, but *Gaia's* past and present, her long life among the spirits and stars. That too.

We could step into that realm, which seems a little scary, heady perhaps. We might ratchet our cognition up a notch from third to fourth. We are immured in three-dimensional reality; this is our world, immutable, we think. But already Gaia holds the fourth onion skin open for us; it teems.

Inside Gaia's planetary form, inside the face and the wings, you may see thousands more like her, but smaller, like an angelic fractal. Some reside in valleys, some in mountains, lakes, ponds, hills, entire nations or landmasses. Think of these as Gaia's handmaidens, or as Earth's legion of landscape angels, maintaining the energy and consciousness and intent for a given area, for us.

Things are happening within Gaia. She's pushing up new flowers, except they are growing from the middle layer, the one with all the lights and geometry, *down onto* the Earth's surface. They pop through with the insistence and resilience of grass growing through cracks in the concrete, and in fact these flowers—they're not really flowers, of course—are growing energetically through the concrete of our fixed views.

What are these flowers that are not really flowers? They are signs on the Earth, secrets Gaia is letting us become aware of at last. Images of the Virgin Mary light up around the globe as a form of adoration from the spiritual hierarchies Gaia comes from—her people. Spacecraft circulate and star beings walk the Earth in bodies of light, evidence of Gaia's other family—progeny of her first marriage, you might say, now let out in the open for us. And marvelous, short-lived forms, light up quickly, then disappear like fireflies across the grainfields, a strange hierophantic picture language, Gaia talking in tongues and somebody writing it down for us to decipher.

From a certain viewpoint, it looks like our planet is going to hell.

From a certain perspective, this reminds one of the Victorian madwoman in the attic. Too crazy to let down to the ground floor. Crazy Granny upstairs. Is Gaia going a little nuts? No, but it might seem that way. She's just upgrading her dialogue with us. Enriching the syntax. Sharing long-withheld, shocking secrets.

Mama Gaia is going through a momentous transfiguration, a life change. Maybe she's talking to herself a bit, mumbling, gesticulating, but it's not like we've even given her an ear for so many years. She's changing, yes, but it's structured, well planned, orchestrated, organic. And like a compassionate mother, she's concerned for how we'll cope with that change, for it will be a transfiguration of every atom of our physical reality.

She's breaking up the concrete; discharging toxicity; eradicating old pictures. Just conceive of it: Everything humanity has ever thought, felt, done here is in Gaia. Can you imagine yourself containing all that? And most of it done under a false impression, a limited view, a minimal and often distorted perception of reality. We've done all these things, killed so many, poisoned so much, despaired ceaselessly, without knowing it all or seeing the full picture. Without understanding where all this human life finally gets deposited.

Now that's all changing. Word of Gaia's transfiguration is moving down the chain of her handmaidens, the legion of landscape angels around Earth. And even we are getting wind of it, catching a few words about it, and noticing it with intrigue or fear, excitement or trepidation, or pretending not to notice or punishing or marginalizing those who do.

Gaia—Earth's Ultimate Landscape Angel

So what is a landscape angel? To explain, we must take one step back to a statement about Gaia. In the 1970s, British atmospheric scientist James Lovelock stimulated world scientific thinking by proposing his Gaia Hypothesis. He said that when you contemplate meteorological, climatological, geological, and botanical factors, the planet exhibits clear signs of being a unified, automatically self-regulating, homeostatic organism.

Lovelock used the ancient Greek name for the planet, Gaia (from *Ge,* "Earth") to signify the planet seen at this holistic level of understanding. He further coined the term "geophysiology" to denote the new science that encompasses Gaia as a self-regulating planet, and geophysiologists as the planetary physicians who deliver planetary medicine. He observed: "If we can think of ourselves as part of a giant living organism and perhaps even a cause of its indigestion, then we may be guided to live within Gaia in a way that is seemly and healthy."[1]

When Lovelock said Gaia as a planetary ecosystem is alive, he meant as a tree is alive or in the way an engineer says a mechanical system is alive when switched on. Although Lovelock did not wish to extend his model to credit Gaia with being sentient, self-aware—or, Heaven forbid, a goddess—many enthusiasts outside the strictures of science did, and thanked Lovelock for the validation of their presumption that the planet is, indeed, alive and aware.

I'd like to thank Lovelock as well, and take his Gaia Hypothesis well beyond his comfort zone, and possibly beyond even that of those enthusiasts. Gaia is not only a goddess, but, more precisely, the landscape angel for the entire planet. The self-regulating planetary ecosystem, including the interlocking domains of the mineral, plant, animal, and human kingdoms, comprise Gaia's physical body. But Gaia as an angelic being is the planet's singular *genius loci,* the spirit of place who holds our geomantic space.

"Landscape angel" is one of many possible terms that refer to a class of angelic beings assigned to maintain the energy, conscious-ness, and evolutionary intent of a given locality. This can be on any scale, from a garden to a lake to a mountain or city—or even larger landmasses, like states or even continents. A landscape angel ani-mates and even broods over a given area. It is extremely alert and observant, and dispenses fine, enlivening auric forces to its physical landscape, stimulating the circulation of life forces by movements of its arms or wings, and often draping an extensive area with, as one psychic said, a "wonderful ovoid of brilliant hues." One landscape angel for a half-acre wood was situated 150 feet above it, enveloping, even insulating, the entire wood with its aura, which radiated and scintillated like the aurora borealis.[2]

Think of these many thousand landscape angels as part of a nested hierarchy, so that the landscape angel for a mountain might be subsumed by the larger scope of activity of the one for the province, and that by the national angel, all the way up to Gaia, who includes them all.

If you want to know about a given locality—say the San Luis Valley of Colorado, a UFO hotspot—you might inquire of that area's landscape angel. Obviously, this is a psychic or visionary inquiry, but the locality's landscape angel is well equipped to know. Later in the book, I report on some geomantic observations of these and other areas, and much of the information came through my exchanges with the particular area's landscape angel who acted as guide, men-tor, and informant.

According to well-known Theosophist writer and clairvoyant Geoffrey Hodson, the landscape angel of a valley, for example, is likely to be aware of every birth and death within its domain, and its aura likely includes memory thought-forms of past deeds in the val-ley. As a creative intelligence, it is charged with overseeing the evolu-tionary processes in the mineral and plant kingdom within its purview, and of being empathetic to human needs and sufferings—"and happy are those who live within its care," Hodson says.[3]

Hodson interacted with a landscape angel in a secluded valley in England in 1926. He described it as beautiful, with dazzling eyes, about 20 feet tall, with a many-colored, brilliant aura whose colors constantly changed "as the auric forces flow in waves and vortices outward from the central form." It would move down the valley, touching everything with its extended aura; dispensing joy, exaltation, and well-being; and quickening impulses to all the nature spirits. This Guardian Angel of the valley, Hodson wrote, imparts a distinctive quality and charm to the valley's psychic atmosphere that potentially affects everyone in its midst, "particularly those who are born and live within the angel's consciousness and the continual play of its aura."[4]

This gives us some vivid impressions of landscape angels. But my vision of Gaia as Earth's ultimate landscape angel included the complex nine-layered geometric middle space between the planet and the angel. Let's consider this "onion" next.

The Name of the Onion Skins: Earth's Visionary Geography

Despite all our sciences and scientific studies, have we *seen* the Earth?

Let's start with the blue-white planet again. See it before you. Now bring to mind some of the sacred sites you have probably heard of: Stonehenge, the stone heads of Easter Island, Chartres Cathedral, the Pyramids of Giza, Mount Fuji, Mount Shasta. Holy sites are distributed copiously across the Earth, and have been recognized and sometimes still maintained by local cultures for millennia. Most visitors to such places affirm that somehow holy sites have a beneficial effect on consciousness; they uplift, inspire, or energize us. They sometimes put us in a creative, philosophical, even mystical state of mind.[5]

To a clairvoyant surveying the planet as a whole, the many thousands of sacred sites can appear as brilliant beacons of light dotting the Earth's surface. Such a viewing may also reveal the intriguing fact that inside the light are structures that resemble temples, palaces, castles, star wheels, star patterns. On this insight alone, we can draw an important observation: Sacred sites have an outer physical aspect, such as a mountain, cathedral, pyramid, or standing stone, and also an *inner* aspect, a light-englobed celestial temple.

For instance, you might look at Montsegur, a craggy prominence in the French Pyrenees that now has only the ruins of a castle but was once the headquarters of Catharism, a divergent Christian sect. That's the outer part. The inner part is that above the five-hundred-foot-high sheer rock is a temple of light.

Take Mount Etna, a massive volcano that dominates the island of Sicily in Italy. Its inner aspect was well described by Homer and Virgil: It is the forge and smithy of Hephaistos, Olympian fire god, assisted in his work by the Cyclopes. Or take Chaco Canyon in northwestern New Mexico: Its outer aspect is a long canyon with many ruins of the long-departed Anasazi Native Americans. Its inner aspect is a massive star wheel, a dome of light extending for miles, and a formidable coiled dragon several hundred yards across guarding the canyon.

Often to make sense of what you see in the inner aspect of a sacred site, you need to check into world mythology for references. I have found that if you take myths seriously as accurate descriptions of a psychic reality, you often gain a valuable map and many clues to a sacred site's *inner* aspects.

The *place* of the inner aspects of the planet's numerous visible, physical sacred sites is the nine-layered onion described previously. This is the realm of visionary geography, also known as the Earth grid, geomantic terrain, or the galaxy on Earth. We could say it is the planet's energy body or Gaia's array of auric layers, chakras, and energy lines. Our planet has subtle aspects to its being, just as humans have.

Visionary geography is an elegant term that indicates that everywhere you look with psychically attuned eyes you see celestial temples, galactic apparitions, angelic epiphanies, and revelations of the Spirit. Adjusting Lovelock's language, we might say this is Earth's *secret* anatomy and physiology. We learn that, as the great Southwest writer Frank Waters aptly put it, "We have not yet comprehended, as have the Indians, the existence of a psychical ecology underlying physical ecology." All living things, including us, have not only outer form, but "an inner spiritual component."[6]

The multiplicity of physical sacred sites, with all the types of ancient megalithic engineering we find strewn about the Earth, marks the spot, grounds the energy, and holds the door open. All of these are tangible markers for our planet's inner spiritual components. We walk through a megalithic enclosure or Gothic cathedral right into this next dimension, the fourth onion skin, the world of Earth's visionary geography.

It's important to realize that the door is held open for us: The Earth's visionary geography is here *for us*. It was designed to be interactive and was designed for us to participate in its maintenance.

As I have detailed in *The Galaxy on Earth* and *The Emerald Modem*, we walk through sacred sites into a galactic landscape. We find all the structures, places, dimensions, intelligences, and processes of the galaxy and spiritual worlds relevant to our potential evolution as embodied humans on a physical Earth. This array of subtle galactic features has been holographically copied and distributed across the Earth's surface and through many of its onion skin layers for our edification. Interacting with them, we continually encounter ourselves. How? It is ourselves as cosmic beings, spiritual beings, wakeful residents of the galaxy before we became inhabitants of planet Earth.

I modify the classical Hermetic axiom to express this: *As above, so below, and in the middle too.* The *above* is the galaxy and spiritual worlds and all their wonders, sublimities, and opportunities for initiation; the *below* is us, for humans, according to most metaphysical traditions, are a miniature of the cosmos, a microcosmos (hence the relevance of astrology). The *in the middle too* is the forgotten mediator between cosmic and microcosmic: Earth and its onion.

Our planet has been provided with a hologram of the galactic array so that we, bearing the same imprint, may see ourselves clearly in this galactic-planetary mirror and remember who we are (spiritual beings) and where we came from.

Importantly, this hologram has multiple dimensions, signified by the nine layers of the onion skin around the planet described. Not all of the geomantic features are in the same layer or dimension. For example, domes are in the fourth, but stargates are in the fifth, and some features are in the sixth and seventh layers as well. This means the Earth's geomantic terrain consists of overlapping subtle dimensions or layers, each requiring more refined psychic ability for us to perceive, much less interact with. This has applications specifically with UFO-ET phenomena. "We live in a multi-dimensional world that is overlapped and visited by entities from other dimensions," wrote a commentator in 1988. "Many of these entities are hostile. Many are not hostile."[7]

Multiple dimensions overlapping our physical reality provide for the spectrum of ET qualities, from hostile to friendly. Similarly, there is a range in the physicality of the events, encounters, aliens, and craft. Some UFO phenomena are seemingly physical, others quasi-physical, and still others are too subtle for sense perception, but discernable through clairvoyance. You might say that some aspects of the ET presence on Earth are close to the surface of ordinary perception, but much is deeper set, dimensionally removed, at a psychic level.

You find this same spectrum with all three signs on the Earth. Marian apparitions almost always are seen by only a very few witnesses. Everyone else has to take the sightings on faith, though sometimes secondary effects, such as strange solar phenomena, are seen by many. UFO phenomena are more frequently noted by multiple witnesses, though abductions seem mostly on an individual basis. Crop circles, by contrast, are visible to all, and no psychic abilities are required. What is elusive about this sign is its makers; typically, the circles appear almost instantaneously and the most that is ever seen of its agent is, sometimes, a luminous pillar or tube of light.

As to how the Earth benefits from the signs, I explain later that the Marian apparitions bless a geomantic node with high celestial consciousness; the UFO sightings, touchdowns, and encounters (which seem to take advantage of preexisting geomantic features as an energetically favorable locale for activities) keep the portals between dimensions open and fluid; and the crop circles have a catalytic effect on the geomantic terrain, seemingly adding something new (metaphorically, at least), a kind of cosmic "electrical" input.

Current News from the Cosmos on the Earth's Message Board

The Earth's visionary geography is a complex web of structures and layers. I have been able to document 92 different types of spiritual structures that may be accessed through outer, physical features.

These 92 different structures or temples have multiple expressions. It's as if the Supreme Being took the Grail Castle, for example, and put it in the cosmic photocopy machine to crank out 144 copies, or 432 landscape zodiacs, or 1,080 copies of Shambhala, and then distributed these copies all over the planet, thus affording everyone fairly easy access to most of the 92 different structures. It's as if the Designer of the array included almost everything interesting ever remembered, even sketchily, in world myth—dragons, cosmic eggs, celestial cities, star beings, golden apples—and hit the copy button.

Most of humanity has forgotten about this pattern—hasn't even heard the rumors of its existence—and we live obliviously on a planet as if surrounded by the results of a massive paper shredding episode. The paper shreds are the remaining megalithic sites, the broken-down, incomplete stone circles or rows, the henges, rings, ditches, solitary stones, sacred wells, holy hills, mounds, effigies, numinous mountains, and the rest. The paper shreds are also the fragmented myths and maps of the geomantic terrain—and their explanation.

Now we enter a time when the galaxy and the spiritual worlds want to communicate openly with us, and they're using this terrain as a message board. They are making three kinds of signs on the Earth: Marian apparitions, UFO encounters, and crop circles. But before we can decipher the messages, we have to understand the message board.

What message board? The message board that the cosmos is using is the planet's vast geomantic array of sites, energy nodes, structures, and processes. In most cases, the three predominant signs on the Earth are inscribed with reference to this visionary geography. Think of it perhaps as premium writing paper because multiple copies of the geomantic features have been part of the planet since the start, inherent and implicit in the Earth's body.

So to make sense of these otherwise baffling phenomena, we need to understand the *specificity* of *where* they take place. The meaning of the phenomena themselves can be teased out when we understand why they take place *where* they do. It's all planned out.

Our interpretation needs to include both the message and the message board—the medium—because considering both together provides comprehension and the chance to respond in kind. Naturally, this is Earth's big secret: that not only do we have a planetary message board, but the cosmos is communicating with us today.

So let's take a moment and get introduced to some of the 92 different geomantic features that comprise Earth's message board. I only cover here, and briefly, those features that come up in later chapters. Also bear in mind that the number 92 is not the final number; I am still identifying new geomantic features.

A Glossary of Key Geomantic Terms
Used for the Signs on the Earth

ALBION: One of many mythic names for an anthropomorphic figure that represents and embodies the totality of creation. Geomantically, it refers to this expression at three levels on the Earth: one for the entire planet, 12 for subdivisions, and 432 for the landscape zodiacs (see entry to follow).

ALBION MINOR CHAKRA POINT: One of 72 secondary energy centers within a large-scale anthropomorphic geomantic figure pertaining to one-twelfth of the planet's surface and serving as a summation and container of all regional geomantic nodes.

ALBION PLATE: A pentagonal (five-sided) division of the Earth's surface, of which there are 12, each receiving a different astrological influence; named after Albion, for he is the "soul" and full expression of the contents of each Plate.

ARC OF ASCENDING CONSCIOUSNESS: Something like a miniature Milky Way arc as we see it from the edge of the galaxy, it is an interactive parabolic curve of consciousness across a ten-mile stretch of landscape. It resembles a walled corridor between dimensions, like walking through the parted Red Sea.

BLAZING STAR: An apparitional form of the Ofanim angelic family (see entry on Ofanim). It is accessed within the human form as a pinpoint of brilliant blazing light, a blazing star, two inches above the navel and two inches inside.

CHAKRAS: Containers for consciousness arrayed in a hierarchical, interdependent sequence along the human spine from groin to head, they embody the planetary spheres or primary dimensions of reality within matter and spirit. There are 72 minor and nine major, totaling 81, and exist on the Earth as well.

CHAKRA TEMPLATE: An experiential copy of the sequence of energy centers or chakras in the human expressed across a landscape of variable size.

CONTROL BUBBLE: A device for controlling the mixture and flow of angelic, celestial, and devic-elemental energies through a geomantic region.

COSMIC EGG: Also called the Egg of Brahma or Mundane Egg, it contains all the elements of creation *in potentia* and in a seemingly chaotic state. It affords an experience of reality before reality was differentiated into myriad forms.

CROWN OF THE ANCIENT OF DAYS: An interactive space for human encounters with an aspect of the Supreme Being, represented as a large White Head or Crown. Smaller versions of the same are called Palladiums.

DOME: An etheric energy canopy, usually many miles wide, overlaid upon mountains and volcanoes, making the site numinous. Domes holographically present the consciousness of individual high magnitude stars and their "star gods."

DOME CAPS: Minor stars (in association with the dome stars) or the light bodies of planets with that star's planetary system, are presented by these subsidiary etheric energy canopies generated by domes.

DRAGON: An astral being in spirallic, undulatory form who contains the electromagnetic field spectrum of light and maintains and protects a geomantic temple.

DRAGON EGG: An energy matrix generated by a dragon that will birth a new, secondary dragon (like progeny) or be used by humans to mirror the unfoldment of their own 81 chakras in a long-term initiation experience.

EDEN: One of 24 original copies and extrapolations of the Garden of Eden template, a model for physical reality of the perfected male-female psyche imprinted at 24 locations.

EGREGORS: Angelic beings that watch and protect the geomantic array of a specified region, usually a state, nation, province, country, or continent.

EMERALD: Prometheus's famous narthex tube in which he captured the gods' fire to give to humans. It refers to the possibility of total illumination of consciousness by a device or esoteric chakra in the chest resembling an emerald. It is often encountered outside at a geomantic site as a holographic projection.

ENERGY FOCUSING NODE: Also known as an Earth minor chakra, it concentrates and distributes energy and consciousness for a geomantic region; it is a country's "navel."

ENERGY FUNNEL: A straight-running channel for higher consciousness states, often marked by tree or stone avenues, with a subtle temple at the end.

EPIPHANY FOCUS: A geomantic node selected each year to receive a weeklong (January 3–9) direct infusion of Christ consciousness; afterward, this charge is still present and potent, and available for human absorption.

GOLDEN EGG: An interactive container by which you release a copy of the Christ Child or golden Higher Self into the landscape as you unfold the same in yourself as well.

HALL OF RECORDS LABYRINTH: One of nine different types

of labyrinths energetically inscribed on the Earth as templates. This one provides access to celestial information, star codings, and other arcane information.

INTERDIMENSIONAL PORTAL: There are 60,600 entries on Earth into another dimension of reality relevant to Earth, the headquarters of the Pleiadian Council of Light, a kind of galactic United Nations.

IXION WHEEL: A training temple whereby you gain exposure to the Solar Logos for the purposes of forging your consciousness into a sword.

JEWEL OF MICHAEL: A higher dimensional meeting place for humans with the Archangel Michael, chief among the 18 archangels in our time and charged with supervising interactions among humans, Earth, and galaxy.

LANDSCAPE ZODIAC: A hologram of the galaxy, with 144 constellations arrayed as a star wheel of variable width upon a flat physical landscape.

LIGHT CORRECTIVE CENTER: A technical, angelically pre-ferred term for the megalithic feature mistakenly called a hill fort: a ditch surrounding a henge, but without any standing stones, and often, enigmatically, named a castle.

LILY: A refined geomantic feature, like a lily of light, created by human illumination resident at a geomantic node and of vari-able size ranging up to several acres.

LUCIFER BINDING SITE: A complex theological situation and a fourth-dimensional model underlies this feature, but in brief, it is a place where a portion of the Light Bearer's essence has been bound, released, or is arriving.

MOUNT OLYMPUS: An assembly point for the 14 Ray Masters (an executive, governmental branch of the Great White Brotherhood) of the Great Bear; remembered in Greek myth as the home of Zeus and his Olympian gods.

OFANIM: A family of angels, known as Thrones (Greek angelology), the Wheels (Hebrew), and Blazing Star or Blaise (my own writings),[8] primarily responsible for the implementation and maintenance of the Earth's visionary geography and for partici-pating in beneficial human-Earth interactions.

OG-MIN CAVE HEAVENS: Arcane enclaves of spiritual beings from the Andromeda galaxy, the previous residence of much of humanity.

OROBOROS LINES: Fifteen planet-encircling (hence, oro-boric) energy lines comprise the planet's energy body armature.

These lines originate in Ursa Major (12), with additionally one each from Sirius, Canopus, and Polaris.

POINTER'S BALL: A doorway between dimensions, appearing as a translucent one-hundred-foot-tall ball or sphere set in the landscape.

PRANA DISTRIBUTOR: One of the planet's 288 subtle energy discharge points where, metaphorically, the Supreme Being exhales life force into Earth.

RAY MASTER SANCTUARY: A dedicated meeting place for a specific Ray Master and humans, and a place to ground that Ray Master's Great Bear energy into the Earth.

SILVER EGG: This egg births the Old Christ, the original Logos, expressed often by way of Egyptian myth as Horus, the all-seeing falcon god.

SIPAPUNI: An emergence point from the Hollow Earth; a physical tunnel of sorts, though occluded, through which humans come and go from the inside to the surface.

STARGATES: Transportation devices for bodies and objects linking selected points on Earth with stars and constellations. Stargates are located in the fifth dimension and are among the more subtle of Earth's 92 geomantic features.

TABOR: A name that refers to an extrapolated hologram of the Emerald onto a landscape site to facilitate spiritual transfiguration in humans.

THREE-STAR TEMPLE: Experiential facility for melding human, elemental, and angelic energies, presided over by one of the 18 archangels.

TREE OF LIFE: Interactive template of the Four Worlds, or primal realms of Air, Fire, Water, and Earth, as mythically represented by the Greek gods Zeus, Hades, Poseidon, and Gaia, respectively, and the physical Earth as a grounding point.

UNDERWORLD ENTRANCE: Portal into the afterlife realm and celestial city of Hades, and of the other named deities of death, as well as the lower astral plane, paradoxically accessed upward by way of the crown chakra.

VALHALLA: Hall of the Slain Warriors in Norse myth, this is an assemblage of the Great White Brotherhood and posthuman spiritual warriors (in Norse, the *Einherjar*) who feast perpetually on the Christ consciousness.

ZODIAC AMPLIFIER: A complex feedback device found at about 80 percent of the Earth's landscape zodiacs that transmits human vibrations from a landscape zodiac back to the host stars and constellations of the galaxy.

Signs on the Earth: New Foundations for a Post-Mythic Existence

The 92-plus geomantic features that comprise the Earth's visionary geography are elements of what I call Gaia's classical grid. It's the original complement, the bones, sinews, arteries, and organs of her galactically imprinted planetary body. For the most part, myth is the language that opens its doors.

When you study a myth carefully and validate it for being a possibly accurate description of reality *at some level,* you find it often presents to you a workable map of the geomantic terrain. The "some level" is the psychic level. Most essential myths, when you pare away the extraneous accretions and misdirections, embody an initiate's map to Earth's visionary geography, how it works, and how to interact effectively with it. Usually, the applications are local.

For example, the myth of Hephaistos, the Olympian fire god, working his forge inside volcanic Mount Etna with the Cyclopes, is acutely descriptive of the geomantic feature of that node (a Mithraeum, or Sun temple, one of eight celestial cities), yet it is also generically descriptive of all copies of such temples. In other words, you can use the Hephaistos-smith mythic tableau as an interpretive template for 143 other Sun temples elsewhere on the Earth, such as at Santa Fe, New Mexico; Machu Picchu, Peru; and Mount Haleakala on Maui. The smith there may not be called Hephaistos, but he is doing the same kind of work.

The original multitude of world myths created a cognitive-conceptual platform for us to appreciate the fact that we live in a galaxy on Earth, and it gave us the tools to decode the system. But nearly all those myths are static, describing the classic grid installation, but not the new one. Only a few, from the Norse (Ragnarok, the Twilight or Final Destiny of the Gods), Hindu (the Kalki Avatar, Vishnu's final Avatar or Descent), and Christian (Revelation: Judgment Day, apocalypse, and the rest), even tried to mythicize our probable future.

Classically, and today still, you follow the geomyths (myths about geomantic nodes specifically referenced to local landscapes) to the appropriate temples in the visionary landscape, get in position, plug yourself in psychically with Earth and cosmos, make your changes in consciousness, and reassemble your cosmic self, and benefit the site by flushing it with human-cosmic energy. But something fundamental has changed in the structure of Earth's geomantic terrain. Something new is being added to it.

The classical grid structure remains intact, valid, and still geomythically interactive with us. The classical structure is based on a nesting of five Platonic Solids—five unique primary geometric shapes that can "grow" in only 13 ways, into one of what are known as the 13 Archimedean Solids. The Earth's classical grid shape, based on the Platonic Solids, is now morphing into one of the Archimedean Solids. To keep it simple, let's just say the planet's overall geometric body is maturing from one with 32 faces, 30 edges, and 20 vertices to one with 32 faces, 60 edges, and 30 vertices. The number of edges is doubling and the vertices increasing by 33 percent—and we're living *inside* that change.

A new geometric shape is being birthed out of the old one. The Earth will end up having two structures, dovetailed and complementary, like a two-story house whose second story looks like the product of an architect's wild imagining. This two-leveled geometric structure is a prime determinant of our life experience on Earth—even of the parameters and possibilities for consciousness—for it is the context and foundation for the geomantic terrain. The 92-plus visionary geography features sit inside this like plants in potting soil.

It puts us momentarily in the position where we're living without myth. The morphing of the Earth's geometry into a new form has no myth, beyond the skeletal and usually grim forecasting contained in the Norse, Hindu, and Christian prophecies, and they are so old as to possibly be outdated. The three signs on the Earth detailed in this book may well be our first new myths. They may serve as scaffolding for us to climb up into this new structure. Tales of Marian apparitions, ET interactions at UFO hotspots, and crop circle epiphanies may be the seeds of a new generation of myth to complement our reborn Earth.

Maybe Gaia, our planet's ultimate landscape angel, in her blue-white body, our Earth, is going through a cosmic initiation, a spiritual upgrade. These celestial signs on the Earth may be the foreshocks of her final change, and since we are embedded physically in her natural web of life and psychically in her visionary geography or onion skin of geomantic nodes, they must equally be foreshocks of our own transformation and consciousness upgrade.

Light in the Blood: Marian Apparitions as Preparations for Our Rebirth through the Earth's Visionary Geography

2 | Everywhere, the Woman Clothed with the Sun—Discerning the Where *of Marian Apparitions*

The Virgin Mary Puts the Mystery Back in People's Lives

She's called the Woman Clothed with the Sun. That label is credited to John of Patmos in Revelation. He foresaw a great sign appearing in the sky in the form of a woman clothed with the sun, with the moon under her feet, and a crown with 12 stars on her head. She was pregnant, in labor, and crying in childbirth. The appearance of the celestial female figure was part of John's overall apocalyptic view of humanity's future. This apocalypse was to include the opening of the seven bowls or seals of plagues, the Day of Judgment, the defeat and entombment of the seven-headed cosmic dragon, and the epiphany and descent of the New Jerusalem.

She is the celestial figure with hundreds of names. Every place she has appeared has generated for her another name. She is the patron of churches, communities, and nations, and her epithets are legion: Bride of Heaven, Blessed Among Women, Dispenser of Grace, Fountain of Living Water, Immaculate Mother, Lady of Victory, Queen of Peace, Mediatrix of All Graces, Mystical Rose. She is the lady of perpetual peace, help, sorrows, mercy, healing, integrity. She is the mother of Christians, Jesus Christ, the Church, the Mystical Body. She is the Perfume of Faith, the Sanctuary of the Holy Spirit, the Virgin of Virgins.

So strong a cultural and religious influence has the Virgin Mary been that the Catholic revival in nineteenth-century Europe has been credited to her. In fact, "visions of Mary became increasingly the most common visions" of that time.[1]

Human expectations of Mary's presence include the belief in her "exceptional powers in times of crisis and her loyalty to those who place themselves in her care." These expectations flavor today's apparitions as much as they did far earlier ones and are the inheritance of "Marian piety and Marian visions of the Christian middle ages." In fact, the belief that one may get privileges or graces through devotional exercises focused on Mary with the goal of developing a special relationship with her underlies "a great deal" of Roman Catholic attention to Marian apparitions.[2]

A thirteenth-century collection of medieval miracle stories called *The Dialogue on Miracles* by Caesarius of Heisterbach listed 64 apparitions of Mary to monks of the Cistercian Order alone. According to one informal count, between the years 40 A.D. and 1999, 363 apparitions of the Virgin Mary have been recorded. The database compiler admits this is but a "partial, working list of some of the more noteworthy apparitions."[3] Of these 363, a few have been officially approved by the Vatican, some denounced, and the rest ignored, left without comment, or awaiting investigation.

The Vatican's validation, or not, seems to have little effect on the vitality of the apparition phenomenon. It keeps on happening. Why?

Life magazine in 1996 in a cover story on Mary said that Mary's appeal was crossing traditional Catholic borders because "the emotional need for her is so irresistible to a troubled world."[4] In a cover story on the Virgin Mary in 1997, *Newsweek* declared that at least four hundred Marian apparitions had been reported in the twentieth century, making that century "a millennial 'Age of Mary.'"[5] The *Los Angeles Times* in 1998 suggested Mary's popularity might be because she is "a comforting conduit of spirituality and a symbol of peace in troubled times" and that her "maternal gaze seems to have an ecumenical appeal."[6] A Yale scholar notes: "The Virgin Mary has been more of an inspiration to more people than any other woman who ever lived."[7] An Italian academic and commentator on the apparitions says there is now "an international Catholic visionary culture."[8]

"The increase in reports of apparitions suggests there is a spiritual hunger today that goes beyond institutional churches," astutely comments Rev. Johann Roten, a Marianist priest and director of the Marian Library and International Marian Research Institute at the University of Dayton in Dayton, Ohio. "There's a need for mystery to be put back in people's lives. Apparitions may be one of God's many answers to these needs." Rev. Roten also observed that while God is not "immediately present" to most people, He entrusts His message to Mary, who in turn entrusts it to visionaries, who pass it on to the public.[9]

That message has certainly been getting around. A tally published by Rev. Roten's organization of about 2,160 reported Marian apparitions shows their distribution over the centuries. The thirteenth century registered the greatest number with 772, followed by 612 in the fourteenth, 315 in the fifteenth, and 275 in the twelfth century. The twentieth century registered 386 Marian apparitions. About these the Catholic Church made no decision regarding 299, made a negative (invalidating) decision about 79, and accepted and validated only eight as authentic: those at Fatima, Portugal; Banneux and Beauraing, Belgium; Akita, Japan; Syracuse, Italy; Zeitoun, Egypt; Manila, Phillippines; and Betania, Venezuela.[10]

Marian apparitions seem to have occurred in recent centuries in waves and clusters, and have been correlated with conditions of exceptional political, social, or economic stress. Notable triggers have been economic crisis, epidemics, wars, food shortages, political persecution, or radical political change. The 1930s in Europe was one such wave. Major Marian apparitions and subsequent pilgrimages occurred in Ezkioga in Spain, Banneaux and Beauraing in Belgium, followed by another subwave through Belgium at seven separate sites; then in 1933, Marian apparitions occurred at 15 additional European sites as well as notable revivals at established Marian sites such as Marpingen, Germany.

During the years 1947 to 1950, at least 65 separate incidents of Marian apparitions were recorded in Europe in nine countries. Then in 1954 there was a renewed rash of 18 apparitions, again Europe, mainly England and France. Estimates indicate that between 1947 and 1954, an average of 12 new Marian apparitions occurred each year, though in the decades 1955 to 1975, this dropped to an average of three yearly, until the 1980s produced yet another Marian wave, including a series in 1983 in Ranschbach, Germany, to which 300,000 pilgrims flocked to behold evidence of the Blessed Virgin of Kaltenbrunn.[11] In April 1987, apparitions of Mary were reported in Hruchiv, Ukraine, followed soon after by apparitions at 13 other Ukraine locations, mostly sanctuaries and monasteries destroyed in previous decades by atheist Russian Communists.[12]

A more radical claim, and one probably quite difficult to validate, was made in 1995 that Mary had appeared 21,000 times in the past ten centuries. Further, scholars report there are two thousand records of ancient Marian encounters in Latin texts, five hundred in verse, and six hundred in Old French prose, and "numerous others" in Anglo-Norman, English, Norse, and Spanish literary documents.[13]

Many apparitions were first registered in Catholic countries, such as Spain, France, Italy, Portugal, Ireland, Belgium, and Poland, but also in some that had a minority Catholic population, such as England. Some occurred in countries that subsequently became Catholic, such as Mexico; some in seemingly unlikely (because un-Catholic) locales such as Bosnia, Vietnam, Egypt, Ukraine, Rwanda, Syria, and Japan; and still others in highly secular or predominantly Protestant countries such as Canada, Australia, and the United States. In fact, since 1987, a preponderance of new Virgin Mary sightings (at least 58 in one count) has been in the United States and in surprising places like Necedah, Wisconsin; Bayside, Queens (New York City); and Conyers, Georgia (near Atlanta).

The Virgin Mary appearances have not been relegated only to predominantly Catholic countries, nor has it been the official priesthood that enjoyed the visitations. Only sometimes. In the majority of cases, the apparitions were made before the laity, the unversed, unschooled, and often, the very young. In many cases, Mary made requests for action, such as to build a shrine or chapel, and later, when these requests were fulfilled, they brought momentous, lasting consequences to those sites. For example:

In 1061, Lady Richeldis de Faverches, a widow living in Walsingham, England, had three Marian visions and was asked to build a replica of Mary's house in Nazareth as a memorial to the Annunciation. In the Middle Ages, Walsingham became one of the greatest Christian pilgrimage sites in Europe.

In 1531, an illiterate Nahuatl-Aztec Indian named Juan Diego had several apparitions of the Virgin Mary at Tepeyac Hill on the outskirts of Mexico City. Mary asked Juan Diego to ask the local bishop to erect a basilica at that spot; today the Virgin of Guadalupe, as Tepeyac was renamed, is a paramount Mexican pilgrimage destination and its basilica can hold ten thousand people.

In 1858, the Virgin Mary appeared 18 times to a 14-year-old French girl named Bernadette Soubirous in the Massabielle grotto in the Pyrenees and asked that a healing chapel be built there. Today Lourdes is world famous as a Catholic pilgrimage and healing site, drawing five million people a year.

In 1879, Margaret Beirne and 13 other villagers of Cnoc (Knock, but also called *Cnoc Mhuire,* "Mary's Hill"), Ireland, beheld a beautiful luminous woman clothed in white wearing a brilliant crown, a rose at her brow, her hands raised in prayer, and surrounded by angels. She was accompanied by Saint John the Evangelist and Saint Joseph in an apparition cast in light upon the church walls that persisted for two hours. Today Knock is Ireland's national Marian shrine.

During the years 1916 and 1917, the Virgin Mary appeared six times to three illiterate children under the age of ten in a rocky pasture called Cova de Iria in the hamlet of Fatima, Portugal. She asked them to help spread devotion to her Immaculate Heart worldwide. Later a shrine was built there, and an estimated 20 million people a year now visit the basilica of Our Lady of Fatima.

Between 1931 and 1936, the Virgin Mary appeared to at least 250 different seers at the hillside Vision Deck and elsewhere in the village of Ezkioga, Spain. So spiritually contagious was the religious enthusiasm generated by these visions, that in 1931 alone, Marian apparitions were reported in 22 other Spanish towns, and between 1931 and 1936, followers of the Ezkioga visions reported Marian experiences in at least 34 additional Spanish communities.[14]

Between June 1, 1961, and November 13, 1965, the Virgin Mary appeared an estimated two thousand times to four young girls in the mountain village of San Sebastian de Garabandal, in northern Spain. She was accompanied by four angels, one of which was identified as the Archangel Michael. Messages regarding spiritual devotion and a preview of humanity's future were provided.

Starting in 1961 and continuing for 13 years, the Virgin Mary appeared some two thousand times before Rosa Quattrini, a Catholic villager in San Damiano, Italy. In her initial apparition, Mary caused a barren pear tree to bloom overnight, it was reported.

On June 24, 1981, two teenage girls beheld the Virgin Mary while they were walking on Podbrdo Hill on Mount Krisevach in the parish of Medjugorje in Bosnia. Later four more teenagers joined their visionary group, beheld the Virgin Mary, and wrote down her messages and predictions. By 1992, an estimated 20 million pilgrims had visited the site—sometimes ten thousand daily—where the apparitions and messages continued on an almost daily basis.

In May 1985, the Virgin Mary started appearing to children at the base of a medieval castle in the Italian town of Oliveto Citra. Over the next year, up to one thousand people would claim to have seen her, and 50 to have heard her messages.

On October 13, 1990, the Virgin Mary appeared before Nancy Fowler at her farm in Conyers, Georgia, near Atlanta, and returned in following years on the same date until 1998. In all, she made 38 apparitions at Conyers. Since 1991, one million people have visited the apparition site (now called Holy Hill), and many have witnessed the heavenly scent of roses, rosaries turning golden, statues of Mary bleeding tears, auras of light around statues and crosses, and the "Miracle of the Sun" in which it appeared to spin, pulsate, turn colors, change shape, and flush golden-yellow and do this for up to seven minutes per episode.

Between January 1993 and the end of 1994, the Virgin Mary made more than two dozen apparitional appearances (with messages) before Ray Doiron at one of the largest outdoor religious shrines in America in Belleville, Illinois.

Miracles of the Sun and Eucharistic Miracles Affirm Mary's Presence

Solar phenomena associated with a Virgin Mary apparition were increasingly noted in the twentieth century. Italian researchers reported that between 1901 and 1970 at least 30 documented cases of such prodigies of the sun were recorded, and that after 1970, a large number occurred at Medjugorje, Bosnia; Kibeho, Rwanda; and almost all the existing Italian apparition sites.[15]

Yet the Miracle of the Sun is but one of many anomalous physical events that accompany or herald a Marian apparition. The following summarizes the range of phenomena reported by Marian visionaries and witnesses over the years: apparitions of Mary and Jesus, visions, prophecies, locutions (messages), physical healings, solar and rosary phenomena, Eucharistic miracles, aroma of roses, stigmata, weeping or bleeding statues of the Virgin Mary.

In the last two thousand years in which the Marian apparitions have been occurring, strange signs and wonders, even physical manifestations, have heralded or accompanied them. These have included: a wooden statue of Virgin Mary, a column of jasper wood, a full-color self-portrait on maguey cactus cloth, a brown woolen scapular, the design for a miraculous medal, roses blooming in winter, healing springs and wells identified, fragrant rose petals or white roses drifting down from a clear sky, unperturbed by winds, a pear tree blooming out of season, churches filling with aromatic incense, plumes of fragrant purple smoke, a crystalline dove shedding light rays over a hill.

Mary has appeared surrounded by a ball of light as bright as the sun; in a blaze of white light; dressed in white, holding a ball topped with a golden cross or standing on a white globe with a green serpent under her feet on the globe; as radiant, luminescent, and transparent; looking like a teenager, wearing a shimmering deepblue dress; as a face in the sun, surrounded by colored lights; on a cloud or pillow, pink roses at her feet; in a white dress with a blue mantle and crown of golden stars, accompanied by four angels; in a violet dress, her breast pierced by three swords; as a nun in white standing atop a church, bowing, moving her arms in greeting; within a multicolored oval aura that emitted brilliantly colored rays; weeping within a large brilliant circle of light that outshone the sun; with a heart of gold enveloped by glittering rays; inside a diamond of light.

At Fatima on two occasions, she manifested as a mobile radiant white globe that dimmed the noonday sun and emitted rainbow rays and raining white globules—as 30,000 people watched. The next Marian-generated phenomenon there was even more astounding. An estimated 50,000 witnesses at Fatima testified that the midday sun suddenly appeared like a silver disk, then began to rotate, dance, and whirl like a pinwheel, crimson streamers flaming on its rim; then it wobbled and zigzagged across the sky and plunged toward the Earth, halted, then reascended to its rightful place overhead, back to "normal."

Extraordinary celestial phenomena were observed by many in 1969 in Fontanelle, a suburb of Montichiari, Italy, in conjunction with a hospital worker named Pierina Gilli and her 36 visitations by the Holy Mother. In a darkening late afternoon sky appeared a large crown of 12 stars; then a shaking red orb that turned on its axis and emitted flames to the Earth, lighting up the sky over Fontanelle with a wheel of fire. On the occasion of another Marian visitation, three rays of light continuously changed colors.[16]

In Zeitoun, Egypt, Mary's appearance was regularly heralded by brilliant, flashing lights, akin to sheet lightning, and one time by aromatic incense filling the church and settling over the area outside it, and another time, by luminous spectral doves gliding through the air around her regular apparitional site. At Bayside, Queens, in New York, hundreds of witnesses captured and confirmed the Virgin Mary's ethereal presence along with light beams and saintly images on Polaroid film, images afterward referred to as the "miraculous photos."

On other occasions, her appearance has been registered in comparatively unremarkable, even shockingly low-key settings: in a grotto by a village's trash heap (Lourdes); in a school dormitory (Kibeho,

Rwanda); in front of a statue of herself (Bayside, Queens, New York); above the roof of a villager's house (Pontmain, France); in a cowherd's ravine in the French Alps (La Salette, France); above a railroad viaduct, then beneath the arched branch of a hawthorn tree (Beauraing, Belgium); on a brilliant cloud above a tree over a pile of rocks in a riverbed (Cuapa, Nicaragua); in a single woman's living room (Amsterdam, Holland); near a small oak tree in a rocky pasture (Fatima, Portugal).

Eucharistic miracles often accompany or in some cases represent the Marian presence. In Akita, Japan, Mary appeared to speak through a wooden statue of herself to a deaf Japanese Sister praying in her convent room. This same queerly animate statue, said to be bathed in light during the Marian presences, subsequently bled watery tears 101 times, and her right hand was observed to ooze a reddish-brown bloodlike fluid that tested AB blood type. In Damascus, Syria, olive oil was extruded from a visionary's fingertips and from an image of Our Lady of Soufanieh (Virgin Mary). In Naju, Korea, tears of blood, water, and oil extruded from a statue of Mary, a Eucharist wafer turned into flesh and blood on the visionary's tongue, and she experienced stigmata.

Sometimes only a single fortunate soul perceived the Virgin Mary, such as Bernadette Soubirous at Lourdes, or a few children such as at Fatima or Medjugorje, while at other times, vast numbers of people witnessed her appearances or at least her effects, such as at Zeitoun, Egypt, where 250,000 saw her on top of a Coptic church. In fact, her apparitions at Zeitoun in 1968 were broadcast on Egyptian television, photographed by numerous professional photographers, and witnessed by Egyptian President Abdel Nasser.

Visions of the Virgin Mary in Betania, Venezuela, began with one woman in 1976, but by 1990, an estimated two thousand people had claimed to see Mary on their own at that location. One 12-year-old girl saw the Virgin Mary above a church in Hrushiv, Ukraine, on April 27, 1987, but between then and August 15 that year an estimated 500,000 people saw her, as she appeared daily at that site, often before up to ten thousand people at a time. Sometimes she appeared but once, as at Knock, Ireland, or eight times at Banneux in Belgium, while at Beauraing, also in Belgium, she appeared 33 times, and in Garabandal, Spain, she made an estimated two thousand appearances, and almost daily, over five years in the early 1960s.

Marian Apparition Sites: New Sacred Spots and Pilgrimage Destinations

Where Mary has appeared, churches, basilicas, chapels, shrines, and sometimes hospitals have often been built as a way of permanently dedicating that apparition site to the furtherance of her presence and message. In Necedah, Wisconsin, the place of her apparition in 1950 was thereafter called the "Sacred Spot." In fact, establishing a sanctified site to which continuous pilgrimages might be made seems to be a central intent of the appearances.

For example, in August 1986, the Virgin Mary started appearing before Patricia Talbot in Cuenca, Ecuador, and this continued daily until October, when it shifted to several times weekly. The Virgin asked Talbot to find a suitable spot in the mountains to create a center to be known as the Garden of the Virgin. Talbot found the place, about 15 miles from Cuenca and the place became the site of the Marian apparitions, drawing crowds of up to 100,000 at a time.

Reportedly, Mary told one of the children who was perceiving her at Beauraing, Belgium, in 1932 that the reason for her appearances was so that people might come there on pilgrimage in the future. At Banneaux, also in Belgium, and Lourdes, she caused springs to appear, indicating they would be healing waters for the sick and infirm, another reason for pilgrimage. Similarly, Bernadette Soubirous reported that The Lady of Lourdes wished to have a chapel built at Massabielle and for people to "come here in procession."

Local Irish tradition says that Saint Patrick on a missionary journey stopped at Knock to bless the village, foretelling that it would one day become a major center of devotion. A Jesuit Mexican missionary, Father Andres Rongier, prophesied in the 1880s that the Nicaraguan town of Cuapa would become famous in the future as a Marian apparition site. Her apparitions did occur, a century later, between May and October 1980.

In Betania, Venezuela, the intent to inaugurate pilgrimage was even more evident. Usually, Marian sites become pilgrimage centers after the apparitions have begun or finished. But many months *before* she ever saw the Virgin Mary, Maria Esperanza Medrano de Bianchini had a vision of an old house, mill, and grotto with clear water. This place *would be* a center of "constant prayer and pilgrimage," a holy site, she understood, but first she had to *find* it. Finally, in 1974, Maria discovered the envisioned spot and dedicated it to the Virgin Mary. On March 25, 1976, the prophesied apparitions began.

Mary reportedly told Maria that Betania would be the Lourdes of Latin America. In 1984, more than one hundred people simultaneously saw the Virgin Mary at the grotto when she appeared seven times, each apparition lasting up to ten minutes. The local bishop petitioned Rome that the apparition site should be regarded as a sacred place, best dedicated to pilgrimage and prayer, reflection, cult, liturgical rites, and the Mass. In 1987, Pope John Paul II officially permitted the apparitional site to be regarded as sacred.

Again, in advance of any public recognition and soon after the apparitions began on September 25, 1983, on November 24, 1983, the Virgin Mary indicated her desired site for a sanctuary to Gladys Quiroga de Motta of San Nicolas, Argentina. The sanctuary site was pinpointed for her by a shaft of light in the darkness on a wasteland called El Campito on the banks of the Parana River. In 1989, the sanctuary opened and, over the course of seven years of visitations, some 1,800 messages from the Virgin Mary were recorded by Gladys. The site has since become renowned for conversions, healings, and vocations.

At both Betania and San Nicolas, clearly specific sites were chosen and pinpointed *in advance* of the apparitions, indicating those sites had particular features suitable for a Marian apparition and its long aftermath. But chosen by whom, on what criteria, and for what overall purpose?

Obviously, one of the outer purposes of site selection for a Marian apparition is to dedicate and preserve that site for the future as a Marian site.

Recently, the Catholic Church established a Catholic Spirituality Center at Conyers, Georgia, and even took over the administration of the site. The purpose of the Center was to further the work of the "new evangelization" declared by the Pope in 1999 and to support the study of the theology and liturgies of Eastern Orthodox churches in accordance with the theological style of the apparitions and Mary's messages there. At her last apparition in 1998, Mary stated that the "graces will continue to flow from her 'home'" at Conyers even though her appearances there would cease and that "her children" should come to Conyers to receive those graces and be "blessed abundantly."[17]

Another purpose is to hallow the ground, to make it a suitably numinous place of intersection between the spiritual and physical worlds. The transcendent realm comes closer to our human domain at Marian-sacralized sites, "bright rents in the heavy curtain that separates this world from the world beyond," now sacred places where as the Virgin Mary was reported to say during her apparitions at Oliveto Citra in Italy in the 1980s, "I and the Holy Spirit work great miracles of spiritual and material grace."[18]

Sometimes when that bright rent is made and the Marian presence is grounded at one site, it spreads to others. The Marian visions at Oliveto Citra in 1984 stimulated secondary apparition sites in Italy, and Mary reportedly told seers she had manifested in at least six other Italian communities in connection with her Oliveto Citra apparition. Further, a powerful apparitional grounding at one new site may restimulate established ones. Mary told seers that she was still present in her sites of earlier appearances, including Lourdes.

Providing a suitable framework for mass pilgrimage to a Marian apparition site may have reached the state of the art at Sabana Grande, Puerto Rico. Ever since she appeared there in the 1960s, thousands of Marian devotees have flocked to the site; now preparations are in hand to erect a statue of Our Lady of the Rosary, allegedly to be twice the height of the Statue of Liberty, and to create a five-hundred-acre "Mystical City" complex, a kind of religious theme park.

Is There a Global Plan Underlying the Marian Apparitions?

The diversity of apparitional locations, the requests for pilgrimages, the identification of sites even before the apparitions—it all suggests a global plan. It's a reasonable assumption that at every place Mary has "touched down" on the Earth plane, a vibrational residue of her presence remains, and this residue is available to us if we wish the spiritual encounter. Clearly, millions of people do wish this, as evidenced by the continuous pilgrimages, masses, services, devotions, prayers, and other activities at them.

But what kind of plan? A plan for what? It's helpful to use an acupuncture analogy. The body has many hundreds of treatment points, possibly a thousand; nearly all have names; they are energy wells on channels or meridians associated with organs; and they have specific locations on the body's skin, front, back, and scalp. Acupuncturists usually have these sites memorized, but they are depicted on detailed body maps resembling the scheme of a big city's subway system.

The point of the acupuncture analogy is that you, the acupuncturist, know this system thoroughly and intimately. You know what happens when you insert little sterilized needles into specific points, or sequences of points. You know in what order the needles can best be placed to get the best therapeutic results, and probably your plan calls for multiple treatments given over a period of weeks or months. You know where you want to go, and how to get there.

So think of the Earth as the patient on the acupuncturist's table. The malady you're treating is lack of Christ consciousness—atheism, disbelief, despair. You know how to remedy this, but it will take a fair bit of time. You'll have to use a special needle, immaculate, perfect for the job—the Virgin Mary. You'll start with certain organs, organ systems, and energy channels most suited to responding to treatment with this specialized needle, but then you'll broaden out into other meridians and acupoints. Like the human body, the planet has many hundreds of treatment points, each with a function, each connected to the whole.

So let's look at 12 Marian sites and see what type of geomantic treatment node each is in the Earth's energy body. Bear in mind that at each of the sites discussed here, and in the many not covered, you *and* the planet get a special formula of Marian infusion, depending on the nature of the geomantic feature and your receptivity. Think of each geomantic context for a Marian apparition as a different type of *filter* for a spiritual presence.

Geomantic Aspects of 12 Marian Apparition Sites

WALSINGHAM, ENGLAND: Let's start with Walsingham, near Norfolk in England. Known for the benefit of the religious tourist trade as England's Nazareth, it offers visitors the Shrine of Our Lady of Walsingham.

The original shrine, built in 1061, was destroyed in the Reformation in 1538,[19] but religious pilgrims have been congregating at Walsingham ever since Richeldis de Faverches had her vision-journey to Mary's original Nazareth home—where the Annunciation of the immaculate conception of Jesus Christ was announced by the Archangel Gabriel—and was asked to duplicate it here as a Holy House. Even today, the approach to Walsingham, through Newmarket, Brandon, and Fakenham, is quietly sacrosanct, known as the Palmer's Way.[20] The Lady Richeldis witnessed three Marian apparitions in all; in one, Mary said the shrine's atmosphere would emphasize the mystery of the Annunciation.

There are two geomantic features at Walsingham that work with the Marian apparitional residue. First, a landscape zodiac, or miniature holographic star map, one of the Earth's 432; this one is about 30 miles in diameter. Set within this interactive wheel of star forms is a Golden Egg, one of the Earth's 666. The Golden Egg facilitates the birth of the Christ Child, or consciousness, in a landscape, as well as in those people interacting with it over time. The Holy House was originally sited in the Maidenwell position of the Golden Egg. Picture a Madonna enfolding a childlike egg in her long arms; her head, heart, and arms are the Maidenwell feature of the Golden Egg—a kind of umbilical cord.

Since the site's dedication in 1061 with Lady Richeldis's Marian visions, the Golden Egg has been hatched, and the Christ Child is expressed in the land. It now works well as an annunciation site for the possibility of the birth of the Christ Child—the Higher Self expressed as a divine child—within the humans visiting. Just to sit for a while within the Walsingham atmosphere can be sufficient, if you wish, to catalyze the process of hatching the Golden Egg within each of us. That the Walsingham Golden Egg is set within a landscape zodiac adds the extra dimension of contacting the Christ Child in the context of the panoply of stars and their energies and qualities of consciousness that comprise the Self.

LOURDES, FRANCE: The geomantic features at Lourdes are twofold. First, the entire area, including the Grotto of Massabielle and Montagne des Espelugues, is under the influence of a dome cap from the dome over nearby Grand Jer Mountain. This dome cap acts as a downward-facing concave dish or parabolic mirror, several miles in diameter and half that distance high, to concentrate the energies of the second feature, a Ray Master Sanctuary.

This can be conceived as a large concave basin on the land upon which fountain and flame the consciousness and energy of the particular Ray Master. In this case, it is Ray Master No. 11, Quan Yin, the compassionate mother aspect of the Virgin Mary complex. Dome cap above, Ray Master Sanctuary below—you have a closed system with a nice feedback loop between star energy (the dome affiliation of the host dome) and Ray Master energy (the flavor of the Ray).[21]

Here the Marian impulse is able to affect an aspect of the physical environment—namely, the water that bubbles up at the spring; ever since Bernadette Soubirous exposed the spring at Mary's request, pilgrims have come to Lourdes for the spring's healing, even miraculous, properties.

KNOCK, IRELAND: Before Knock became Ireland's premier Marian pilgrimage site, it did not seem to have any features that would recommend it as a sanctified geomantic site. A windswept village, it overlooked flat country in the southeast of Mayo County in the west of Ireland; in the 1870s, prior to the visitation, Knock was impoverished and virtually unknown, "a remote, inaccessible spot, a place of 'forgotten fields and forlorn farmhouses,'" and barely a dozen homes huddled about a small church dedicated to Saint John the Baptist.[22]

Straight west overland from Knock about 30 miles is Cruach Padraig, Saint Patrick's Stack or Mountain, a mountainous cone of quartzite standing 2,510 feet over Clew Bay. Cruach Padraig is Ireland's holy mountain and the focus of an annual summer pilgrimage centered on August 1. Here, many centuries ago, Saint Patrick is credited with driving the snakes out of Ireland and overcoming Corra, the Great Swallower, a female demon who lived inside the peak.

The Marian apparition occurred only once at Knock, on a rainy, late afternoon on August 21, 1879, but it was unforgettable, according to the 14 witnesses who testified they'd seen it. The south gable of Knock church was irradiated with a brilliant golden light. Within this luminous globe were three figures standing just above the ground, seemingly like statues, except they were moving: the Virgin Mary, Saint Joseph (her husband), and Saint John the Baptist. Behind them was an altar with a large cross, and in front of that a young lamb, and at least two hovering angels. Mary wore a crown with glittering crosses with a rose at her forehead; her hands were extended apart and upward, as if saying the Mass, her eyes focused heavenward.

To her right was Saint Joseph, his head bowed in reverence. To her left was Saint John the Baptist, dressed like a bishop, a large open book in one hand, the other gesturing as if emphasizing a point. In today's parlance, we'd say the apparition had the quality of a hologram; in 1879, one of the witnesses walked up to the apparition and could discern the words on the book's pages. None of the figures said anything or delivered any messages; Mary was afterward known at Knock as Our Lady of Silence. No matter. Within a week, miraculous cures were reported at Knock, and the pilgrims started arriving.

Today the village of Knock is organized around the Basilica of Our Lady, Queen of Ireland, which opened in 1976 and can accommodate 14,000 people. The wall of the original church that was the site of the 1879 apparition has been enclosed in glass and is contained within the Basilica as an object of veneration. It's estimated that 1.5 million people visit Knock every year, attending Mass, performing the Stations of the Cross, the Mysteries of the Rosary, and other Catholic devotional activities.

At least three geomantic features at Knock provide a suitable context and receptacle for the Marian apparition. First, a Ray Master Sanctuary occupies the religious center of Knock; it is dedicated to Ray Master No. 10, the deep yellow whose expressions have included Lao Tzu and Saint Patrick. This fact accounts for why Saint Patrick reportedly blessed Knock in the fifth century, foretelling its future as a Marian shrine: He was already there through his Sanctuary. He was also activating or at least tuning up the Sanctuary as part of his overall geomantic work with the energy features at Cruach Padraig.

Second, the landscape about and under the Basilica holds a Tree of Life template. This template, imprinted long ago, was activated by a kind of preset timer at the time of the Marian apparition, or perhaps the apparition itself activated it. The Basilica, and the original church, is set in the second tier of the Tree of Life, in the Second World called Briah, while the Third and Fourth Worlds flow over a broad open walkway leading up to the building; the First World, Assiyah, is behind the Basilica.

Third, the Knock site has a chakra template, about the same size as the Tree of Life, or about one-half mile long. The heart chakra position occurs where the Basilica stands and in the Second World of the Tree of Life template.[23] Sitting in the Basilica, essentially in the energy residue or holographic numinous memory of the 1879 apparition, pilgrims get a fusion of heart chakra and Second World energies and consciousness.

Approaching the Basilica from a distance, you have the opportunity to walk through the chakras and the two lower worlds of the Tree of Life—and all of this under the spiritual auspices of the Ray Master Sanctuary. You walk through the first three energy centers or chakras, aligning yourself with the energies templated on the landscape here, and through the first two Worlds, arriving at the Basilica and the threshold of the heart chakra and Third World.[24]

FATIMA, PORTUGAL: The Marian apparitions at Fatima, Portugal, were preceded in 1916 by three appearances of the Guardian Angel of Portugal in a hilly area outside town called the Chousa Velha, used for sheep grazing. Fatima was then a hamlet, elevation three thousand feet, about 110 miles north of Lisbon. A male angelic figure, reportedly of dazzling splendor, appeared within a light whiter than snow, as the children called it, describing himself as an Angel of Peace and the Angel of Portugal. He appeared before the three children, aged six to nine. He gave them Holy Communion and prostrated himself before the Eucharist, offering a prayer to Mary and the Christ. In retrospect, he was preparing both ground and visionaries—geomantically, all of Portugal—for the Marian appearances to come.

The next year, the same children experienced the apparitions of the Virgin Mary in the Cova da Iria, a rocky pasture within the

Chousa Velha; between May 13 and October 13, 1917, there were six appearances as well as unusual, anomalous physical effects, described previously. Today, the basilica of Our Lady of Fatima stands near the Cova da Iria, as Mary requested.[25]

Among the many unusual physical effects that accompanied Mary's Fatima apparitions was the shower of rose petals that vanished on touching the ground. Vedic literature recounts many instances in which flower petal showers accompanied celestial visitations or expressed auspicious affirmations by the observing gods of events either in the spiritual worlds or on Earth. The Vedic accounts also report that the gods would shower great personalities with flowers, such as roses or white blossoms, to mark victories or other key events.[26]

The startling appearance of Portugal's Guardian Angel as a herald of the Marian apparitions is actually a clue to the site's geomantic function. The Chousa Velha area is one of the Earth's 72 minor chakra points, or Energy Focusing Nodes. Each of the 72 original landmass subdivisions of the Earth's surface and its corresponding folk or people were assigned a Guardian Angel. These beings are also known as Tutelary Princes of the Nations and egregors. The Fatima children beheld Portugal's egregor at Chousa Velha because that is his grounding point for Portugal, his geomantic base of operations for that nation (Portugal's umbilicus). The geomantic feature is the Energy Focusing Node, or minor Earth chakra; the attendant deity there is Portugal's egregor, or National Guardian Angel.

The Portugal Guardian Angel of course was already positioned at the Energy Focusing Node of that landmass before the 1917 apparitions. But once the apparitions occurred, that egregor's function was expanded to include protecting and nurturing the Marian residue set within that country's spiritual umbilical point.

During one of Mary's apparitions at Fatima, she gave the children what they later described as a vision of the Hell realms and the suffering of souls. They seemed to gaze into an ocean of fire, full of roiling devils and shrieking lost souls. They reported that Mary said, as commentary to this upsetting vista, that God wanted to establish devotion to Mary's Immaculate Heart *at this place* as a way of saving the tormented souls in Hell.

Geomantically, this is apt, because where the church now stands is a Lucifer Binding Site. It's as if they dropped the church on his head and pounded him into the ground. Obviously, the Lucifer energy was already at this site, and most likely bound from an earlier time, which somewhat explains the children's fearsome Hell vision, not an experience widely reported at other Marian sites.

As most Christians (mistakenly) equate Lucifer with the Devil and the Hell realms, and as the Virgin Mary stated she wanted to help redeem the Hell souls through her devotion at Fatima, this situation is expressed geomantically by the Virgin Mary's compassionate presence at a Lucifer Binding Site (the portal to the Hell realms in Catholic belief) under the auspices of Portugal's egregor.

Geomantically, this is, ideally, an excellent situation for both the landscape and individuals using this site for purposes beyond those described by Catholic liturgy. A Lucifer Binding Site is a place in the landscape that helps you confront your own Shadow, the unexpressed, repressed, denied aspects of yourself. Such a site contains equivalent rejected cultural material from the society at large and, ultimately, from all of humanity since its inception on Earth. It is a vast astral dumping ground for all the unwanted parts of the human collective psyche, conveniently demonized as Lucifer, the proud fallen (and punished) angel in conventional theology.

But as you start to address your Shadow (and possibly, under training or supervision, the collective Shadow) at a Lucifer Binding Site, then here at Fatima, you have the benevolence of the compassionate goddess as a balm for your efforts and possible difficulties. Lucifer, if he is to be unbound at this site, will, when it happens, also have the benefit of Mary's presence as a spiritual restorative and healing agent.

Mary's presence at Fatima is further enhanced by the presence of a Ray Master Sanctuary at this site. As one clairvoyant described it, Mother Mary's "Retreat" is located in the etheric above (or within) the physical site in a temple with a healing flame burning on an altar. "There is a stream of light that flows like a mighty waterfall from the etheric temple to the physical focus [the Basilica] and to the present hour pilgrims are healed by the 'waters' of the healing flame." Images in "living spirit fire" of angelic orders and perfected

Christed Ones under the supervision of the Archangel Raphael are also present.[27]

EZKIOGA, SPAIN: Starting in June 1931, two young children in the Basque village of Ezkioga (then spelled Esquioga; 1931 population: 550) of northern Spain saw the Virgin Mary on a hillside above the town. Soon others had similar visions nightly for several months. Many people had multiple visions, as many as 30 in the case of a 17-year-old female seer.

As word spread throughout this region of Spain, pilgrims flocked by the thousands to Ezkioga and its Vision Deck, a platform erected on the hillside at the epicenter of the apparitions. By the end of 1931, an estimated one million had come, sometimes as many as 15,000 to 20,000 people on a single evening; on four occasions, when physical miracles had been predicted, 80,000 people were present. In some respects, the Ezkioga apparitions seemed a gift to the Basques. "It is possible that more persons gathered on that hillside on July 18 and October 16 [1931] than had ever gathered in one place in the Basque Country before."[28]

Unlike many of the other Marian apparition sites, at Ezkioga the visionary encounter with Mary was not so much dependent on the seership or grace of a few individuals. Rather, it seemed the site itself evoked the visionary experiences. In the first month of the apparitions, over one hundred different people reported apparitional experiences. Typically, a resplendent cloud of light heralded Mary's appearance to the chosen psychics; the cloud or nimbus of light would then open to reveal her in the middle crowned with stars. One seer described light in the form of a halo with a radius of 12 feet; in the middle of that brightness appeared Mary dressed in mourning, as the Virgin of the Sorrows, the Dolorosa.

During 1932, many of the Ezkioga seers began a new phase of what they called passive sacrifice in which they experienced mimic crucifixions. This "mystic fad" began in January and peaked on Good Friday a few months later. On that day, dozens of children and adults "writhed on the Ezkioga stage in simultaneous agony feeling imaginary nails being driven through their hands and feet and lances piercing their sides."[29] Previously, and peaking on Lent, many Ezkioga seers had led groups up the hillside as they recited the

Stations of the Cross; the seers reported experiencing these stations as if they each were Christ.

No record exists of any diocesan priest having a Marian vision at Ezkioga, and while many local priests were supportive of the events and the seers, the Church itself actively sought to discredit, invalidate, and even shut it all down. The original seers, the children, were put in an insane asylum for tests of sanity, though they were later released with a clean mental bill of health.

Both priests and apparition participants and believers realized that Mary's appearances on the Ezkioga hillside and the respectful, sometimes ecstatic response of thousands of pilgrims, had rendered it a sacred landscape. A Franciscan monk noted "the place itself had been converted into a living shrine." The surrounding mountains were its walls and the "immaculate vault of heaven" its roof. Antonio Amundarain, a priest from Zumarraga, a nearby town, said: "The apparition site has begun now to be regarded with veneration and the greatest respect; it has become a place of prayer, of recollection, of greater faith and piety."[30]

From a geomantic viewpoint, Mary was settling her apparition upon *prepared ground*, at a site with predetermined visionary geographic features. Between her repeated apparitions there and the positive response of the thousands who stood on the Ezkioga hillside, the site's inherent sanctity was grounded and amplified by the numinous events that took place between 1931 and 1936.[31]

Ezkioga's inherent sanctity or preexisting geomantic structure has four parts: dome cap, energy funnel, Silver Egg, and Albion minor chakra point.

The dome cap is several miles wide, broad enough to accommodate the village and the hillside; it originates from a dome over a nearby mountain. The dome cap gives Ezkioga its initial, numinous ground; it establishes the area as holy space, as a sacred site awaiting its epiphany and human recognition.

The energy funnel starts in or below the village and runs up the hill; although its route was not marked in recent times with a double row of trees, as has been customary in many energy funnel sites, the well-worn pilgrimage path up the hillside more or less serves the same purpose.

The subtle temple at the end (or beginning) of the energy funnel corresponds approximately with the physical placement of the Vision Deck upon which the visionaries had their Marian encounters and, later, their mimic crucifixions. The temple itself is much larger than the deck, of course—probably, if transposed to physical dimensions, the size of the entire hillside. But the Vision Deck is placed essentially in the physical correlate of the temple's inner sanctum.

Into this superposition of Vision Deck and energy funnel temple came the Virgin Mary in her fourfold expression. There slowly turns the pedestal with the four deific faces of Kali, Durga, Quan Yin, and Mary. Very few if any of the Ezkioga seers reported seeing Mary in her Madonna-with-child guise. Here at Ezkioga, the Christ is present in his mature, adult form, in what the ancient Egyptians would have called the Elder Horus and the Greeks, Dionysus. The Elder Christ is present here by virtue of the hatched Silver Egg at the hillside.

Geomantically, each of the 1,080 Silver Eggs around the Earth hatches the same thing: the Elder Horus, which is the mature Christ in his far-seeing aspect. At some point in the recent history of Ezkioga, an initiate hatched this Silver Egg, which is to say, underwent the appropriate interactive energy exchange with it so as to facilitate the emergence of its true, inner essence, the holographic presence of the Elder Horus or Christ. It seems fitting, even logical, that many of the Ezkioga visionaries felt drawn to enact the Stations of the Cross and the mimic crucifixions at the hillside; these inner experiences are a kind of foundation or on-ramp to an encounter with or higher dimensional experience of the Elder Christ.

For Elder Christ, think, post-Ascension, or pre-Ascension, before or after the incarnation—the Christ in his ultimate, eternal cosmic essence. Here, the Virgin Mary's role (in actuality, the fourfold goddess) is as conductor of souls to the Christ reality. Unlike other Marian apparition sites—where, for example, Mary is presented in her Madonna guise, as the on-ramp to the birth of the Christ Child within the pilgrim—here things stand at the opposite end of this continuum. The Christ is already achieved; he's been to Earth and ascended.

Yet here he is again, sword in hand, with a nimbus of hundreds of flaming red Seraphim angels around him, the same angelic host that provided his holy escort during the Ascension. It's not surprising that, in the latter days of the Ezkioga visionary cycle, some seers added an apocalyptic flavor to the apparitions. Some reported Mary had spoken of chastisements and balancings of accounts against sinners, cities, even countries.

They took their Catholic catechism seriously; it said Christ will return to Earth to exact the Last Judgment. So if he's seen at Ezkioga, the Last Judgment must be at hand. One Spanish visionary reported a prophecy attributed to Christ that "the hour of my Reign in Spain approaches." Ezkioga visionaries started seeing angelic hosts brandishing bloody swords, or fighting demonic hordes or human infidels on the mountain ridges around Ezkioga. Even the least glimpse of the tableaux of the Elder Christ with sword in a corona of flaming Seraphim could inspire apocalyptic, retributory psychic pictures like these.

The general tone of the Ezkioga visionary reports and their interpretation and commentary by supporters throughout Spain gave the apparitions a certain Basque-centered flavor, even purpose. The apparitions occurred just before the dreadful Spanish Civil War, which erupted in 1936 just after the Ezkioga apparitions seemed to conclude. Many commentators gave the entire apparition spectacle a quasi-political or spiritual-political spin, and even this rather obvious human filtering of a transcendent event has a geomantic base.

Ezkioga is a minor chakra point (one of 72; the left elbow) of a large-scale regional geomantic figure called an Albion, whose subtle form stretches across France, Spain, Portgual, and the British Isles.[32] There are 12 such figures on Earth, and each is a composite of the entirety of the human collective over time; it is also a mirror of what esoteric traditions and many myths call the Anthropos or Cosmic Man, all of creation expressed as a transcendent universal human.

These Albions are presently perceived to be sleeping, but the one just described, which I call the Virgo Albion (because it's under the astrological influence of the constellation of Virgo) is slated to be the first of the 12 to awaken through geomantic activation. Events at Ezkioga were an important contributory awareness spark injected into this vast geomantic form. Whether or not the eventual awakening of the Virgo Albion fulfills the millennialist expectations of the

1930s Basque Marian seers, in light of this geomantic explanation it's not hard to understand how such expectations could arise.

GARABANDAL, SPAIN: Consistent with the theme of confronting and assimilating the Shadow as at Fatima is the geomantic nature of the Marian site at Garabandal, Spain. This is a mountain hamlet of only a few hundred people at an elevation of two thousand feet; the village sits in the Cantabrian Mountains in a dry, rocky, almost treeless valley as if clinging to the sides of two adjacent hills. The apparitions occurred in a rock-lined waterway, dry except during heavy rains and known as the *calleja,* or ravine. At the top of the *calleja* is a place now known almost devotionally as The Pines, a low hill crowned by a cluster of pine trees.

The church has not officially "authenticated" the apparitions here, and between 1961 and 1987, the diocesan bishop urged Catholics to ignore the events at Garabandal (the ban was lifted by his successor). Even so, thousands of pilgrims come annually to the shrine of Our Lady of Carmel.

At Garabandal, we find two geomantic features: a Prana Distributor and an Underworld Entrance. The Prana Distributor (288 on Earth) is the planetary expression of a spiritual feature Judaic mysticism says humans have within them: 288 Sparks. These are described by Qabalists as variations on the utterance of the Divine Name, sparks of God-Light. Geomantically, the Prana Distributor is a means of infusing the Earth's visionary geography with cosmic life force, where, to use a metaphor, God can gently exhale Spirit into the Earth's light body. A Prana Distributor preserves a spark of the original, pure Light of creation. You might think of it as a spiritual waterfall, full of uplifting celestial negative ions.

The second feature, the Underworld Entrance, presents itself unusually, as if turned inside out. Persian mysticism speaks of the Chinvat Bridge, or the Bridge of the Separator. After death, you cross this bridge: If your sins are heavy, the bridge narrows and you fall off; if your sins are light, you make it across. You are assisted by what the Persians call the Daena, an angelic maiden who represents the original purity of your soul before and after all incarnations.

At Garabandal, you encounter the Chinvat Bridge (a pale blue edifice) at the *calleja* where it crosses it perpendicularly. At the end of the Bridge is a huge golden lion's face that seems to be inside a physical rock mass. The lion's mouth is open wide, and you pass through its mouth, through the larynx, into what I call the Cave of Your Astral Body. It's probably the same as the Greek and Egyptian Judgment Halls. The judgment is your own review of the contents of your astral body, the light and dark, beatific and beastly, things you've done. It's all there: everything you've barely or not even been aware of in your present life, and the cumulation of the same from all your lives—your undigested karma.

This is acutely relevant in light of the forecasts given by Mary to the Spanish children in the 1960s. The children reported that Mary gave notice of an imminent "world-wide warning from God" to be seen and felt interiorly by everyone around the planet. The Warning's purpose would be to "correct the conscience" of the world. It would be a "revelation of our sins" as each person would have an "interior experience of how they stand in the light of God's Justice." It would be a purifying experience, to "see in ourselves our conscience."

The Warning would first be seen everywhere in the air, then be immediately transmitted into the inner experience of every human, the children were told. The Warning would prepare everyone for the Great Miracle to occur in The Pines and leave there a "Permanent Sign," visible yet supernatural, which would endure there as testimony "until the end of time." It would be something never before seen on the Earth. If humanity failed to get with the program after these three events, then God would send what Mary called "the Chastisement," which involves inescapable fire that even immersion in water cannot subdue.

The emphasis on the correction of conscience ties the Marian prophecy at Garabandal directly to the site's geomantic Underworld Entrance feature. Time spent in the Cave of Your Astral Body is certainly an invitation to review and correct your conscience, even to birth it in the light of heightened awareness. Esoteric traditions maintain that you normally experience the contents of your astral body after death, but through the Underworld Entrance (and at Garabandal, with the additional compassionate support of the Marian presence), you may do so while still living and embodied. That is particularly valuable because the weight of your "sins" (karmic residue, the astral body contents) were created while you were embodied and likewise can only be expiated while you are living.

SAN DAMIANO, ITALY: At San Damiano, a mountain village 45 miles southeast of Milan, Italy, Rosa Quattrini reported a series of Marian apparitions beginning in 1964. The Virgin appeared in Rosa's vineyard above a barren pear tree, which subsequently bloomed as a confirmation by Mary of her presence there. Over the next 20 years, Rosa recorded approximately two thousand Virgin Mary encounters and accompanying messages, typically on Friday afternoons.

In 1965, Mary indicated the precise spot in the vineyard where Rosa should have a well dug for the purposes of providing miraculous, healing water to the faithful who would come to San Damiano. A "great source of graces will come out" of this pure water; it will be a "water of salvation for numerous souls," Mary told Rosa, who noted that the Madonna on this occasion was accompanied by Archangels Michael, Gabriel, and Raphael. This water, sanctified by Mary at this spot, would cleanse the body and soul of all pilgrims, even free one from obsessions, Mary told Rosa. The well was dug and the water made available. On one holy day in 1971, it produced 50,000 liters (13,000 gallons).

As at Lourdes, the provision of sanctified, healing waters at a previously unknown and unvisited site grounded the Marian presence there and gave the public a visible, tangible reason for making a pilgrimage to it. It is probably currently impossible to quantify and thus "prove" the Marian apparitional influence on the water, but in some sense those consuming the blessed water were enabled to take into their body a kind of spiritually amplified substance.

At San Damiano we have an example of the Virgin Mary enhancing a site's preexistent geomantic and numinous features by adding something new: Marian sanctified water. Rosa later reported that Mary had named her apparitional site her "Garden of Paradise" and envisioned there a "City of the Roses" to serve especially the needs of orphaned children, the pious elderly, and the sick. It would have 15 altars (to symbolize the 15 mysteries of the Rosary), and be a large "sanctuary."

This is a fascinating and valuable clue, for here Mary has indicated the site's geomantic and spiritual function, both present and future. Mary has provided a vision of the site's eventual (or desired) unfolding beyond its initial geomantic recognition and activation in present times as a holy site. It will be, someday, a Marian site plus an additional feature, the City of the Roses.

The Garden of Paradise reference, judging by Mary's quoted remarks to Rosa, is meant to be a physically symbolic rendition of the Garden of Eden, with its tree, well, and running waters—"the garden of origins," Mary told Rosa. She also said: "This place [the apparitional site] has a double vocation. It is a call and a point of arrival. It is a sending and a starting point." The site was consecrated by God; it is the pilgrim's "refuge in my heart," a place of prayer one day to be "big and great," and Mary will always be here "with the angels and the saints."[33]

The geomantic interpretation of the San Damiano site confirms Mary's prevision of the site's probable or desired future development. First, it is a Ray Master Sanctuary, a prepared template, almost a landscape serving dish, for the Marian presence. Once she touched down in current times, the Sanctuary (visually it looks like a broad concave dish with a central fountain inside a temple) imprint and its radiating potential will remain for a long time.

Second, the Sanctuary is complemented by the dual presence of a Pointer's Ball and an Arc of Ascending Consciousness. The Pointer's Ball is a conduit into other dimensions, a portal or dimensional crack between our spacetime reality and others, in the spiritual worlds and other physical ones. The Arc of Ascending Consciousness is like an on-ramp to the Ball, a preparatory, ambulatory approach to the Ball. You could more or less walk the physical route of the Arc across the greater San Damiano landscape. As an energy feature, the Arc resembles a curved, enclosed energy corridor several miles long, terminating at San Damiano.

Given the presence of these three geomantic features at San Damiano, you can begin to see why Mary called the place a point of arrival and sending. The Pointer's Ball feature would largely account for that. The three features together are sufficient to create such a field of heightened numinosity—a Paradise bubble, if you wish, and hence Mary's stated Garden of Paradise template—that you could, if psychically open to it, walk from our present time into an already achieved future (Mary's City of the Roses), which is presented in its light form at that site and awaiting its eventual and matching physical manifestation there.

My psychic impression of this site is that Mary should be taken at her word. This site, with its combination of three geomantic features, would be marvelous for healing and mystical immersion in the transcendental reality of Mary's Sanctuary on the "Other Side"—that is, in the spiritual worlds. The intent here is to have some or all of the subtle features grounded in the physical with approximate structures and land use features, so that visitors may participate in a blended reality of the physical and spiritual.

According to Rosa's report, Mary said her Sanctuary, in its spiritual reality, is already decorated with flowers, mostly roses, to represent all the peoples of the world, "the multiple graces of the divine love," and the possibility of each human soul being "transformed into a divine rose."[34]

MEDJUGORJE, BOSNIA: Since June 24, 1981, when the Marian apparitions and messages began, Medjugorje has welcomed an estimated 20 million pilgrims to its Hill of Apparitions, in the early days at the rate of ten thousand daily. This is the local name for Crnica Hill (also called Mount Podbrdo), above the hamlet of Podbrdo; Medjugorje itself means "area between two mountains," the other being Krizevach Hill (Cross Mountain or Hill of Calvary),[35] above the hamlet of Medjugorje, a mountain community of about 3,500 Croatians.

As with some other Marian sites, the spiritual activities at Medjugorje were seen in advance in a vision. Sister Briege McKenna, an Irish nun, was visiting Bosnia in May 1981 when in a vision she saw Father Tomislav Vlasic, her host, in a "twin-towered church sitting in a chair and surrounded by a great crowd." Underneath the chair there flowed "streams of powerful healing water" out onto the people and the landscape, she reported. A month later, the apparitions started.[36]

The Marian apparitions have occurred at Crnica, but hundreds of healings, some quite remarkable, have been registered at Krizevach. Mary is said to pray there every day. The two sites, plus a third (the parish Church of Saint James, the village's patron saint), comprise the "prayer zone" of Medjugorje and are the focus of a steady influx of pilgrims. Evening Mass is said every day in the prayer zone, and in 1999, an estimated one million visitors took Holy Communion. Under the steady influence of Mary—they call her *Gospa* here—Medjugorje has become known as the "world's confessional," a sacramental center where people come to reconcile in penance with themselves, others, and God.

Since the apparitions began, the Virgin Mary has transmitted a series of messages to what were then, in 1981, six Croatian children. Since then, it is said she has revealed ten secrets about the forthcoming fate of the world and a kind of eschatological schedule for the Final Days that will include three "warnings" and a demonstration or "permanent sign" to be left palpably at Medjugorje. One prime mission of the apparitions, Mary declared, was to prove God exists.

Mary has been quoted by the Croatian visionaries as describing Mount Podbrdo as "a Tabor." The Transfiguration of Christ is believed to have happened on Mount Tabor in Israel, and it's said three of his disciples witnessed the Christ in his newly expressed glory.[37] Applied to Medjugorje, one interpretation is that "the special privilege" granted to the disciples at Tabor "was being extended to the Medjugorje visionaries, and through them, to all who open their hearts to God." In another communication, Mary said "this parish is elected by me and is special" and "different from others" such that she was bestowing "great graces" to all those who prayed there from their heart.[38]

The apparitions of the Virgin Mary, declared Prof. Paul M. Zulehner, a pastoral theologian from Vienna, in 1988, lead one to the scriptures and the heart of faith. "The Blessed Mother is not an end in herself but a sign-post" for people wanting to "live the Word of God" and celebrate the Eucharist, and to carry that "eucharistic devotion" home with them from Medjugorje. Zulehner also observed that the site is a "mystagogy" that leads people into the depths of a mystery in which God opens the human heart from the outside. The result, potentially, is a "mystical renewal in the encounter of man with God."[39]

Zulehner's remarks are particularly interesting in light of

Medjugorje's geomantic situation and function. First, there is a dome over Crnica Hill and Krizevach (this being a higher continuation of the same landmass), corresponding to a star in the constellation Lepus (the Hare). The 48 dome caps generated by this dome (several miles wide) are capable of distributing the spiritual events and energies at the Medjugorje dome out across the land. The Lepus dome over the Medjugorje prayer zone sanctifies the entire area. Everything for perhaps a five-mile radius out from the two hills is under the spiritual amplification and numinosity emitted by this dome—a huge temple of light.

Second, the Crnica-Krizevach Hill complex is the site of a Hall of Records Labyrinth, one of the planet's 12. The labyrinth itself is removed from the physical dimension but to psychic perception resembles a traditional labyrinth. At the heart of the form is the Hall of Records, a depository of information pertaining to the Earth and its relations with stars, planets, and galaxies. Experientially, this is a highly esoteric and refined geomantic feature, and at first blush seems remote from the overlay of Catholic dogma and ritual at the site.

But let's recall the intriguing references cited about Medjugorje being a mystagogy, a training ground for encountering the Mysteries, and that the apparitions of the Virgin Mary were not the end in itself, but a sign-post to a deeper, eucharistic understanding of spiritual mysteries and God's reality. Let's say that Mary is the stylus that plays the record in this labyrinth. The content of the messages, the exhortations to prayer, mass, and communion, and the vast layering of piety, expectation, and Catholic belief upon her apparitional presence gives people a form or container to approach the Mysteries, something people can, if they choose, *see through* to the truth of her presence *there.*

In effect, Mary stands at the center of this Hall of Records labyrinth, and she conducts you in. She is the doorway, the psychopomp, the transparency, pointing to something beyond her, although most tend to see her as the altar. To an extent, the revelation of Medjugorje is not yet manifest; the information in the Hall of Records labyrinth has not yet been "downloaded" and distributed, though the Marian presence has now been well distributed through the dome cap network as a preparation for the next phase.

Mary is also a guide for a profound experience available here. When she referred to Medjugorje as "a Tabor," a site of transfiguration, she was indicating its third geomantic feature, and a sublime one at that. Here it is helpful (though dogmatically unconventional) to conceive of the Transfiguration of Christ as a demonstration of a stage of initiation and development available to all humans.

As one authority on the esoteric interpretation of Christ wrote, Master Jesus "re-enacted all the five human initiations for the benefit of humanity." The Transfiguration is the third initiation, but the first major one (the first two being threshold experiences), and here "the personality is irradiated by the full light of the soul and the three personality vehicles are completely transcended."[40]

We tend to look outside ourselves, especially when a Marian apparition hallows a site such as Medjugorje, and deify the outer revelation, but the real message of Mary at Medjugorje and why she calls it a Tabor is that its energies can facilitate the emergence of the Christ light *in* every person there. Then the revelation is the epiphany of light, the glory (within the matter of the body) when the Christ light suffuses and changes the entire living body. Here the experience of individual transfiguration is guided and "birthed" by Mary.

In fact, the Marian apparitions were partly a ruse to draw world attention to this site and to get people coming to it in our present time. Once there, Mary is available as a mentor, psychopomp, and compassionate mother for the fiery transfiguration process. Geomantically, you could say the Tabor is a concentration of Spirit, a fire seed, at the energetic center of the site, which heats up the indwelling Spirit in each human visitor so that eventually—days, years, lives—it transfigures the person entirely.

The Tabor is a geomantic feature found at other places around the Earth. To me it looks like a golden teardrop-shaped seed with a human figure inside. The tear also resembles a broad shallow plate slipped in horizontally through the mountain. The figure inside is variously known as the Monad, Spirit, God of Your Heart, Higher Self. In everyday terms, this means the continuity of consciousness that you (as an embodied individual) stem from, that which initiates all the incarnations you have ever had, or will have, and the reasons why.

The Tabor of course is not your Higher Self, but the archetype of the figure. It is a template, a model, of the completed transfiguration of ego to Self to stimulate that same process in you, if you wish. You certainly are changed when this energy of higher awareness and purpose infiltrates your mind and body. Think of the Tabor as an *irresistible* impetus to transfigure, to invite the God of Your Heart to enter your life and start to breathe through it, expanding you.

The Tabor is also describable as an Emerald, a feature I discuss in chapter 3 in the context of the Christ experience of Transfiguration at Mount Tabor.

In terms of a geomantic use of Marian apparition sites, you could, for example, facilitate the birth of the Christ Child within you by spending time at a Golden Egg site, such as Walsingham. Later, after this new living impulse has matured a bit within you, you could deepen its suffusion through your body by spending time at a Tabor Transfiguration site, such as Medjugorje.

It's a slow process; I have described it like time-lapse photography. It could take a long while, or could happen instantaneously. You can sense evidence of this possibility in some of the comments made by visitors to Medjugorje, as paraphrased here:[41] Its miracle is conversion, the rediscovery of faith, reunification with God; its function is the celebration of salvation in the Holy Spirit; one experiences here the closeness of God, the grace of redemption, a touch of Heaven; it is a place of holy exuberance, of spiritual lightning bolts, where Mary harvests souls for Christ in the perfect parish.

OLIVETO CITRA, ITALY: On the evening of May 24, 1985, in the Italian hilltop village of Oliveto Citra, about two hours southeast of Naples, a group of boys, aged eight to 12, reported an apparition of the Madonna at the gates of an abandoned medieval hillside castle. They had first seen a luminous trail streak across the sky and mistook it for a falling star. Then they saw the Madonna with a babe in arms. Soon a young woman saw the Virgin Mary outside the castle gate, with all the expected features: indescribably beautiful, dressed in white, wearing a blue mantle and crowned in stars, and holding the Christ infant in her arms. This young woman experienced 30 more apparitions of the Virgin Mary until her father forbade it.

Unlike most Marian apparition sites, not one seer or even a small group of seers would ultimately run point on the visions and messages. Over the course of at least five years, the Madonna appeared to new seers every day, and in different, even contradictory ways, as if to defy deliberately the dogma of her expected appearance. Within the first year of her apparitional debut, Mary was seen by an estimated seven hundred to one thousand people, and 50 said she spoke to them.

She told a woman that first night in May, "I have not chosen you alone, because many will see Me, but only those who have the courage to believe will remain."[42] In fact, one fascinating aspect of the Oliveto Citra apparitional sequence was its nondoctrinaire or even antidoctrinal content and style. There was no single charismatic psychic mediating the visions (such as Bernadette Soubirous at Lourdes or the handful of children at Fatima or Medjugorje) or acting as the central point of reference, authority, or validation, so "every pilgrim was impelled to experience, in ways more or less sharp and evident, this connection for him or herself."[43]

Of course, people in authority always seek to control apparitional phenomena, and soon the Queen of the Castle Committee was formed in Oliveto Citra to adjudicate the authenticity of reported visions. The parish priest looked favorably on the apparitions because of their fruits: conversions, increased religious observance, and an enhancement of the spiritual tenor of the village. Within less than five months of the first report, at least 10,249 pilgrims had visited the tiny community of Oliveto Citra (1980s population: about 4,000) and signed a visitor's register; two hundred prayer groups had formed throughout Italy to recite, at the same time, daily prayers from Oliveto Citra; and the medieval castle and the village itself became sacralized.

The castle had already gained a reputation for apparitions, including that of a "lady in black," certain nocturnal processions of the dead—and as the place of former "disgusting deeds" of the medieval castle lords (which is to say, a place that carried a polluted psychic residue from past dark acts and abusive energies). Legends of apparitions of spirits in distress arose out of this.

The apparitional form of the Virgin Mary is actually not the prime geomantic feature or reason for visiting Oliveto Citra. She is its psychopomp. It's not surprising that the hill and ruined castle had a reputation for distorted numinosity; often European castles were sited at places that had a reputation for being what today we call a sacred site, and a dome cap sits over this hill and all of Oliveto Citra, giving the enclosed area its prime spiritual charge. But it is what is inside the hill (and in another dimension) that should draw our attention.

Mary stands at the entrance to a golden rotunda inside of which is a geomantic feature I call an Ixion Wheel. It is an initiation chamber for induction into the mysteries of the Solar Logos, the throat chakra, and Christ speech. You lie down on your back in the chamber, which is shaped like a cross set into a wheel or round table; the feature is a structured receptacle for receiving the Solar Logos stream from the Sun. This may also be experienced as a sword stroke, the "sword" being the Word focused and concentrated and inserted into you.

You would use such a feature as part of your multiaspected initiation into the Christ mysteries; the Solar Logos is the Christ or Word made manifest through speech. So here the purpose is to facilitate that speech-inspiring infusion. At Oliveto Citra, you receive the blessings and orientation by Mary acting as the soul guide to the inner temple and your facilitator; then you experience the Solar Logos aspect of the Christ through the Ixion Wheel inside the temple.

With the Virgin Mary appearing and speaking to many of the faithful at Oliveto Citra, it would be easy to assume that her apparition was the focus. But from a geomantic point of view, it is more like Mary reopened the temple. You pass through her apparitional energy field as a psychic *preparation* for the main event inside, which is *your* experience of the Solar Logos, a Christ aspect.

No one charismatic visionary emerged as the prime interlocutor between Mary and the community of pilgrims; rather, everyone had their own individualized experiences. This is fitting for the Christ speech Mysteries with respect to the experience of Pentecost. In that experience, each of the 12 Apostles was so filled with the Holy Spirit that he could speak as the Logos, could communicate in "tongues"— which is to say, individualize his Christ speaking to fit the context and spiritual level of his listener—with the result that witnesses could not tell the Apostles apart from the Christ because they sounded like him. Without the dogmatic structuring of the Marian interface at

Oliveto Citra, users of that site can potentially have their own individualized encounter.

CONYERS, GEORGIA: The geomantic terrain and a Marian presence have been creating another possibly perfect parish at Conyers, Georgia, since 1990. The Holy Hill, a slight incline on the property of Nancy Fowler, was declared by Jesus (according to a visionary report by Fowler in the early 1990s) to be "Holy," despite its appearance as a "little, insignificant, very ordinary hill."[44]

Taking advantage of the relatively level landscape at Conyers is a landscape zodiac about ten miles in total width (including both halves). The Marian apparitions and messages, the special light and meteorological effects, and the devotions and attitudes of the many visitors there are set in the context of this circle of stars and the stations of the zodiac.

In this respect, the Stations of the Cross and the other liturgical activities at Conyers are performed on the geomantic stage of a star wheel of the cosmic Self, which is the ultimate expression of a landscape zodiac. We might think of the perfected expressions of the 12 astrological signs as the 12 Apostles, and the totality as the Christ. All of this is performed while in the "field" of Mary, who is summoner, host, psychopomp, and nurturer in service to this site.

Also present at Conyers is an esoteric though vital geomantic feature called a Control Bubble. There are 238 of these on the Earth. Think of the Bubble as a sphere containing dials that adjust the flow of consciousness in an area.

Normally, the Bubble adjusts the mixture of angelic, elemental, and cosmic energies moving through a terrestrial landscape. The Conyers Bubble can additionally regulate the flow of Marian consciousness through the geomantic network, thereby subtly influencing a territory that is considerable, given how few Bubbles there are globally. The Marian energy, with the steady presence of human devotional consciousness at Conyers, also acts as "plant food" for the zodiac and seeds for further potential Christ awakenings.

BELLEVILLE, ILLINOIS: The apparitions at Belleville in the 1990s are intriguing to study because here Mary settled into an already prepared Catholic shrine occupying two hundred acres overlooking the Mississippi River Valley near St. Louis, Missouri. The site has many devotional stations and facilities, including a Lourdes

Grotto, chapels, rosary courts, amphitheater, church, and sculpted spire—a veritable Mary theme park. More than one million people enjoy the multifaceted facilities every year.

Overall, the place is called the National Shrine of Our Lady of Snows, and was founded by the Missionary Oblates of Mary Immaculate in 1958.[45] In early 1993, Ray Doiron—in his early sixties and, as he puts it, "a one-hour-a-week Catholic like everybody else"—began seeing the Virgin Mary at Belleville. He may have been a casual Catholic, but he had had his own kind of preparation, which included three near-death experiences and a mystical experience of Jesus.[46]

Actually, the first apparition seemed to emanate from his television, but after that, Mary appeared to Ray in the Lourdes Grotto; when people heard of these visits about six months later, Mary shifted her appearances to the spacious amphitheater, which seats 2,400. During Mary's monthly apparitions to Ray, up to eight thousand people would sit in the amphitheater sharing vicariously in the presence. Typically, she would appear like clockwork, or as if summoned, at the point when the assembled people prayed the mystery of the Visitation, which is the second set of ten Hail Mary beads on the rosary. Ray would see her, record her messages, then after a 45-minute visit, report it to the crowd.

Ray says Mary is young, regal, and beautiful. The Light glows from her and in her, and "her whole body appears to be an eternal light" that radiates all around her. "Something so bright, it is as if I am looking straight into the sun," Ray said. "Our Lady was asked, 'Why are you so beautiful?' She said, 'I am beautiful because I am love.' She told me because She is free from sin and that is the way we will be also in Heaven, in our glorified body."[47]

The Oblate Missionaries prepared the apparitional site for several decades before Mary appeared, but it had been prepared long before that in an earlier cycle of geomantic activation. A very long time ago there was a Light Corrective Center, about one hundred yards across, at the National Shrine. Where the main shrine and amphitheater now stand, there once stood the Center. (You can still see these centers in the British Isles: a broad flat grassy extent surrounded by one or more ditches.) Evidently, all physical traces of this geomantic feature have been erased over time, but here's an impression of what it looks like with the Marian presence:

It looks like a pale blue diamond golf ball set on a tee in the ground. The golf tee is formed by many hands raised in supplication, about to receive something precious. That something is Mary as a large, even vast, smiling face inside a 20-faceted diamond of pale sky-blue hue. Once on the tee, the Mary diamond slowly and continuously revolves, or perhaps it's the face that turns. All Light Corrective Centers have a particular geodesic polyhedra (Platonic Solid) present as an energy signature or template; here it is a 20-sided icosahedron. The Marian diamond settles into the prepared iscosahedron like a hand in a glove.

The selection of this site as a contemporary place for Marian revelations is best understood by knowing something about its past. It was once associated, energetically and geomantically, with the extensive mounds and ruins of the ancient Native American city complex called Cahokia, outside East St. Louis, which in turn, despite archeologists' conservative estimates and concepts, was associated with the Atlantean culture more than 150,000 years ago.

Now, as then, the Marian presence sits on the tee of the Light Corrective Center as a revolving beacon to be seen for miles by psychic eyes and to be enjoyed subliminally as a spiritual food by those sitting in the amphitheater.

A Continuity of Female Deific Apparitions at Tepeyac Hill

I save this early Marian sighting for last in the discussion because it shows the layering of deific attribution at a single site and highlights the possibility of a continuity of different, or differently seen, spiritual presences in the same place. It also shows how cultural and theological filters may influence the way celestial beings are perceived and described and how they're presented in a culture.

Tepeyac Hill, located three miles northeast of Mexico City, was once the site of veneration of the Aztec goddess variously called Tonantzin, Coatlaxopeuh, and Coatlicue. Then on December 9, 1531, a baptized Nahuatl Indian named Juan Diego (called *Cuauhtlaohuac*, or "Singing Eagle") on his way to church in Tlateloco climbed Tepeyac Hill and experienced an apparition of the Virgin Mary. This was the day after the Feast of the Immaculate Conception.

He heard birdsong atop Tepeyac Hill, and then a woman's voice calling out his name; after climbing up the 130 feet to its summit and standing amidst the mesquite and prickly pear cactus in the cold winter's morning, he saw her.

She spoke to him in his native Nahuatl dialect and asked him to petition the bishop to build a *teocalli,* or temple, here in her honor. Her language of discourse was significant as the Spanish colonialists administering Mexico had forbidden the speaking of Nahuatl. She said she wanted to show her compassion to Mexicans and to all who sincerely asked her intercession.

That afternoon, Diego beheld the Virgin Mary again at Tepeyac, and she repeated her request. Meanwhile, the bishop, hearing the unlearned peasant's fantastic report, was skeptical and wanted proof, a sign, of the visitation.

On December 12, Diego climbed the hill a third time, though reluctantly. Initially, he was trying to avoid seeing her again as he needed to tend his dying uncle, so avoided the hill. But Mary appeared, assured him of his uncle's healing, and asked him to climb Tepeyac and, against logic, collect some freshly blooming roses. It was winter after all, and no flowers were supposed to be in blossom. But the roses were, and Diego wrapped them in his *tilma,* a kind of serape or poncho made of maguey cactus fiber.

Meeting later with several bishops to give his report on Mary's request, Diego opened his *tilma,* spilling the roses to the floor. If it wasn't astonishing enough to see fresh roses in December, inside the *tilma* was a full-color portrait of the Virgin Mary, painted as it were miraculously on the highly perishable fabric. She appeared as a dark, pregnant teenage Aztec princess; the chief colors in her image were deep gold (in the rays), blue green (in Mary's mantle), and rose (in the flowered tunic). Apparently, the *tilma* captured her image just as Juan Diego saw her on Tepeyac.

The bishop agreed to build the church, and today, more than 450 years later, Mary's image is still intact—vibrant, in fact—on cloth that should have disintegrated after, at best, 20 years. The *tilma,* uncracked and unfaded, protected by glass, and framed in gold and silver, is now the centerpiece at the Basilica of Guadalupe in Mexico City, a shrine built in 1976 that draws 12 million visitors annually and holds up to 20,000 at a time for Mass. This superseded the two earlier shrines erected there in 1533 and 1709.

By 1539, the legend goes, upward of eight million Mexican Aztecs were baptized as Catholics on the strength of the Marian image in the *tilma*, or possibly because they believed their Mother Goddess Tonantzin had returned to Tepeyac and herself converted to Christianity as an example for her followers. Or perhaps the Catholic clergy threw a Christian cloak over her? Tonantzin may be the pagan mother at Tepeyac, but the "real mother is Nuestra Senora. She is the only one," a contemporary Mexican woman told traveler Eryk Hanut. Another commented on how Mary remained, is still present. "The Tilma is her daily physical presence here. She came in 1531 and has stayed ever since."[48]

Did the apparition call herself the Virgin Mary? Not exactly. How did she end up being called the Virgin of Guadalupe? By a spelling mistake, it seems.

The historical records for the event say she called herself Tequatlaxopeuh (a name in Nahuatl) or Coatlaxopueh, which means, approximately, the one who crushes the head of the serpent or who triumphs over the rule of the serpent. Juan Diego understood Mary to say she would crush, stamp out, and abolish the stone serpent, which religious authorities interpreted to mean sculpted images of Quetzalcoatl, the Feathered Serpent of Aztec myth to whom the Aztecs reportedly were even then making 20,000 human sacrifices annually. Apparently, there was once a statue of Quetzalcoatl in the Temple of Tonantzin atop Tepeyac.

And Guadalupe? Apparently, these Nahuatl names, or at least Coatlaxopueh, to the untutored ear sound like *quatlaupe*, which to a Spaniard is like Guadalupe, a Spanish name meaning "wolf's river" or "the waters of the wolf." A Black Madonna made of wood and presented to the Bishop of Seville in 580 A.D. was thereafter known as the Spanish Guadalupe. The original Basilica of Guadalupe is located in Caceres in Estremadura Province, Spain. I'll come back later to the possible Nahuatl identity and function of Tonantzin-Coatlaxopueh.

The geomantic situation underlying Tepeyac is complex. First, Tepeyac Hill is a dome cap that originates at either Popcatepetl (elevation: 17,887 feet) or Iztaccihuatl (elevation: 17,343 feet), two adjacent volcanoes about 30 miles southeast of Mexico City.[49] Bear in mind that Mexico City sits at ten thousand feet. Both mountains have large domes over them, and these domes overlap to form a fish-shaped vesica piscis form, which in turn acts as the double-domed gateway for a landscape zodiac whose heart was Tenochtitlan, now Mexico City.

A third domed mountain is Tlaloc (elevation: 13,615 feet), also a volcano, a little to the north of the other two. Together, the three domes generate up to 144 dome caps throughout the Valley of Mexico and provide an intense degree of spiritual illumination for that area, including all the star points in the zodiac. The dome cap over Tepeyac Hill is associated with a minor star within the constellation of Virgo, the Virgin, known to the Greeks as Astraea, goddess of justice and daughter of Zeus (King of Olympus) and Themis (a Titan). Tepeyac Hill is also a star-fall site within the Mexico City landscape zodiac.

We get some clear insight on the attribution to Coatlaxopueh as the crusher and subduer of serpents. Within Tepeyac Hill, or, more properly, in the same space but in a subtler dimension, is one of the Earth's 1,053 minor dragons. Mary or Tonantzin or Coatlaxopueh is standing on the dragon insofar as in her apparitional form she appeared on the top of the hill, but it is not correct to portray her as a crusher, subduer, or slayer of the dragon. They don't need slaying; rather, they need activation so their energy can infuse the landscape.

Further, this minor dragon has released numerous dragon eggs into the area bounded by the dome cap, which is perhaps a few miles across, and the landscape zodiac as a whole, which is much broader. Each egg offers an individual the opportunity for interaction, alignment, and mastery. Metaphorically, you "slay" the dragon or lower self by encountering and *assimilating* its energies and conditions of consciousness in stages under the watchful, supportive presence of the Mother Goddess of Tepeyac Hill. The dragon is also correlated with the vital life force energies called kundalini, usually described as a serpent coiled three and a half times around the base of the spine.

So did Juan Diego see the Virgin Mary or Tonantzin? Are they the same celestial personage who changed her appearance to suit changed cultural conditions and global plans for spiritual unfoldment? Or did Tonantzin and her wilder, scarier aspects get softened into the already familiar Mary?

Amusingly, whatever the correct name is, it still is meaningful, for Mary-Tonantzin, depicted as pregnant, is the carrier of new life. There is still, as several commentators have noted, a strong *goddess* presence here. "The name Guadalupe, which means 'hidden river,' alludes to the great invisible flow of life and spirit which permeates and waters all humankind."[50] A recent pilgrim to Tepeyac commented in support of this: "The hill was starting to feel like a classic sacred site of emergence, one that facilitates the spirit of the Earth to burst into the tangible realm."[51] As one observer commented, "Surely, the Virgin of Guadalupe is Rome's most successful adaptation to local religion and culture."[52]

Let's sort out some of the mythic attributions. Tonantzin was the Aztec "Our Mother," a goddess of motherhood, but the name might be an alternative for Cihuacoatl, who handles this role. Cihuacoatl, also Aztec, was the "Snake Woman," the most powerful of Aztec goddesses (her roars signaled wars). Yet she was also a lunar fertility goddess, celebrated with phallic symbols at annual harvest festivals.[53]

Tonantzin was also considered the same as the Aztec deity Coatlicue, "Goddess of the Serpent Petticoat" or "She of the Serpent Woven Skirt." This figure is the Mother of all the gods, even of the Sun; she's also called a Moon goddess with five aspects and the primary Earth goddess in whose existence matter and spirit are fused to support her function, which was to incarnate the spirit in tangible matter. Thus Coatlicue is regarded as the mother of humankind, but she has both benevolent and malevolent aspects (just like the polarity of Quan Yin and Kali, Aphrodite and Durga). She gives life, and she takes it back.

In one famous sculptural representation, Coatlicue stands on huge taloned feet and wears a dress of woven rattlesnakes and a necklace of severed hearts and hands. Blood gushes from her severed throat and wrists, and in place of a head, there are writhing coral snakes. Two great snakes emerge from her neck and face each other, creating "a face of living blood. A monument of cosmic terror, Coatlicue stands violated and mutilated," as if demanding retribution.[54]

This is a fearsome variation on the Mater Dolorosa motif, and it is also a potent expression of the "negative elementary character" of the Feminine. Jungian theorist Erich Neumann drew a parallel between Coatlicue and the Hindu Kali, as well as other dark goddesses of "sheer frightfulness." He said: "So great is the inhuman, extrahuman, and superhuman quality in this experience of dread that man can visualize it only through phantoms." Even so, behind the dreadful appearance is the archetypal feminine and maternal.[55]

Frank Waters, well-known writer of Southwest topics, novels, and Native American interpretations, who was present at Tepeyac Hill in the 1940s for the annual pilgrimage, sensed that to the Mexicans, Our Mother, though dressed up as the Catholic Virgin Mary, was still Tonantzin, mother of the Aztec gods. "This was the idol behind the altar, the kachina within the mask, which the people still worshipped. Tonantzin's new Spanish name of Guadalupe did not deceive them."[56] It just provided cover for their ongoing "pagan" worship.

Some authorities on Aztec religion propose that the full, complete Female Self as expressed through the various deities was split into good and bad aspects, and that Tonantzin (and her Catholic guise as Mary), split off from the other, darker guises, was the only safe, good mother form left.[57]

Of especial relevance to the geomantic nature of Tepeyac Hill, specifically its dragon and dragon egg aspects, Coatlicue lives on Coatepec, which means Mount Serpent or Snake Hill, with her daughter, the Moon-goddess Coyolxauhqui, and her four hundred star god sons, the Centzonhuitznaua. These are four hundred stellar deities in the Southern Hemisphere, sometimes called the "Four Hundred Southerners." The star reference, of course, is suggestive of the landscape zodiac. Often, in myths, to *kill* really means to *activate*, so to slay the Four Hundred Southerners could mean to illuminate the many hundreds of stars templated in the land. The snake reference is quite likely to the resident dragon, which, after all, is an undulatory, kundalini-like energy feature—dragons are often called winged snakes—obviously present at Tepeyac Hill long before Juan Diego arrived.

Coatlicue, a virgin, became pregnant immaculately while on Coatepec when she placed some white feathers in her bosom or swallowed them. Or she placed a ball of feathers in her waistband. From this pregnancy, she birthed the plumed serpent god Quetzalcoatl, armed with a blue shield and spear, hummingbird feathers on his left leg, and a feather plume. Her child is also called—or it's her second offspring—Huitzilopochtli, for the Aztecs, the Sun born as a fully armed war god who then slew many or all of the Southerners.[58]

So in the varying descriptions of the goddess of Tepeyac Hill—as benign mother deity, disturbing snake goddess, pregnant teenage Nahuatl spirit, or Virgin of Guadalupe better known as the Virgin Mary—we see the possibility of the fourfold perception of the four spiritual beings who comprise Mary—Quan Yin, Kali, Durga, and Aphrodite, as they're known in various myth systems.

The Marian apparitions continue to happen, and it seems at an accelerated rate, highlighting new and unusual, even unlikely locations, at least at first glance. As the next example shows, some of the new Marian sites may have surprising geomantic significance and the Marian presence acts as a kind of inauguration of the site, long dormant geomantically, into activity in the present time. This next example also gives us a glimpse of a Marian presence without the customary external Catholic symbolism and dogmatic interpretation attached.

Table 2-1. Geomantic Features at 12 Marian Apparition Sites

Site	Features
Walsingham, England	Landscape zodiac, Golden Egg
Lourdes, France	Dome cap, Ray Master Sanctuary
Knock, Ireland	Ray Master Sanctuary, Chakra template, Tree of Life
Fatima, Portugal	Energy Focusing Node (minor Earth chakra), Lucifer Binding Site, Ray Master Sanctuary
Ezkioga, Spain	Dome cap, energy funnel, Silver Egg, Virgo Albion minor chakra
Garabandal, Spain	Prana Distributor, Underworld Entrance
San Damiano, Italy	Ray Master Sanctuary, Pointer's Ball, Arc of Ascending Consciousness
Medjugorje, Bosnia	Dome, Hall of Records labyrinth, Tabor
Oliveto Citra, Italy	Dome cap, Ixion Wheel
Conyers, Georgia, U.S.	Landscape zodiac, Control Bubble
Belleville, Illinois, U.S.	Light Corrective Center
Guadalupe-Tepeyac Hill, Mexico	Dome cap, minor dragon, dragon eggs, landscape zodiac

Inaugurating an Angelic Theme Park with a Marian Imprimatur

Here is an unusual and unconventional report of a recent Marian sighting.

It took place in south-central Norway in the summer of 2000, about ten miles from a town called Roros on the eastern edge of the Rondane Mountains.[59] By its outside appearance—an abandoned copper mine with extensive external tailings spread out over perhaps one hundred acres—Storvatz, the place where we sat for an hour, was an unlikely one for a vision of the Virgin Mary.

The landscape had been ripped open, its mineral wealth scooped out, and the place left in ruins. And it had a curious legend: Four centuries ago a Norwegian hunter killed a moose here and where the animal fell, copper fragments were revealed, suggestive of a huge copper deposit underground. The king of Norway granted this lucky hunter mining rights, and his descendants spent the next several centuries pillaging the site until the copper ran out. There were no trees in sight, no sign of anything green or growing, and the huge mounds of earth and copper tailings seemed dead and inert. Yet we had come here by specific angelic invitation—"Sit where the moose was killed," they said.

A colleague and I were working with a group trying to contribute some healing energy to this site in cooperation with the angelic world. This work (and the Storvatz copper mine site) was in the context of earlier landscape work having to do with a large geomantic feature nearby and extending through the Rondanes.

I had visualized and projected a large pale-blue shallow dish about two miles wide to lie under the abandoned copper mine. From the underside of that to the center of the Earth, I had next projected a grounding cord, a kind of wide, open drainage pipe, down which the cumulative toxicity of centuries of human misuse and its consequences at this site could drain. Clearly, the landscape was in pain and required relief, like a wound that needed to ooze out its pus.

From out of Shambhala (a paradise of enlightened adepts on the Earth, according to Buddhist legend) came 26 golden angels, each in a golden robe, each with a golden sword. They stood on the rim of the blue dish, towering above everything, and inserted the tips of their swords into the landscape. These angels were of the Elohim family, and we had worked with them before. Between each of the Elohim was a vertical golden shaft or cylinder of the same height, brought here specially from Shambhala.

There next appeared a vertical structure resembling a golden grain silo; inside was a corkscrew of energy twisting and turning dynamically like a golden spindle. I later understood that this was a manifestation of the Solar Logos, the inside spiritual intelligence of the Sun and an aspect of the Christ. The rapidly rotating spindle distributed solar rays across the blue dish and landscape, like a wet golden retriever shaking off its water droplets in a magnificent shiver. The motion of the spindle established an energy link between the cosmos and Earth.

Next, on suggestion of our angelic mentors, the Ofanim, my colleague visualized and projected a golden wand in his hand, which he inserted into the center of the effulgent golden circle formed by the Elohim and cylinders. "It was like putting the wand into butter," my colleague later commented. "I saw an illumination enter the Earth, like tendrils of light moving through the planet much like *qi* moving through the meridians in the body in response to the acupuncturist's needles." Following this, he saw form over the landscape an umbrella of all the major colors and their subtleties, and then these very bright rays entered the Earth like rainbow rain.

Meanwhile, I became aware of a presence approaching. It felt like the Earth feminine and the cosmic feminine were meeting, blending. At first, this approaching feminine presence was indistinct, undefined to me, but then it started to congeal into an image, a Madonna dressed like the Virgin Mary—but with an Asian face. She was very young, barely 20, yet ageless. She stood statue still, as motionless as a sculpted figure on a pedestal, but the pedestal was turning, though excruciatingly slowly.

The Virgin Mary figure stood about one hundred feet tall, both ethereal and vivid, like living alabaster, and somehow her face was almost at eye level with me, though it was not looking at me all the time. She turned ever so slowly, observing the site, but as she turned, I sensed she had more than one face or appearance.

65

The Virgin Mary or Catholic face seemed to alternate with the more Asian countenance, resembling depictions of Quan Yin, the Buddhist goddess of compassion. I sensed there might be a couple more guises as well. Later, I understood these other two faces were Durga and Kali, both from the Hindu pantheon—Durga a warrior goddess, Kali, a death crone. As this fourfold Mary turned, she radiated a lovely pink light out across the blue dish and landscape.

Later, as we drove back to the hotel, one of our group put on a CD. It was a man singing *Ave Maria.* I hadn't mentioned my Marian sighting to anyone.

I suppose if it had been an earlier time, say the nineteenth century, I might have started, either by intention or inadvertently, a Mary cult at Roros, followed by the erection of a majestic cathedral and pilgrimages of the faithful hungry for an infusion of the Marian presence. Why had the Virgin Mary, in her unsuspected, even unsettling, fourfold guise appeared at this abandoned copper mine outside Roros in August 2000?

"To seal the work you had facilitated," the Ofanim explained. We had been interacting with a geomantic feature within the Rondane Mountains—a landscape zodiac, an imprint of some of the zodiacal stars on the etheric landscape measuring, in this example, about 50 miles in diameter. The copper mine at Storvatz, along with Roros and another site called Os, comprised a primary zodiac amplifier, the feature found at 360 of the planet's 432 landscape zodiacs. The amplifiers establish a feedback loop between the actual stars above and the virtual stars below in the star wheel. The three-part amplifier for this zodiac occupies an area that at its furthermost point at Storvatz is about 30 miles from the periphery of the zodiac in the Rondanes.

Think of the zodiac amplifier as three broad steps leading up to the doors of a great cathedral. On the first step on your way to the temple—assuming you use this vast Norwegian temple sequentially or properly—you get a living infusion of the Virgin Mary. As she has imprinted this first aspect of the zodiac amplifier with her own essence, we could say the Virgin Mary provides the spiritual imprimatur for anyone intending to interact creatively with this vast geomantic workshop. Enter the Rondane temple by starting at Storvatz and you get a delicious Marian infusion of the blended cosmic and terrestrial feminine.

The Rondane zodiac is under the astrological influence of Aquarius, our imminent new cosmic energy. The zodiac is also the Earth's primary inner heart chakra, called the *Ananda-kanda*, which has eight petals. These eight petals or vibratory fields are represented geomantically by eight celestial cities in this area.

Further, the mythic Yggdrasil, or Norse Tree of Life, is located here, as are Mimir's Well (one of the 12 Crowns of the Ancient of Days); Nidhoggr (one of the 13 primary dragons, plus at least eight named minor dragons); four of 26 Garden of Eden templates (only 12 are still extant on Earth) and the original, primary patterning one; at least six gnome eggs; two stargates; several domes; a Valhalla, or Hall of the (spiritually) Slain; a Hollow Earth entry point (called a sipapuni); and more.

Even the moose-killing site has additional geomantic significance. The moose is an expression of the egregor, or National Tutelary Angel and Guardian form, for Norway. Its grounding and access point is at the site of the copper mine at Storvatz. To say a seventeenth-century hunter killed a moose here, in addition to whatever historical factuality it might have, is a sign for the national egregor grounding point being here.

The moose egregor is a kind of interactive spiritual container for the lived history and evolving consciousness of the Norwegian people on the landmass of Norway. It is one of 72 such National Tutelary or Guardian Angels originally assigned to the Earth and its landmass divisions. The egregors of other countries have different forms, such as the eagle for the United States and rooster for France; we encountered Portugal's egregor or National Guardian Angel at Fatima, as discussed previously.

All these features sit in an overall geomantic site that has remained pristine, untouched, and virtually unobserved since Hyperborea, millions of years ago. The Rondane temple is like a fabulous present from the Earth, held in trust for millennia until the present time when it can be revealed and celebrated.

Why did Mary have four faces? "These are four aspects of the compassionate goddess, each facing a different direction. They are

Quan Yin, Lady Nada, Kali, and Durga," state the Ofanim. Lady Nada is perhaps better known in her other guises as Aphrodite, Hathor, the Irish saint Brigit, and Mary Magdalene. Obviously, the phenomenon of a Marian apparition has application and meaning beyond the Catholic context. It's a question of theological and psychic filters.

The Ofanim suggest that to see the Virgin Mary only as the Christian Mother of Christ is often to miss 75 percent of her full apparitional reality. I say "often" because in many cases, the four goddesses manifest in the revolving pedestal format, but sometimes, the being of only the Virgin Mary (only 25 percent of the full presence) will manifest at a particular place to serve a particular purpose. On these occasions, she will be like a fusion of the *Anima Mundi* or World Soul and the *genius loci,* the spirit of a place or "place soul." It is understandable that the psyche will interpret the energy according to familiar visual and cognitive categories, be it Virgin Mary for Christians or Tara or Quan Yin for Buddhists.

From the spiritual world's viewpoint, the content of the "Virgin Mary apparition" is a fourfold expression of the compassionate goddess, whose names derive from the Hindu (Durga and Kali), Buddhist (Quan Yin), and Christian traditions (Virgin Mary). In Buddhist lands, especially Tibet, visions of Quan Yin or the Green or White Tara (a Tibetan variation of the same being) are fairly common, though they don't have the eschatological import they do in the Christianized West, where an apparition of the Virgin Mary is fraught with two thousand years of Christian-flavored history and *expectation.* In Hindu India, Kali is generally feared as a gruesome death crone, and Durga is a female warrioress from myth. I'll discuss the attributions of these goddess figures later.

Evidently, no cathedral or basilica is planned by the angelic hierarchy for the copper mine property at Storvatz. The Marian apparition residue will be enshrined and perpetuated by other means in the future, through what the Ofanim whimsically called "an angelic theme park." Certainly, in the meantime, the Marian touch is not going away. Once touched, the Earth remembers the Marian presence and continues to transmit it back to all interested parties as well as across its planetary network of geomantic sites.

The crucial point to keep in mind here is that the *where* of the Marian apparition is of high significance because it is always geomantically embedded.

A Global Net of the Mothers of Christ

Our 13 examples of the geomantic context of Virgin Mary apparitions suggest that in each case the apparitional presence sets down into a preexisting energy feature of the Earth's visionary geography, either a site already recognized as sacred or one made so by the visitation. Given the vast history of the Earth, it is also quite likely that many of the Marian apparition sites were once, long ago, numinous and recognized as such, and then over time forgotten.

In the course of the Marian apparitions of the last two thousand years, the Virgin has appeared and charged the landscape with numinosity in an increasing diversity of cultures, many of which are not Catholic, although they may have small communities of practitioners in this faith. Further, the apparitions in recent decades have been accelerating in locales far distant from the power center of Catholicism, Rome, and its major outposts, countries such as France and Spain. Significant apparitions have been registered and cultic followings have emerged in India, Brazil, Vietnam, China, Ukraine, Egypt, Japan, Korea, Rwanda, Syria, Argentina, Ecuador, Nicaragua, Philippines, Israel, Lebanon, Bosnia, and others.

We could look at this in terms of the phenomenal evangelistic spread of Catholicism through its holy figure, the Virgin Mary. But we could also look at it geomantically and consider the *planetary* effect of these hundreds of apparitions.

First, there is the infusion of the Marian energy from the hundreds of Marian pedestals into the Earth as a whole, living organism, like hundreds of acupuncture needles implanted across the Earth's skin. Second, you have the different flavors and filters of the Marian energy because of the differentiation of geomantic interfaces across the Earth. You have the Marian energy under domes, with dragons, Golden Eggs, landscape zodiacs, and other features.

So this celestial energy is being infused into the Earth in these two ways, and it's all happening *behind* the facade of Catholic dogma, ritual, and belief. Regardless of what the visionaries report that Mary said or did, this steady, wordless geomantic global suffusion is happening. I say suffusion because after the infusion from the apparitions, the geomantic terrain of the Earth is subtly changed, suffused with the Marian presence. The Earth's visionary geography is the carrier for this suffusion, the interface between the Marian spirituality and the planetary terrestrial consciousness.

Just because a Marian apparition, or infusion, happened hundreds of years ago does not mean its impact has waned or its energy dissipated. Earlier sites were merely early ones on a long list of planned apparitional infusions. The plan assumed an additive and cumulative effect from all the apparitions over time. It also postulated an end time, that is, a time when the apparitions would stop. Some of the Virgin Mary visionaries, such as at Fatima, Garabandal, and Medjugorje, have quoted Mary as saying an end would come to the appearances and would be marked by certain specific signs and events. We can reasonably assume that the completion of the Marian apparitional timetable will coincide with the Marian infusions into the Earth reaching a maximum, desired level.

It could be argued that the time schedule for the Marian apparitions has been the entire Piscean Age, an astrological window lasting about 2,100 years, ending sometime in the twenty-first century with the advent of the Aquarian Age. Another view popular among Marian devotees is that her continuing, escalating apparitional calendar is part of a "pattern of divine activity in the 'last days' immediately preceding the Second Coming of Christ."[60]

Catholics tend to see the Marian apparitions as evidence of a divinely appointed plan to history, a kind of preplanned apocalypse, in which the Virgin Mary has been assigned a pivotal role by God, involving intercession, intervention, and mercy. They also see her as the chief adversary of the monolithic Devil, or Satan, in the End Times. The increasing incidence of Marian appearances and her conspicuous interventions in history, this view holds, are signs that the "last days" are upon us and a new Marian Age is imminent.

It's also intriguing to note that, as far as we can tell, the Marian apparitions are a relatively recent event on the Earth, happening only since the advent of the Christ. This may seem obvious (how could the Virgin Mary return if she hadn't first been the embodied mother of the Christ on Earth?), but not if you take it out of the Catholic theological context. The spiritual being (or beings) who is the Virgin Mary may have appeared on Earth before, possibly many times, and influenced many people, but not in this guise or with this long-range intention.

It all changed with the Christ incarnation, after which the apparitions assumed a new objective, almost an urgency. As I explain in the next chapter, some metaphysical authorities such as Rudolf Steiner propose that with the Christ incarnation, the Mystery revelations, once interior, secret, and very arcane, were turned inside out and made public—were even, in the long term, democratized, made available to many. If the Mystery initiations underwent this profound change, all the supporting figures would have new roles too.

All of this is happening beyond the control of the Catholic Church. From a geomantic viewpoint, it is irrelevant whether the Vatican ratifies a Marian apparition as authentic, such as at Lourdes (1858); or suspect, such as at Lipa, Philippines (1949), knowledge of which was suppressed for decades; or Necedah, Wisconsin (1949),[61] which was repudiated by Church officials; or many of the other recent sightings about which the Church has not yet ruled. The infusions happened anyway.

The Church cannot force its theological interpretation of the Virgin Mary on a transcendental event. Obviously, it can't stop the Virgin Mary from showing up around the world.

It can, and often does, invalidate, discredit, or simply resist apparitions for a long time (like those of Bernadette Soubirous at Lourdes)—and then acknowledge them, or vilify them, discount, discourage, or ignore them. As the statistics show, only a small percentage of reported apparitions get approved by the Vatican. Even more problematic for theological control is that in some notable cases (Garabandal, Necedah, Fatima, Medjugorje, and others), the reported Marian messages have made critical remarks about the clergy and the Catholic Church.

The Marian apparitions are a source of contradiction and uneasiness for Catholic clergy, especially when the supernatural is thereby made visible, says Mariologist Rene Laurentin. "The clergy, true to its tradition, does not welcome an apparition as good tidings. They see it as a rather unsavoury event." Their first reaction is to look immediately for the flaw and seek to "cover up, suppress or limit the impact of the unusual phenomenon." Institutional church authority tends to feel itself and its power structure "under attack" by apparitions.[62]

There is such a thick layer of interpretive Catholic dogma about all the Marian apparitions (those credited and those denied), as well as miracles, locutions, withheld secrets, and apocalypticism, that viewing the sites geomantically—by definition, outside a Christian filter—sometimes seems the only way to get a clear, unbiased look at what is going on through these sites.

From a geomantic viewpoint, the moment the Virgin Mary grounds her energy at a site through a visionary's *seeing her* (itself a grounding event), then the Earth has one more Marian infusion point. What Mary says, or doesn't, and how much her appearance, recommendations, and prophecies are in accord with Church dogma is of less consequence than the *fact* that she infused a given site, even if it's seemingly only somebody's backyard.

It's easier to get a perspective on the Marian apparition phenomena outside the confines of Catholic doctrine. She is not returning to hundreds of planetary sites merely to confirm and validate Church theology, though sometimes this happens. As Mariologist Rene Laurentin sensibly explains, an apparition, even without Church recognition or sanction, can be salutary to the faithful. It helps one recall, convert, "actualise the gospel," reinsert it into our current times as a living testament. Marian apparitions are "tangible signs, in proclaiming the immediacy, the presence, the familiarity and the power of the gospel," he says, and we ought to "welcome them joyfully as God's grace."[63]

Even so, there is no obligation for higher spiritual realities to conform to our traditional descriptions and models. They can change and adapt to changed historical and social circumstances, such as our present time. The traditional molds may be outmoded and even counterproductive today, almost two millennia after the Christ incarnation. From the viewpoint of the spiritual world, the Marian apparitions have their own agenda, intention, calendar, start and finish points, and meaning. All of that may well be different from our enculturated and theological expectations. Maybe the apparitions are here to overthrow those.

In most cases, the Virgin Mary touches down once at a given site ("once" meaning for a specific time period, even if it spans many months), then does not return. But the Marian infusion remains at that site as a psychically detectable spiritual atmosphere, in which visitors may immerse themselves and which is strengthened over time by the positive attitudes and beliefs of those visitors.

At Marpingen, Germany, a solidly Catholic village near the Luxembourg border, Mary came back 123 years after her first appearance. Marpingen, once called the Lourdes of Germany, was the site of repeated Marian apparitions in July 1876 as registered by three eight-year-old German girls. Afterward, thousands flocked to Marpingen and many claimed miraculous cures from a nearby spring. The apparitions continued intermittently for 14 months.

Many years later, after considerable wrangling among church, civic, and governmental authorities, a chapel and Stations of the Cross were set up in the Härtelwald, a hilly forest about one mile southeast of Marpingen, where the principal apparitions occurred. The girls reported seeing a "white figure" and "woman in white" who identified herself as the Virgin Mary and asked that a chapel be built and that water be used from a nearby spring for healing.

Then in May 1999, it started all over again, as three adult women living in Marpingen (aged 24, 30, and 35) reported Marian apparitions there, and, again, thousands of pilgrims flocked to Marpingen, sometimes ten thousand a day. It didn't concern the pilgrims that the Church, decades earlier, had judged the 1876 Marpingen apparitions to be "inauthentic." The question of authenticity raged again amongst the local civic and Catholic diocesan authorities and pilgrims in the 1999 reprise of Mary's appearances. There was also tension in April 2000 between local health authorities who deemed the holy spring water to be unfit for public drinking and the supporters of Mary who had urged pilgrims to drink the water because Mary had dedicated it to heal people as "God's gift."

Bear in mind, with the Marian apparitions seen globally, you're adding spiritual energy to a system at a rate it can assimilate it without being overwhelmed. The pace of Marian apparitions—infusions—has accelerated greatly since the 1940s, which should tell us our collective ability to assimilate this high-energy infusion is growing too. It also suggests that the phenomenon of Marian apparitions is building toward some culmination or defining moment or critical mass.

Here's a psychic impression I had recently while considering the latter: Upon the Earth, seen from a distance in space, there are hundreds of navy-bluish pedestals upon which a humanlike figure of light stands, her arms outstretched, as if receiving or giving something to the world, or both, in one gesture. Yet she seems expectant, awaiting something, ready for it. In other places, new blue pedestals with the celestial feminine figure upon it are emerging from out of the Earth, like seeds rapidly sprouting into plants seen in time-lapse photography.

What is Mary waiting for? She's awaiting the birth of the Christ Child.

Not the only, unique Child; that has already happened. But the one in us.

The hundreds of Virgin Mary pedestals (they are also like pillars) are linked, as if the outstretched arms are holding up a translucent webbing, a global net. It is not a netting in a physical or even energetic sense; rather it is a uniformity of expectation, a prepared place. The navy-blue Virgin Mary pedestals are, as I've written elsewhere, like a net of mothers, fishing for the Christ infant in the etheric seas that surround the planet, their hands raised in readiness.[64]

The multiplication of the Marian tableau into hundreds of copies is part of a planet-wide *preparation* for the gradual manifestation of the Christ Child. You could see this as a descent of the Christ from the ethers around the planet, a kind of Second Coming, or as the mass birthing of the Christ Child from within humanity throughout world cultures, one person at a time.

But the imminent birth of the Christ Child will not be a mere repetition of the first birth two thousand years ago. There will be not only one, but thousands, and eventually, many billions, one for—and in—each human living on the Earth.

It will be a Second Coming of the Christ, but not in the literal way we've been led by Christian theology to expect. St. Louis-Marie Grignion de Montfort (1673–1716), a French Marianist, said Mary was in the background in the first Christ event, but in the Second Coming she would be prominent. Mary's God-appointed powers would be especially noticeable in the final days of the Devil's reign over humanity, he said. Perhaps he had it right when he wrote that through Mary "Jesus Christ may be known, loved, and served."[65] The acceleration of apparitions would be the *sign* that this knowing was to start, he suggested.

The only qualification I make to de Montfort's prediction is that this time the adoration of the Christ will be an *internal* event. We will watch with validation as a new body of consciousness mothered by Mary gestates within us. Christ did it once and once only for the planet and humanity; he showed us how. Now, in the second coming, we each do it ourselves, but *inside* ourselves. The goal is to rebirth ourselves not as Christians but as individual faces of the Christ.

The global net of the Mothers of Christ is in place, ready to receive the newborn infant—the Christ awareness born in individual humans. From this psychic-geomantic viewpoint, Catholic dogma about the Virgin Mary is less important than the energetic reality of her multiplied presence around the Earth.

Globally, we have hundreds of Marian-infused sites and, annually, millions of people making pilgrimages to these places hoping to touch that infusion. In many cases, people think that what is central are the outer events and phenomena, that the Virgin Mary appeared here and caused miracles of the sun or heavenly roses to appear, but that's just the window dressing to draw people to the site and hold their attention while they absorb the infusion like a rare, healing air.

3 | The Message of the Virgin Mary's Global Presence—Understanding the Why of the Apparitions

Over the many centuries of her appearances on Earth, the Virgin Mary has passed on many messages to her visionaries. But what is the message of the continuing *fact* of her apparitional reality? That's the focus of this chapter.

Inside and Outside the Theological Filter on Mary

Mary has said a great deal to her visionaries over the last several centuries of her appearances. Most of it has been in accordance with Catholic dogma, though a small amount has taken a critical stance on the priesthood and the Vatican; has revealed secrets about the world and its future, still publicly withheld; and has even taken other seemingly political and advocacy positions. My intent here is not to review or critique the content and tone of the messages, but I think a certain prudence and circumspection regarding them is in order. Bear in mind that many of the Mary visionaries are children or teenagers, usually not educated or only minimally so, and sometimes barely literate. Very few of the long list of Mary seers have been trained clergy versed in dogma. There is no evidence that any of the adult visionaries were psychic before the apparitional experience. It's one thing to *see* something extraordinary such as the apparitional form of the Virgin Mary, which can be a matter of spiritual grace, and this seeing is credible and worthy of our belief—or at least, the suspension of our disbelief. It's another to somehow later remember pages of Marian dictation in formal, even theologically correct, language.

As a journalist and clairvoyant, I have interviewed people and angels, have had visions and seen beings, and have received messages. I know how hard it is to remember the content of either visions or messages if I'm not taking notes or tape-recording events as they happen. There is no evidence that any of the Mary visionaries ever found themselves with notebook and pen when they beheld Mary. I find it hard to believe that untrained visionaries could have remembered and translated into reasonably lucid prose many lengthy messages from Mary, and to have them come out mostly in accord with conventional Catholic dogma.

Granted, only a handful of Marian apparitions have been officially authenticated by the Vatican, and usually after great resistance. Yet the majority of her statements, to a non-Catholic, sound as if they could have been issued by the Church and seem to reinforce Church dogma and practice.

Why should Mary's messages be in accord with Catholic dogma? Isn't that too convenient? It's worth noting that, in general, the more her attributed messages departed from the theological mainline, the greater the likelihood that those messages, and in fact the claim for her apparitional presence at a given site, were marginalized, discredited, or repudiated. Maybe the ones most deserving of our attention are those in which a different Mary peeks through a crack in the rigid theological curtain.

The Church might respond that her messages are in accord with dogma because the Church holds the true revelation of the Christ (and Mary's role) and in her apparitions she repeats that dogma because it is the truth reflecting itself. Perhaps—though it's a circular argument. Mary repeats Church dogma because that dogma is true. Maybe.

What might Mary's apparitions mean without a theological filter? It's been my experience that spiritual beings—angels, ascended posthumans, the gods and goddesses of various pantheons—tend to grow weary of (or bored with) human categories, hierarchies, and descriptions and look for new guises, new angles of presentation, new messages or ways of conveying them.

We could say that the active players in the spiritual world are by definition iconoclasts; they like to shatter the images of them we have cocreated, and make new ones. As the centuries and astrological ages progress, it's imperative to devise and distribute new, more timely containers for revelation so that we, the recipients and users of these containers, do not grow conceptually stagnant and unable to get the fresh, new, living spiritual input.

The Four Compassionate Goddesses in Slow Motion on the Mary Pedestal

Let's start with a view of the Virgin Mary from outside the confines of Catholic dogma, human expectation, and received tradition. This comes from the Ofanim, an angelic order with the commission to work with the Christ energies with and on behalf of people.

As mentioned in the previous chapter, in many cases the apparition of the Virgin Mary is actually a composite of four celestial figures—four faces of the compassionate goddess: Quan Yin (known to Chinese and Buddhist cultures), Durga (known to Hindus), Kali (also Hindu), and Ray Master Nada (virtually unknown as such).

Here the Ofanim's description clearly departs from Catholic dogma. Catholicism claims that the physically embodied woman, the Virgin Mary, who immaculately conceived and bore Jesus the Christ, bodily ascended into Heaven at the end of her life. Subsequent apparitions of her to embodied people on Earth presumably have been of this same ascended posthuman body making herself momentarily visible to a select group.

According to the Ofanim, Marian apparitions since Mary's bodily Assumption have not necessarily been of the once-living woman, the mother of Jesus, in a supra-bodily, spiritualized state. Rather, the apparitions have been by a quartet of spiritual beings whose apparitional presence is meant to fulfill a *role* and embody an ongoing *message*. Presumably, these four did not appear together prior to the Christ incarnation. They manifested copiously on their own and through their own mythic or religious guises, but working together as a group of four is a new thing.

I'm proposing that after the Christ Event[1] (the incarnation, crucifixion, ascension), the composition and identity of the Virgin Mary changed; her role did not. Her identity changed because now the intent is different. Before, it was the birth of the one planetary Christ. Now, the intent is the birth of the individualized Christ in every human. So the Virgin Mary is altered for this.

She can appear as the conventional Virgin Mary, but she doesn't have to.

Centuries of theology have confused the issue. The numerous Marian apparitions, because their form and content have seemed to match Catholic theology and expectation, have shifted the emphasis from the sheer and startling fact of her recurring appearance here on Earth. The moment Mary shows up, her presence is claimed by the Catholic theological filter, even if the Church denies the apparition's validity. Preexisting dogma continually shunts Mary *outside* us, as something to adore, worship, follow, put up on a pedestal. But what if the purpose of the apparition is to deliver the reality of Mary *within* us, to turn us not outward to received dogma but *inward* to revelation?

What is the simplest, most true statement we can make about the Virgin Mary? She is the mother of the Christ. That is her *role* in the great cosmodrama of the birth of the Christ on the Earth. The Christ has been born on the Earth, and Mary filled her role as his mother then. So why her continual apparitional return?

If we turn the fact of the apparitional revelation inward, we see her role *now* is to facilitate the birth of the Christ *within* each of us. *Now* she comes for us. She appears increasingly, and in multiple locations, to reinforce the idea that we find the Virgin Mary within ourselves so as to birth the Christ Child afresh, and millionfold.

I develop this interpretation more as the chapter progresses. For now, let's get a sense of who these four compassionate goddess figures are.

Durga is a name from Sanskrit and means "the Unfathomable One," "Impenetrable" (like a mountain fortress), or "Beyond Reach." This is one of the oldest and most widely used names for the Divine Mother, known as the consort of Shiva, one of the Hindu trinity of high gods (the other two are Brahma and Vishnu).

Durga is often shown as a golden-hued woman with a gentle and beautiful countenance. She has ten arms: in one, she brandishes a spear, which she uses to pierce the giant Mahisha (details follow); with another, she holds the tail of a serpent (reminiscent of Coatlaxopueh at Tepeyac Hill in Mexico City, the one who crushes the head of the serpent); with a third, she holds the head of a defeated giant whose breast is being bitten by the serpent.

Usually, Durga is shown standing on the back of a fierce lion, expressive of her formidable power to punish or bestow grace. Her task is to kill the demon of ignorance, but she also nourishes the poor and blesses all those who seek realization of God, giving them love and knowledge in their quest.[2] Durga is praised for saving humans from difficulty, for being the sole refuge of humanity, and as the pure lightener of burdens.

Often Durga is depicted as a fearsome female warrior, a bloodthirsty destroyer of old, inimical gods called Asuras, sometimes called Antigods. These were considered the archetypal enemies of cosmic order; they were agents of entropy, disorder, and chaos. Durga has ten arms, or ten forms through which she delivers the gods and humans from the influence of demons.

These ten forms are sometimes called the *Mahavidyas*, Durga's ten different aspects, as expressed in Hindu belief. The Mahavidyas reveal knowledge *(vidya)* and are sources of wisdom for humans; they may be consorts to the gods, or to Shiva, but they are not submissive, passive consorts, but independent, even dominating women. Most of the ten Mahavidyas are fierce, even frightening, warrior goddesses, armed with the powers of magic to combat on Durga's behalf all demonic enemies.

The Mahavidyas appear or are produced by Durga when she has

to confront the principal demons or other enemies of the gods and the cosmic order. As the primary battle queen, her commission is to uphold and protect the cosmic balance. "Though she is eternal, the goddess becomes manifest over and over again to protect the world," declares one ancient Hindu religious text.[3]

In one version of the story, all the gods together created Durga to overcome an otherwise invincible destructive giant called Mahisha, King of the Giants. This giant scared even the gods with his one hundred million chariots and innumerable horses, men, and elephants. He had claimed Heaven for himself, and scattered the original deities, who wandered the Earth homeless.

The gods beseeched the goddess (called Uma, Parvati, or Mahamaya) to fight on their behalf. Streams of glory emanated from the faces of all the gods and flames were emitted from their eyes, and it all flowed into Mahamaya until "she became a body of glory, like a mountain of fire . . . a mountain of effulgence."[4] Their concentrated powers flared out like jets of fire that "united into a blazing sphere which took the shape of the goddess." The new composite warrioress, her body compounded of the essence of all the gods and equipped with their powers, had three eyes, wild black hair, and 18 or even a thousand arms.

To support her in battle, all the gods loaned her their celestial weapons (trident, discus, conch shell, thunderbolt, mace, rosary, quiver of arrows) and, with these, she destroyed Mahisha in a formidable struggle in the Vindhya Hills. Mahisha assumed many forms, including an elephant as large as a mountain and a buffalo, symbolic of death, but with the arsenal of the gods' magical weapons, she destroyed him. Afterward, she assumed the defeated giant's name (Durgama) and was known as Durga (the feminine form), although to the gods, she was *Mahisha-asuramardini*, "The Destroyer of the Buffalo-Demon."

One can't help but speculate that in Coatlaxopueh (Coatlicue), the original Aztec female goddess perceived at Tepeyac Hill, we find traces of a Mahavidya, a fierce aspect of Durga. Remember, Coatlaxopueh was known as "She who triumphs over the rule of the serpent," and in her guise as Cihuacoatl, she was "Snake Woman" whose roars signaled the advent of war. Here the serpent stands for all the enemies of the cosmic order, the usurpers of the gods' residence and powers, and Durga as Coatlaxopueh restores that rightful order.

It's important to note that Mary told one of the Medjugorje visionaries that Satan was given the entire twentieth century to have his way with humans, but with the dawning of the twenty-first century, that hegemony would end. Mary has also been quoted by different visionaries as saying God appointed her to be Satan's chief adversary in this time period. The escalating incidence of Marian apparitions throughout the twentieth century might be interpreted as Durga in her Mahavidya guises making assays against the formidable agent of evil and disorder. Of course, you have to look behind the gentle and genteel facade of the Catholicized Virgin Mary to see the warrioress Durga guise. Studying the layering of deities at Tepeyac is helpful.

One of Durga's Mahavidyas is Kali the Black, the death goddess in Hinduism. Kali is most often depicted as a black-skinned woman with four or five arms; she is hideous, emaciated, dreadful, naked, and she smiles wildly. She wears a belt of severed human hands and arms; corpses of children are her earrings; she wears a garland of freshly decapitated heads; each of her ten hands holds a weapon, each an instrument of destruction; her tongue protrudes hideously from her mouth, ready to lap human blood; her teeth are sharp and fanglike; snakes writhe around her neck; her eyes are flaming, bloodthirsty red; and her face and breasts are smeared with blood, and blood trickles from her mouth and upraised sword.

Kali, the ferocious, terrifying aspect of the female goddess as world ruler, leaves destruction and death in her wake. "As goddess of death, Kali has to destroy everything, including her husband [Shiva], since no visible thing is eternal."[5] Yet, as a Mahavidya, Kali herself is a revelation, for if nothing visible is eternal, then what is beyond the visible, the transcendent, must be, and to know Kali is to have a profound realization of this truth, of the state beyond manifestation. It is appropriate that Kali is Shiva's consort, for he too is the Destroyer; he destroys the fixed forms and static universe created by Brahma and sustained by Vishnu; he shatters convention and illuminates consciousness.[6]

Kali may be scary, but her image is symbolically rich. She is black because this is the color in which all distinctions of color are dissolved. She's naked because she has divested herself of all the veils and illusions of existence, and her only garment now is Space. She represents eternal Time, and since she stands before manifestation or is seen through the visible, she gives life and takes it. She stands on the corpse of her slain consort, Shiva, who in this image represents the Unmanifest, the nonexistence, eternal night, "the static but potentially dynamic state that precedes manifestation."[7]

Kali is the powerful outsider, the breaker of boundaries, the totally wild woman, sexually powerful, even voracious, immodest, aggressive, repulsive, full of energy, extremely dangerous. She denotes freedom from the norms of society and conventional existence; she shatters them to reveal ultimate reality. Her wild, disheveled, unbraided hair denotes the dissolution of the visible world; her sword is the dawning of knowledge "that cuts the knots of ignorance and destroys false consciousness (the severed head)."[8]

Yet she is not all death. As a Mahavidya, Kali's hands form two mudras or ritual hand gestures, one to remove fears, the other to grant boons. This informs her devotees that she can allay the fears of those who invoke her and that she can bestow the lasting gift of the accurate perception of reality leading to liberation from all constraints of matter and spacetime. As the preeminent death goddess, Kali destroys ignorance; she dissolves illusion; she destroys attachment.

Kali is usually ranked as first among the ten Mahavidyas of Durga. Second on the list is Tara, generally portrayed as a benevolent, compassionate, even playful goddess who guides her devotees through troubles. Through Tara's guises, we work our way back to the Chinese personification of Quan Yin. But there is another deity behind Quan Yin called Avalokitesvara, "The Lord Who Surveys or Looks Down." In the descriptions of Tara and her guises, we have probably the closest approximation of the four goddesses to the Virgin Mary of Catholicism (except for the Madonna with child aspect).

It's a little complicated, but the chain of appearances goes Avalokitesvara (India: Hindu and Buddhist) to Quan Yin (Chinese:

female valence) to Tara (Tibet: White and Green Tara [but also Chenresi]; and in India) to Kwannon (Japan).

Avalokitesvara is a Bodhisattva, or benevolent savior deity, whose compassionate regard for existence is portrayed by his 11 heads and one thousand arms. He can see in all directions and aid a great many in need at once. His name also means or suggests the Lord *(ishvara)* "Who Hears the Sounds or Outcries of the World" or the "Sound *[svara]* That Illumines the World." His compassion is limitless and through his thousand arms he helps all in need. In the palm of each of his thousand hands is an eye signifying his all-seeing aspect.

In China, Avalokitesvara, a male-valenced Hindu-Buddhist deity, shifts to the feminine side altogether as Quan Yin. Her name means "Who Contemplates the [Supplicating] Sound of the World." Technically, Quan Yin began, in terms of iconic representation, as a male deity, then under the influence of Taoism and Tantra assumed a more feminine guise. Quan Yin manifests in any conceivable form whenever a sentient needs her help to relieve suffering or alleviate danger.

Quan Yin holds a child in one arm, or accompanies a young woman holding a fish basket, stands on the clouds or rides a dragon before a waterfall. She rescues shipwrecked passengers from a sinking ship amidst high flaming waves, an image taken to denote her ability to free souls from the illusions of matter and the snares of ignorance (in Hinduism known as *samsara* or *maya*).

In Tibet, Avalokitesvara morphs into Chenrezi ("Looking with Clear Eyes"), the compassionate bodhisattva and patron and protector of all Tibet. He has 11 heads, one thousand arms, sits on a lotus, and is the focus of meditation. But Tibetan religious culture also elaborated the personification of Dolma ("Savior") or Tara as a feminine emanation of Avalokitesvara. Eventually, her cult articulated 21 different forms for Tara, varying in color, bodily posture, attributes, and her degree of peaceful or wrathful manifestations.

In one account, Tara is born when Avalokitesvara, about to achieve nirvana (highest illuminating consciousness) and leave the spacetime plane, hears the laments of all created beings at his imminent departure and sheds a tear of compassion. That tear is Tara, the essence of the essence of compassion. Often Tara appears dramatically to rescue her devotees from perilous circumstances, including imminent death; almost in opposition to Kali, Tara is the cheater of death. She protects, preserves, and saves life, even bestows longevity.

Among Tara's epithets are *Jagaddhatri* ("Mother of the World" or "World Nurse") and *Sarvavamaya* ("She Who Creates Everything"), and she is often depicted in Hindu icons as having large, full breasts and a swollen belly, possibly pregnant.[9] If not specifically pregnant with a child, she is, at least symbolically, expressive of the first maternal impulse toward creation, as if she were filled with the universe and were about to push it out into individuated life. In Tara, we see also the Catholic devotee's belief that the Virgin Mary will compassionately intercede in individual human affairs when needed and called upon.

The fourth face of the compassionate goddess is also a Mahavidya, next in importance after Tara, known as Tripura-sundari, Sodasi, and Lalita. Each of these names illuminates a key aspect of her essence. The first name, Tripura-sundari, means "She who is beautiful in three worlds." But the word Tripura also refers to sound and its function in the cosmos.

This goddess's invocatory mantra is a cluster of three syllables, and is identified with the entire alphabet, source of all sounds, words, and language. Thus she is equated with "reality expressed in terms of speech." Her specific mantra is understood to correlate with the cosmos, just as a seed contains in potential the entire, full-grown plant. Her mantra of 15 Sanskrit syllables contains the "fullness and essence of ultimate reality" accessed through sound; it is a full expression of the goddess's essence and, for the initiate, a reliable way to experience the revelation of her presence in meditation.[10]

The name Sodasi translates as "She who is 16," which means Sodasi is perceived as a goddess who is perpetually 16 years old. Some experts also interpret this to mean the goddess who has 16 good qualities. The comparison with descriptions of the Virgin Mary's perceived age are obvious: She is always described as being a teenage girl, between 16 and 18 years old. The third name, Lalita, also correlates straightforwardly with the Virgin Mary. Lalita means "She who is lovely" or "the lovely one." The word also has both tender and erotic nuances, an attribute in keeping with Tripura-sundari.

She is depicted as lavishly adorned with fine clothing and ornaments. She is beautiful and erotically appealing. She is said to suffuse desire throughout creation and all creatures, even with a mere glance. Not surprisingly, then, she is known as The Desirable One, She Who Is Filled with Erotic Sentiments, She Who Overflows with Desire and Pleasure. Clearly, she is the Hindu equivalent of Aphrodite, the Greek love goddess.[11]

In other presentations, Tripura-sundari is shown with four arms, each hand holding something—a noose, a goad, arrows, and a bow. She sits as a queen on a throne or on a lotus atop the prostrate body of Shiva; she is adorned in costly jewels from the crowns of Brahma and Vishnu; her body is lustrous like pure crystal; she has the marks of a married woman upon her and her breasts are full. Sometimes she is called "She Who Gives Life" and "The Mother Who Oversees Birth." Her qualities seem to range, then, from virginal teenager of 16 to lascivious young adult woman to still-young mother.

Previously, I referred to this fourth face of the compassionate goddess as the Ray Master Nada, a Sanskrit word that means "Sound." I will discuss the Ray Masters and their relation with the Virgin Mary apparitions next, but for the moment it's important to appreciate that Nada, a word that encapsulates a key aspect of Tripura-sundari (and her Egyptian equivalent, Hathor), also connotes sounding, droning, roaring, howling, and screaming. Nada also means "roaring bull" and by association with the related word, *nadi*, it means river, stream, and rushing, stream of consciousness and stream of rushing sounds.

In Hindu thought, Nada is often part of the term *Nada Brahma,* which means "The World Is Sound" or "Brahma's Sound." Brahma, the prime creator god in Hinduism, is equated with the cosmos itself, his body, so Nada is the underlying sound that creation emits. "Nada Brahma is one singularity: the primal sound of being. Being itself."[12] And that's the sound of Tripura-sundari.

The Role of the Ray Masters in the Great Bear—and the Virgin Mary

Now let's look at the context in which these four compassionate goddess figures who comprise the Virgin Mary arise. These four deific figures are members of what the Western metaphysical tradition calls the Great White Brotherhood. This is a kind of cosmic

United Nations of posthumans and other spiritually advanced beings from across the galaxy. Posthuman means a human who has spiritually developed beyond the necessity of continued incarnations and who is able to operate effectively at a larger scale of activity—the cosmos.

The Great White Brotherhood is understood to influence, even direct, human conscious evolution on Earth, and elsewhere, to have regional "offices" on Earth, such as Shambhala. This is the elusive planetary city of the gods of humanity as described in Asian and Buddhist literature. The Brotherhood makes contact now and then with humans and even works with them as mentors on particular projects. The "white" in Great White of course is the luminal essence of the members in that their manifestation essence is as light and as bodies of light.

Central to the operation and essence of the Great White Brotherhood is the constellation called Ursa Major, the Great Bear, with the familiar Big Dipper. We all know that the Big Dipper, understood as the tail and lower back of the Bear, has seven bright and named stars. Hindu myth says that each of the seven stars is the home of a *rishi*, or divine sage. Each of the stars is given the name of one of those seers, including Bhrigu, Pulastya, Pulaha, Kratu, Angiras, Marichi, and Atri. These rishis are said to be "mind-born sons" or *Brahmaputras*, of the great creator god Brahma, created long ago at the start of creation. Each rishi has a "wife" or consort in the Pleiades, a star cluster in Taurus. This gives us 14 rishis.[13] They are said either to live in the Great Bear stars or to be those stars themselves. The Great White Brotherhood is also centralized in the Great Bear, even originated there.

The rishis are on hand for every cycle of creation, though they may change their names, genders, and guises, and are charged with upholding and imparting the cosmic laws. They are eternal powers who appear every time a new revelation of cosmic laws and principles is needed. They are seers because they see—know and embody—the manifold cosmic laws and express them. "The stability of the world results from the rituals performed thrice daily, at dawn, midday, and sunset, by the seven seers, and the recitation of the sacred triple-song (Gayatri) by all the twice-born at the same hours."[14]

In the Western metaphysical tradition, the rishis are sometimes called Ray Masters, notably in the work of Alice Bailey published in the 1930s to 1950s.[15] The "rays" in Ray Master refer to specific streams of influence, certain consciousness and evolutionary themes transmitted from each Great Bear star to humanity over time. This spectrum of themes in consciousness and evolution can also be described in color terms, as the seven major rainbow colors and their subtleties. For example, there are rich deep blue and pale sky blue; scarlet and pink; emerald green and pale spring green. The 14 Ray Masters each represent, manage, and transmit one of these colors and its full range of activity throughout the created worlds, which means multiple galaxies (see table 3-1).

It's said also that each human soul has its own unique identification with a single color and that this color represents a fundamental initiatory theme and consciousness nuance. When a person begins a spiritual process of initiation into the cosmic mysteries, this pre-arranged color identification specifies which Ray Master (or sometimes which group of them) will supervise their initiation. For example, the Ray Master of the lilac ray handles the energies of transmutation, while that of the gold ray complements that work by imparting discrimination and discernment in the transmutation process of alchemical inner changes in consciousness and identity.

Geomantically, the Ray Masters have at least two types of Earth-human points of interaction. The first is called a Ray Master Sanctuary (there are 1,080 of them on Earth) at which a single Ray Master may interact with humans; the Greek god Apollo, a Ray Master, had such Sanctuaries at Delos and Delphi, for example. Collectively, the Ray Masters have assembly places, recalled in Greek myth as Mount Olympus; there are 108 of these on the Earth, remembered under different mythic names across the cultures. When appropriate, individual Ray Masters enter human incarnation for a lifetime to help catalyze or support certain pivotal human events. Several Ray Masters were physically present with Jesus, also a Ray Master, in the guise of Mary Magdalene, John the Baptist, and several apostles.

Of further interest is the fact that each Ray Master is capable of 1,746,000 simultaneous manifestations, which means being present

---

Table 3-1. Colors and Selected Guises of the 14 Rishis or Ray Masters or Lords of the Seven Rays of Ursa Major

Ray #1—PALE SKY BLUE: Apollo, Arjuna, Master El Morya

Ray #2—PALE ORANGE, PALE GOLD: Durga, Artemis, Sekhmet, Diana, Master Kuthumi, Maitreya Buddha, John the Baptist, Pythagoras, St. Francis of Asissi, *Virgin Mary*

Ray #3—PALE RED, PINK: Master Lady Nada, Mary Magdalene, Aphrodite, Hathor, Narada, Freya, St. Bridgit, Joan of Arc, the Mahavidya Tripura-sundari (Sodasi, Lalita), Radha, Sita, *Virgin Mary*

Ray #4—PALE SPRING GREEN: Hilarion, St. Joseph (Jesus' father)

Ray #5—DEEP VIOLET, ULTRAMARINE VIOLET: Serapis Bey, White Flame

Ray #6—SCARLET: Master Jesus (carrier of the Christ), Santanda, Subhuti, Hephaistos, Goibniu, Wayland

Ray #7—LILAC, PALE INDIGO: St. Germaine, Francis Bacon, William Shakespeare, Herakhan Baba

Ray #8—PALE VIOLET/BLUE VIOLET: Pallas Athena

Ray #9—RICH, DEEP BLUE: Kali, Persephone, Paul the Venetian

Ray #10—DEEP YELLOW: Lao Tzu, St. Patrick

Ray #11—PALE YELLOW: Quan Yin, Tara, Chenrezi, Avalokitesvara, Dolma, *Virgin Mary*

Ray #12—GOLD/DARK ORANGE: Master Lady Portia, Benjamin Franklin

Ray #13—RICH INDIGO-PURPLE: Maha Chohan

Ray #14—EMERALD GREEN: Djwhal Khul, the Tibetan Master

---

in that many different places (and in that many different guises too) at the same time in the galaxies.

Since the Christ Event, four Ray Masters have assumed a female guise and have been appearing collectively, though sometimes alone, as the Virgin Mary. Since the Event and the advent of Virgin Mary apparitions, we may conceive of this arrangement as four Ray Masters, representing the four aspects of the compassionate goddess or World Mother, surrounding a fifth, Ray Master Jesus, original *carrier* of the Christ on the physical plane of Earth. As colors, we could picture this as a circle—as in the revolving pedestal of four Marys—divided into quarters, each a color: pink, deep blue, yellow, and pale orange, with bright scarlet at the center.

Maybe a little bit of this chromatic reality has already been noted by Marian seers. A Franciscan father at Medjugorje reported seeing an "incredible pink-violet cloud" out of which emerged "the magnificent figure of a woman." She gradually disappeared on high, her apparitional vehicle "losing little by little its splendid pink-violet color."[16] At Oliveto Citra, Italy, seers (mostly children) reported that the place in the sky where the Madonna had appeared in the clouds on July 20, 1985, had suddenly flushed bright red. Earlier in the twentieth century at Fatima, Portugal, on October 13, 1917, seers reported astounding solar phenomena including a dance of colored lights like a wheel of fire. Shafts of yellow, green, red, blue, and violet colored the clouds, trees, rocks, and crowd.

Pink, violet (similar to deep blue), yellow, blue, and red are five of the colors potentially associated with the Ray Masters mentioned.

What is often called the World Mother or Universal Goddess is often characterized in three or four essential qualities of femininity: virgin, maiden, whore (Nada, Aphrodite); benevolent matron-mother (Quan Yin); death-crone (Kali); and warrior-protector (Durga).[17] As suggested above, Christian orthodoxy does not prepare us, cognitively or even conceptually, for this expanded perception of Mary. We may expect the virgin-maiden and matron-mother guises, but not the whore, warrior, or death-crone. Her reality is all four.

Turning the Mystery Initiations Inside Out into a Public Demonstration

Let's step even further away from conventional Christian interpretations for what we might call a metaphysical and experiential model. The Christ Event—the spectrum of initiatory demonstrations from birth to ascension—is enacted *once* on every planet in the universe that supports self-aware, conscious beings, human or otherwise. This is done for the mutual benefit of the planet—understood to be a self-aware cosmic being in planetary form—and its inhabitants, embedded in the life of the planet's consciousness by way of that planet's energy grid or visionary geography, as explained earlier in the book.

It may sound a bit odd to put it this way, but the Christ Event on Earth was not intended to be the founding spark for the Catholic Church as an institution and Christianity as a religion. In other words, ultimately, the Christ Event was meant to spark human individuals across the planet, regardless of gender, age, nationality, ethnicity, or religious affiliation. It was not meant to establish an orthodoxy of belief, practice, and ritual, but to be an *initiation* into the greater realities of identity, consciousness, and galactic, even universal, life.

Austrian clairvoyant Rudolf Steiner explained that the advent of the Christ Event on Earth utterly transformed the ancient Mystery initiations. The Christ appearing on Earth and demonstrating the five stages of initiation turned the Mystery initiation inside out, so that what was once arcane and interiorly perceived was now external and cognizable by everyone. The Christ Event matured the human initiation experience and took consciousness to a new level. It was a "re-portrayal of symbolic rites enacted during the process of the old Initiation, but fulfilled now at the higher level of full Ego-consciousness."

Here's how Steiner explained it: "The goal now, since the Mystery of Golgotha [the Christ Event], was that a man should undergo Initiation while maintaining full awareness of the Ego ["I" consciousness] functioning in him during the hours of waking life." The essence of the post-Christ Event initiation is that the human "I" (Ego) remains "as fully awake in the higher worlds as in the external physical world." This was "truly the greatest advance that has ever taken place or will ever take place in the history of the Earth and of humanity."[18]

By "I" consciousness, Steiner means the ability for each of us to say "I" to ourselves. Other traditions call this "the witness": It's the part of your awareness that stands behind all sense perceptions, observing, noting, being aware. It's not exactly the inner monologuist in your head who maintains a running commentary on things; rather, when this monologuist shuts up and is still, it's *that* point of quiet, self-awareness to which Steiner's concept of I-consciousness refers.

We take this for granted today, but long ago, when humans were more naturally psychic, they would enter the astral or spiritual worlds entranced, in a dull, dreamlike state in which they could not tell themselves apart from the content of the visionary world. A human did not know he as an individual was experiencing the spiritual world; he could not say *I am here witnessing these events.* Thus he lacked "I" consciousness. Through many centuries of having our human attention focused on the body and the physical world, we have, collectively, learned to recognize ourselves as individual human beings.

I-consciousness means we can be aware of ourselves as individual humans cognizing the outer or inner world. Now, Steiner suggests, the spiritual goal of human evolution is to bring this established I-consciousness into the spiritual worlds, so we can wakefully and individually see what's going on there. Part of that perception will be the revelation of spirit in matter, of seeing the interpenetration of the material world by the supersensible, and to see it in daytime, waking I-consciousness. *Then* the human-I can take the next step and receive the Christed initiation as suggested in the statement "Not I, but the Christ in me." The human-I gets infused with the Christ-I, ushering in a radically new level of identity, perception, and world understanding—flesh made Word.

You can see why it's necessary for the Christ to initiate a planet and its higher conscious life only once. In fact, the history of a planet and the struggle of its self-aware conscious life to achieve greater awareness can be divided into two phases: before the Christ Event, in which the Mystery initiation is interiorized in the astral body, and after the Christ Event, when you can stay awake during it in your physical body and its parameters of perception. The Christ Event is the pivotal catalyst that demarcates the before and after states of consciousness as well as the before and after phases of that host planet's conscious evolution.

Planet and the collective human psyche are *both* involved—in a reciprocal processing of this momentous upgrade to matter-based consciousness. The host planet, conceived of as a sentient, self-aware being (popularly called Gaia) in the solar system, benefits from the Christ infusion as much as humans do. Gaia provides the reciprocal resonant context for humanity to process its own collective initiation.

This visionary experience includes the birth of the Christed "I" or Ego within the human, an alchemical process of transformation involving the five stages of initiation that Jesus the Christ exemplified in the birth, baptism, transfiguration, crucifixion, and ascension. Steiner called this visionary experience collectively the Mystery of Golgotha or simply the Christ Event, and he emphasized that the whole point was to inspire individual humans to *repeat it*. To facilitate this extended process of infusing the human I-consciousness with the Christ is why the Virgin Mary is touching down on so many repaired geomantic sites all across the Earth. It's groundwork for our own radical transformation in consciousness.

Steiner explained that as humans take the Christ impulse into themselves—he did not mean, necessarily, that they become Christians—over the course of time, and perhaps even lifetimes, they will gradually acquire the "forces and power of this Egohood" of the Christ and manifest the higher faculties of cognition, spiritual perception, and clairvoyance, enabling them to see Christ in the higher spiritual sphere in which he is working. Think of the Christ impulse, grounded forevermore in the Earth, as a kind of clairvoyance food. It enables us to develop the cognitive powers of our own Egohood, the cosmic Self within each of us that Christ exemplified, thereby enabling us to perceive him during daytime, waking consciousness, grounded individually in our own body.

When we are able to behold the Christ where he is working in the spiritual worlds, we will realize the Second Coming of the Christ is not what we thought. There is no need to come again; the Christ never left the Earth. The planetary initiation that the Christ Event precipitated is permanently part of Earth reality now, anchored into the planet on the physical and subtle levels. Steiner declared that the preeminent psychic event of the twentieth century and beyond would be the perception of the risen Christ *already* in the subtle or etheric aura around the Earth.

As Steiner explained, the Christ is the embodiment of the cognitive power that will enable us to see and know this each on our own. We no longer need the old forms of clairvoyance (astral dream states) to develop our Ego or priestly mediations on our behalf. Now we can develop the Ego on our own as part of our "Earth-mission," as the spiritual powers of the "Son of Man" start to stream into us. "This Ego is to be recognized in its highest form in the Christ," the Ego archetype to be given over to us.[19]

Steiner foresaw that as the twentieth century progressed, humans would increasingly manifest a natural etheric clairvoyance. Mystical experiences would increasingly become the common heritage of humanity, even in people with no previous training, and there would be a renewal of interest in the Christ Event.

Everywhere you looked, it would be like Saul's momentous conversion experience on the road to Damascus: first a disbelieving, cynical atheist, then a converted psychic and Christ initiate because he saw Christ with his own eyes. Increasingly, individuals would see and know the Christ on their own, unmediated by priests, dogma, even ritual. When many start having this Damascan Road experience, then we can say the Christ has "returned" to the Earth—certainly he will have returned to human perception.

Of course this raises the question: What does the Christ *look* like? Presumably Saul perceived the Christ-infused Rabbi Jesus in his risen celestial form, accompanied by 1,080 fiery Seraphim. Or perhaps he beheld Christ as a stupendous cosmic being, as the mystic warrior Arjuna saw Krishna (Christ seen through the Hindu filter) in the *Mahabharata*. Amidst a battlefield, Arjuna beheld Krishna's astounding universal presence, his thousands of "varied divine and multicolored forms" possessing unlimited mouths and eyes, the countless celestial ornaments and weapons, all overwhelmingly brilliant, "as if hundreds of thousands of suns had risen simultaneously in the sky"—the all-encompassing energy of time itself.[20]

Arjuna, ecstatic and bewildered, saw in Krishna's universal form "the unlimited expansions of the universe situated in one place although divided into many, many thousands." Contained in this form were all the demigods, sages, and living entities. There was no limit to its glory, no beginning or end, and even the planetary systems and their gods were "perturbed" to see this "terrible form." The revelation of Krishna's true form was overwhelming for Arjuna: "Covering all the universe with Your effulgence, You are manifest with terrible, scorching rays . . . burning this entire universe by Your own radiance" as all the great warriors assembled for battle "enter blazing into Your mouths."[21]

The remarkable thing about this story is that Arjuna and Krishna, in human form, were both traveling in the same chariot. Then Krishna, still present beside him, revealed his universal form to Arjuna in response to his request.

In a sense, both Arjuna and Krishna, seated next to each other, were the cosmic Christ. The Christ is both cosmic and terrestrial in guise. Here's why: At some point in our process of initiating our I-consciousness, we will confront the paradoxical revelation that *the face of the Christ is your own.*

Though he didn't use the term "fourth dimension," Steiner's prophecies regarding humanity's unfolding of clairvoyance suggest that's what we'll see. Steiner said humans in his future (our present) would ascend to a cognition of the spiritual worlds to "see the physical world permeated by a new sphere."[22] Through the development of capacities we already have in the I or Ego, "and with the help of Christ, you can find the path leading into the spiritual worlds."[23] Further, a number of humans would experience "the strange condition of having Ego-consciousness but at the same time [have a] feeling of living in a world essentially different from the world known to their ordinary consciousness."[24]

This is much like the aberrations in spacetime continuity that people experiencing UFO-related experiences recount, that they sensed themselves in two or more places at once or living parallel lives or in other "strange conditions."

Alternative Perceptions of the Cosmic Christ from Outside Christianity

We have seen possible ways of conceiving of the identity of the Virgin Mary outside the proscribed dogma of Christianity. Now let's do the same for the Christ.

The Hindu description of the universal form of Krishna as presented previously is a suitable starting point, but first a clarification. Christianity schools Western culture in believing that Jesus the Christ appeared once in the flesh on the Earth and that before this advent there was only a prophecy of the eventual arrival on the planet of the messiah who hadn't arrived yet. Rudolf Steiner's psychic interpretation of the Western Mystery initiations suggests that this is only partly true.

Initiates were able to travel in psychic vision to where the Christ was and have their mystical encounters with this cosmic being there. Steiner said that the Christ worked with several Elohim (an angelic family) in the Sun. The Christ, assuming many different culturally determined guises, appeared fairly often to initiate vision in the supersensible worlds close to the physical realm. The psychic and mythic accounts of these human-Christ encounters make it sound as though the Christ was physically present in some of his guises (such as Rama, Krishna, and Dionysus) on the terrestrial Earth, but I think it more likely the encounters took place in an intermediary visionary or imaginal realm.

The essential point, in Steiner's interpretation, is that the encounter with the supersensible cosmic Christ was the prime focus of the Mystery initiation.

My research suggests that some of the cultural guises the Christ has assumed include the Hindu preserver god Vishnu and his various incarnations or descents such as Rama and Krishna; the ecstatic Greek god Dionysus; Egypt's Elder and Younger Horus; and the Norwegian sacrificial god Balder. To avoid possible confusion, by Christ here, I do not mean the Ray Master Jesus who for a time embodied the cosmic Christ on Earth in a physical human body. Rather, I mean the Christ as a cosmic being or universal "fact" as Steiner liked to say.

Let's start with the Hindu Vishnu and his descents, Rama and Krishna. In Krishna's majestic revelation of his universal form to his initiate-disciple Arjuna, he showed in terrifying vividness that he was the destructive force of time. Arjuna was appalled to see thousands of warriors rushing into the flaming mouths of Krishna, who devoured them like a meal. They are all already dead because they are alive, Krishna said. I am all-devouring time itself. Arjuna understood that Krishna is the supreme personality of the Godhead in the transcendental world, that he is "all-pervading, and He is the Soul of every soul . . . magnanimous and unlimited . . . the shelter of the whole universe."[25]

Arjuna was able to see everything in existence through Krishna, even the prime creator gods such as Brahma and Shiva and the energies they worked with. All the gods, divine sages, innumerable planets and suns were *inside* Krishna's form. Not surprisingly, one of the most frequently used epithets for Krishna in this vision is all-pervading: He pervades all of space, and all its contents are in him.

This makes more sense when we remember Krishna is a "descent," or emanation, of the larger god, Vishnu, whose name itself suggests "to pervade."[26] Vishnu preserves and maintains the Creation; the other two prime Hindu gods either create it (Brahma) or destroy it (Shiva). So Vishnu is the inner cohesion of manifest existence, the centripetal energy that holds everything together.

As the preserver god, Vishnu fulfills his task by periodically making descents or emanations into the worlds of form and substance. Hindu myth says he has had nine major descents, and 12 minor ones, with a tenth major one scheduled for our future, when he'll appear as the Kalki Avatar.

In the case of Vishnu's emanations as Rama and Krishna, as recorded, respectively, in the *Ramayana* and the *Mahabharata*, two of India's oldest, most favorite epics, both were undertaken to correct major imbalances in human society, usually through a cataclysmic battle between two forces. In his incarnations as Rama and Krishna, Vishnu had a consort: Rama's Sita, who was abducted by Ravanna, and Krishna's adoring Radha, who was not abducted.

In Sita and Radha, it is likely we have female emanations of the same Ray Master (Nada) who is in perpetual consort-Ray affinity—we might say, the scarlet and pink, the major and minor hues—with the Christ (Vishnu) and his emanations, to which we should add the biblical Mary Magdalene as his consort. It is considered heretical, and Christian moralism certainly downplays this, but we can see this same, seemingly eternal consort relationship played out again in the relations between Master Jesus and the "whore" Mary Magdalene.

Hindu tradition retains the original, playful, erotic, adoring side of this relationship.[27]

In Egypt, Horus is the divine son of Osiris and Isis, and is sometimes shown as an infant seated in the lap of his mother, whose hieroglyph means "throne." One of Horus's oldest names was *Har,* which means "the High" or "the Far-Off," referring to his ability, in his falcon form, to see things far away—omniscience, in other words, itself an act of pervading all space and time. Horus was twofold, the Younger Horus and the Elder Horus, and he had two eyes to match. The right eye is white, the Sun, while the left is black, the Moon. With this cosmic face, Horus protectively oversaw all of Egypt and was also called *Harakhtes,* "Horus of the Horizon."

A little more about the Two Eyes. Horus the Elder was the left, Black Eye, called *wedjat,* and this represented his wisdom aspect and his association with Thoth, the Egyptian deity of wisdom, arcana, and Mystery initiations. Horus the Younger (as in the infant in Isis's lap) was the right, White Eye, associated with the Sun god, Ra. The Elder Horus initiated one into the sublimities of the eternal Mysteries; the Younger Horus guided one into the ecstasies of spiritual rebirth.

The ecstatic Greek god Dionysus has much in common with Krishna. Krishna had his adoring *gopis,*[28] his young, lascivious female lovers and adorers, while Dionysus had his Maenads, the frenzied, body-ripping female devotees.[29] Dionysus, of course, is the Olympian god credited with introducing grapes, wine, and drunkenness to human mortals, but a subtler, less literal understanding of this might be more revealing. I find it a richer interpretation to construe this as the infusion of the human body with the Christ blood and its spiritual essence—a eucharistic communion of sorts. The Dionysian intoxication would be akin to the wild, almost delirious abandon of Krishna's *gopis,* in which Dionysus represents (and offers) "ritual madness and ecstatic liberation from everyday identity."[30]

Norse myth focuses on the sacrificial aspect of Christ as the god who dies—in fact, he is the *first* god to die. Balder is the son of Odin, the high god (equivalent to the Greek Zeus), and he lives in a heavenly palace, entirely free of taint and impurity, called Breidablik ("the far-shining one"). Balder's name itself, though its etymology is vague, suggests light; it may derive from or be related to the Old

English *Bældæg*, which means "the shining day." Balder died as a god when Loki, the Norse trickster god, induced another god to throw a branch of mistletoe at the unsuspecting Balder. His mother had gotten all living creatures except mistletoe to refrain from harming Balder, who had dreamed of his own death.

Balder as a spiritual character is only minimally sketched in Norwegian lore. What is foremost is the fact that he was the first god to die, which of course concisely summarizes the conventional understanding of the Christ Event. With Dionysus, we glimpse the ecstatic, spiritually inebriated state of Christ-energy infusion; with the more stately, even abstract, Horus, we see the far-seeing wisdom aspect and the possibilities of a rebirth of oneself into a divine child; and with Krishna, we appreciate the erotic delight of unfettered consciousness and, of course, the awesome revelation of his universal form.

There is another nuance to the cosmic Christ that links these threads. The Ofanim state that the Christ, also called the Logos or Word,[31] is all the spaces in between the points of light (stars) in the universe. "The Logos is the Word manifest. The Logos is an empty space between things." Picture the many billions of stars in our galaxy and others; all of these stars are separated by vast empty distances reckoned in light-years; yet these empty spaces between the stars comprise a fabric that links and *pervades* all of spacetime and imparts meaning and purpose—the catalytic Word—to all creation. That's the Christ.

Here is a theologically neutral way of describing how the Christ permeates and pervades all of space, the space between the stars. It comes from Einstein's general relativity theory, which he developed to account for gravity.

Einstein postulated that space and time form a unified fourth-dimensional matrix called spacetime through which light travels at a uniform speed. Recent explanations of Einstein's model have us picture spacetime as a thin stretched rubber fabric onto which we place a bowling ball (a star: mass and/or energy). The ball, from its weight, deforms the flatness of spacetime and creates a curved gravity well; it curves spacetime around it so that time flows differently in its vicinity, usually slower than the universal norm.[32]

The many billions of stars are the mass curving the fabric of spacetime, but this spacetime fabric is also the all-pervasive Logos.

Therefore, we can say that the Logos is in part the fourth-dimensional stretched fabric of spacetime; the Logos uniformly pervades this fabric as the space between the gravity wells of stars. It is both the flat and curved spacetime fabric of reality, the speed of light and its alterations by mass. You could say the Logos pervades spacetime as the Elder Horus (uncurved, flat, original, uniform spacetime) and as the Younger Horus (the deformed, curved, newborn spacetime shape). The Logos is thus the rationality of spacetime.

We could also say that the Logos, the thin rubber sheet of spacetime, is the Light moving uniformly and without disturbance at light speed. Where it encounters a gravity well, created by a body of mass or energy (a star), and the flatness of spacetime is deformed into a curvature, the Light slows down some.

Gravity causes time to slow down. Mass (matter) causes light to slow down. This slowing down of light (time) around a star is like the death of Balder; he falls out of his unbroken bliss of heavenly life in Breidablik into the experience of humans and our mortality. We can see why Arjuna saw in Krishna's universal form the flaming mouths of all-devouring time. Krishna, as the original, smooth-moving supreme personality of spacetime, as the Logos, devours all mass because all mass (stars, humans) is eruptions within the Logos's uniform fabric. This is also why Arjuna saw all of creation, the stars and planets, as inside Krishna.

The Christ (as Krishna) is the connectivity, the pervasive awareness that binds spacetime and all its gravity wells (objects of mass) together. It sees and knows them all, for they are all within the Christ's field of being. So as you develop the Christ Child and make your cognitive way into 4D and the spacetime fabric, so too will you start to see panoramically like the Christ. You will see the stars and their beings and know what they're doing and why. How could it be otherwise, for your consciousness pervades and holds it all together.

This insight gives us another way of understanding the meaning of the Christ Event on Earth. The entirety of the Earth's visionary geography is the terrestrial equivalent of the spacetime fabric of the universe by the amended Hermetic formula "as above, so below, and in the middle too." The prominent features of the Earth's energy body—most notably, the domes—arise out of this preexistent fourth-dimensional spacetime fabric around the Earth. The domes in fact are mirror versions of the stars above, creating gravity-time wells in warped spacetime upon the Earth. We know them as numinous sacred centers, usually at and over mountains.

The setup of the planetary initiation by the Christ is elegant: The Logos embodied itself as a human (Ray Master Jesus bearing the cosmic Christ), in effect, turning himself inside out, then initiated the Earth's own spacetime fabric. Imagine a rich drop of blood uniformly staining a white blotter scarlet; the Christ infusion of Earth similarly "stained" all of Earth's spacetime geography.

Ascending Mary's Global Net of the Mothers to the Spacetime Christ

So what is the purpose of the Marian apparitions on Earth? Contrary to Church dogma, Mary does not come to announce humanity's judgment or chastisement or to renew Christian faith and piety.

According to the Ofanim, her appearances have to do "with the rendering of the neural connection in the right side of the brain and not so much to do with Christianity. But if that is the filter, then it has everything to do with Christianity."[33] The intent of the continuing apparitions is to help humans "go beyond the reflection of self to something greater, to the Christ within." As I have suggested, the proliferation of Marian apparitions is a basic groundwork for the birthing of the Christ Child, or Christ-infused I-consciousness in us.

The proliferation of Marian apparitions prepares the collective human psyche for an experiential and cognitive upgrade. It does this by infusing multiple geomantic nodes across the Earth with her essence, which, in practical terms, is an energy or enhanced consciousness that facilitates our second birth so we may generate something beyond our three-dimensionally defined selves.

The Marian visitations across the Earth are softening the hold of the "male" analytical psyche on consciousness, melting the hard edges of logic with the warmth of the compassionate goddess. They are nurturing "female" intuitive consciousness as the "womb" for higher cognition and clairvoyance, so we can go beyond reason to the Logos, have a higher knowing of context and purpose.

Further, just as Ray Master Jesus appeared on Earth to transmit the energies of the living cosmic Christ, so do the four Ray Masters manifesting as the Virgin Mary transmit the energies of the Divine Mother, Mrs. God, the Mother aspect of the Mother-Father God or Cosmic Feminine. So through the many Virgin Mary apparitions across the planet (at geomantic nodes that amplify and distribute the contact), the Great Mother touches the Earth.[34]

The implementation of this evolutionary agenda through the Earth's sacred sites with the Marian-imparted spiritual impulse is highly efficient. Obviously, only a minute percentage of humanity at present is actually having the Marian apparitions firsthand, but millions can receive virtually the same spiritual impulse by visiting the Marian sites. Even more can receive the impulse merely by hearing about these apparitions or the reports of pilgrims; and still more will register the impulse in their subconscious merely by being on the same planet and physical reality as these happenings. In starkest terms, merely to hear that such a thing is happening can have a powerful effect.

Once Mary has touched down at a site, her presence remains there to inspire and catalyze future generations of pilgrims. Through the geomantic diversity of the sites, the impulse enters the planet and collective psyche through many different structures and filters (refer back to table 2-1). Our consensus reality starts to transmute under its sustained influence. To use a different analogy, Mary rings a celestial bell on Earth, and all the sacred sites she touches or impinges upon carry and amplify the reverberation.

Presently, millions of people have registered the Marian impulse in their subtle bodies, and even if many of them have since died, they still carry the Mary contact in their souls as an indelible imprint and catalyst for spiritual evolution. Subtly and gradually, the fabric of planetary reality is being shifted by the gentle, persistent, persuasive force of Mary's repeated presence.

And remember, it's the *four* aspects of the compassionate goddess that are infusing themselves into planet and psyche. That includes the "virgin"-mother, but also two or three aspects of the cosmic feminine many of us resist—warrior, death-crone, and what we might call the Magdalene-Aphrodite "love" aspect.

We must take the next step. Mary is appearing outside us as a sign on the Earth to inspire us to find her within us, to manifest the living Virgin Mary *inside* each of us. We don't need to make a new religion or cult out of it; we don't even need to use it to renew Catholicism or to believe in divinely ordained miracles. But we do need to heed this sign on the Earth and act on it. As outrageous as it may sound, each of us needs to become a Virgin Mary within.

The Ofanim suggest that the nature of human psychic experiences in our time, and increasingly so into the future, will involve an "externalization of the inner hierarchy." This complex observation is based on the fact that the human, in body and mind, is a replica of cosmic structure, processes, and the angelic and hierarchical (posthuman, transcended human) kingdoms. In short, whatever real deities exist outside us also exist inside us. If there is a Virgin Mary external to us, there is one internal to us. Now it's time to see her within.

Up until now, we have assumed the outer one was the only one; now the revelation of the outer one serves to illuminate the inner one. Now the structures and beliefs of our inner spiritual world will be displayed before us as if we've been turned inside out and we barely recognize ourselves. That's not surprising. Rudolf Steiner once said that should we encounter our own astral body in the dream world we would not recognize it as our own, as ourselves. It would appear to be so strange, even bizarre, possibly scary, that we'd assume it was a formidable denizen of the dream realms and probably try to run away.

You might be wondering, so what and why bother? What if I don't feel like birthing the Christ Child, or don't even believe in the terminology? It's your choice, of course. But consider: This energy infusion and its ramifications are under way on our planet, affecting all aspects of where we live, down to the molecular and atomic levels, slowly, inexorably changing reality. Wouldn't it be prudent to be proactive with this inevitable planetary transformation rather than resist it and become the effect of its changes?

The Marian apparitions are a sign that the change is under way, that our reality is being reconfigured in front of us. So to birth the Christ Child, as the seat and possibility of heightened awareness, we must first locate his mother, the Virgin Mary, in us. Obviously, this is a symbolic, alchemical transformation that's being asked of us, or *offered* us.

We must get past the conceptual roadblock of virginity equaling no sexual intercourse. The Virgin Mary is not "virgin" because she conceived Jesus without human male intermediation; she is virgin because she represents the unpolluted, untainted human soul, cognitively clean and clairvoyant, capable of birthing a higher seeing—Christ awareness. It has nothing to do with sex; that is a confusing, mistaken literalization of a spiritual process.

Paradoxically, in our interior, individual experience of "being" the Virgin Mary and "birthing" the Christ Child within us, we are impregnated by the Holy Spirit and undergo a virgin birth, just as Catholic doctrine declares.

In the old Gnostic metaphor of spirituality, the teaching function of the Virgin Mary was represented by Sophia, the goddess of divine wisdom. Sophia was that part of the supreme Godhead—the Gnostics called it the Pleroma, or absolute fullness of existence and reality—who wanted to behold God. Think of the Pleroma as the fourth dimensional, virginal fabric of smooth, flat spacetime, before the light "fell" into matter, mass, and experience, creating curved space.

Since she was with and in God, she could only behold God by stepping outside that context, by leaving the Pleroma and "falling" into the lower realms of matter. She did, and for a time she was known as the Whore Sophia because she was tainted with the concerns of matter. Here, think of the fallen whore Sophia as wandering around the slower, gravity wells of curved spacetime.

Let us not overlook the obvious: To the nonpsychic schooled in the Western parameters of scientific reductionism and atheistic materialism—all of us to some degree are affected by this—reports that a spiritual being is appearing more or less in our three-dimensional world is an astounding fact. Potentially, it shatters our fixed conventions of reality. It's a salutary shock to the Western mind and body, indoctrinated out of miracles. Marian apparitions demonstrate the reality of spiritual presence in our world and remind the soul in the body that it is not forsaken, godless, and bereft on Earth.

In esoteric early Christian practice and, of course, in Gnostic ritual, the emphasis was to purify the fallen Sophia within each person, to make her the Virgin Sophia once again. That was understood to mean a purification of the astral body, the seat of the taints, karmic residue, and repercussions of having fallen into the realm of matter, mass, and gravity—human incarnation. To regain the status of the Virgin Sophia meant—and still does, in initiatory terms—to have cleansed the astral body and undone the fetters it imposes on clairvoyance. For how can you behold the glories of the Pleroma, God, or Heaven, if your psychic apparatus—the psychic organs or chakras in your astral body—is polluted?

Think of purifying the Whore Sophia and restoring the Virgin Sophia as something like climbing out of the gravity well of curved spacetime onto the flat, pure, flowing Logos eternity of original spacetime.

Let's remember that, ultimately, Christianity is not a spectator sport. Even though the conventions of Christianity seem to school us into taking a passive, observer's position as the priests perform the highly finessed spiritual arts of intercession with the Christ and God on our behalf, the setup actually calls for each of us to get out on the playing field and birth the Christ consciousness on our own. To become active players in the Christ-human interaction, we have to do two things: Create the mother and birth the child—within us, individually.

Making the Christed Initiation a Participant's Game One Person at a Time

On a practical level, how do we take advantage of this Marian impulse? How do we start fulfilling the angelic agenda for human and Earth evolution and go beyond the reflection of self to something bigger, the Christ within? The Earth's visionary geography already has an interactive feature assigned for this.

First, let's note the elementary level purpose of this new Marian impulse. Her apparitions at such a variety of sites around the planet return the Christ experience and our potential to participate in it to the Earth. Arguably, Christianity, as we know it, has been divorced from the Earth and earthy reality, and it has tended to put us at some distance from our own earthiness, the body of flesh. When you correlate the Marian apparitions to the variety of geomantic nodes and their planetary function and the whole interconnected network they form, then you start to reconnect Christianity—the genuine, pure Christ impulse that preceded its institutionalization—to its planetary roots and context.

To participate in this new impulse, ideally, we bring our body to a Marian-infused geomantic node. Then our flesh and the planetary flesh join in the Christ.

Second, Mary is highlighting and activating premium sacred sites relevant to the agenda of expanding the Christ impulse in our times. Many of the Earth's holy sites are famous for past reasons; they are not all necessarily intensely relevant for our current conditions. Many Marian apparition sites are not on the official catalog lists of culturally recognized holy sites, but should be; many have become acknowledged as such because of her apparitions there.

Bear in mind the Earth has many thousands of holy sites, preset for activation and deactivation in accordance with a master geomantic calendar for Earth. Some sites may seem mundane, unnoticed for millennia until their time arrives; a Marian activation marks their online status and they become sacred and noticed as such by us. Other sites (such as Belleville, Illinois) may have been "on" in the deep past, then forgotten, then activated again with a new geomantic mission, to carry the Marian impulse into the twenty-first century.

So time spent meditating at and accessing the higher realms through Marian-infused sites, no matter how obscure, remote, disputed, or even discredited, should be a worthwhile first step. She's already pointed out where the numinous action is, so why not go to these places?

Third, there is a feature called a Golden Egg, and there are 666 of them across the Earth. At least one Marian apparition site profiled in chapter 2 (Walsingham, England) has a Golden Egg, and many other sacred sites around the planet have one (see table 3-2). The purpose of a Golden Egg is to "hatch" or birth the Christ Child as an expression of the Higher Self within the human. If you visit a Golden Egg site in which the outer, geomantic expression has already been achieved—the egg is hatched—then you can immerse yourself in the "outer" exemplification of the achieved state as a way of coming into resonance with what you want to experience and embody inside yourself.

Table 3-2. Selected Locations of Interactive Golden Eggs

Vesle Solukletten, Rondane National Park, Norway

Tetford, Lincolnshire, England

Burrowbridge Mump, Burrowbridge, Somerset, England

Goetheanum, Blood Hill, Dornach, Switzerland

Acropolis, Athens, Greece

Edfu, Egypt

Mount Holyoke, Skinner State Park, Hadley, Massachusetts, U.S.

Pyramid of the Sun, Teotihuacan, Mexico

Wawel Hill, Cracow, Poland

Glastonbury Abbey, Glastonbury, England

Burley Hill, Oakham, Rutland, England

Shrine of Our Lady of Walsingham, Walsingham, England

The Golden Egg is laid out like a two-dimensional tableau of Madonna and Christ Child across a stretch of landscape typically three to five miles long. It has three parts: (1) a kind of egg holder; (2) the egg itself, seen as a golden sphere; and (3) a Maidenwell, the Madonna aspect that clutches the egg's crown to her chest.

I call this feature a Maidenwell in honor of a place-name site where I first experienced it with the Golden Egg at Tetford in England. The local topographical map identified a small section of hillside as Maidenwell, but the actual hamlet of the same name was perhaps a half-mile from there. Physically, Maidenwell is a grassy field with a prominent lookout; interiorly, it is a state of fluidic, multi-aspected, higher clairvoyance; and, geomantically, it is a well of motherly love and nurturance with long, embracing arms that embrace the Golden Egg (Christ Child), occupying several miles of landscape down the hill.

Ideally, visit a Marian apparition site with strong geomantic credentials (see table 2-1) and absorb the vibration of the Marian presence there. Then visit a Golden Egg (see table 3-2), and walk it from egg cup to Maidenwell. The nurturance the Madonna gives the Christ Child (your new self to be born) is the "milk" of diversified, fully operational clairvoyance—far-seeing cognition.

As you walk the three primary geomantic stages of the Golden Egg, identify each landscape site with yourself; bring it into your body so that the first phase, the egg cup, fills your first two chakras, the Golden Egg itself the third through fifth, and the Maidenwell your sixth and seventh chakras, the seats of clairvoyance. That will make it easier to sense the Mary nurturance that enters the crown of the Christ Child born of the Golden Egg—it'll be in *your* crown.[35]

Further, if you have the opportunity, immerse yourself in the energies of two other geomantically heightened Madonna sites: Maiden Castle in Dorset and the Merry Maidens in Cornwall, both in England. Neither is known as a Virgin Mary or Madonna site, but both will amplify your participation in Her energies.

Maiden Castle is a huge, grassy oblong, flat hilltop occupying 7.4 acres just outside the city of Dorchester in southwestern England. It is surrounded by several deep ramparts and archeologists call it a hill fort. The Merry Maidens, near Penzance, also in southwestern England, is a stone circle 78 feet wide consisting of 19 stones, each four feet high, and set 12 feet apart on the perimeter of what archeologists call a perfect circle. Of relevance to us here is the meaning of the Maidens. The Maidens represent aspects of the cosmic or divine Mother, the Virgin Mary's ultimate archetype, the Mother behind the Mother.

The 19 Merry Maidens—the spiritual presences and templated energies grounded by the physical stones—represent what the Ofanim term the 19 phylums or groups of aspects of the cosmic

Feminine, the total of which is 94. You can get the initial infusion of these 19 aspects at the Merry Maidens stone circle; this means an intense immersion in the great sea of their clairvoyance.

We might usefully think of them as the 19 basic expressions of the Virgin Sophia, as pristine—virginal—faculties of clairvoyant knowing. "The feminine aspect, all the coherence of what you may term right-brain activity, the powers of clairvoyance, clairsentience, clairaudience—all are available at this site," the Ofanim explain. Each of the 19 stones amplifies an aspect so that the interior of the circle is a sea of maidenly clairvoyance. Then you can deepen the activation of your clairvoyant faculties by time spent at the House of the Mother, Maiden Castle, where the full panoply of 94 aspects is available for you to experience.

Again, the practical emphasis here is finding ways to create the Virgin Mary within ourselves, in accordance with the Ofanim's observation that the purpose of her multiple external manifestations is to unify the brain hemispheres and balance the intuitive and analytical functions of consciousness so that we can then be in a position to birth the Christ Child within and experience the radical enhancement of awareness, identity, and global responsibility this entails.

But what is this Christ Child we're supposed to be birthing? Obviously, it's a symbolic pregnancy—or is it? It's the rebirth of the self on a foundation of initiation. The child represents the newborn, new-founded consciousness, who enters the human Earth world fresh with cosmic perspective and identity. It's the second birth, the spiritual one, voluntarily and wakefully gone through.

Generically, it's the "fruit" of most initiation experiences across the cultures—the possibility of inner self-development and self-evolution. According to a sensitive reading of the Gospels, each of us, internally, "is a *seed* capable of a definite growth." As we stand conventionally, we are incomplete and unfinished. "A man can bring about his own evolution, his own completion individually." Or not, if we don't want to. "But it is only the inner, *unorganised* side of a man which can *evolve* as does a seed by its own growth, *from itself*." Our second birth belongs to the "*man in himself,* the private, secret man, the internal man."[36]

As humans, our birthright is to have this seed of Christ consciousness within us, but we have to choose wakefully to sprout it. If we decide this, then the Marian-imprinted sacred sites and Golden Eggs await us as aids in the process. And Mary keeps appearing as a sign on the Earth that it's time to get started.

What do we "get" if we birth the Christ Child from out of ourselves? Let's recall the previous description of Christ and flat and curved spacetime. Christ is the self-aware, all-seeing space between all the stars, the logoic connection among them, the original pure, flat, spacetime flowing at the speed of light, or Christ consciousness, *aware of everything* in the spacetime world. That is what we *get*, at least to start with: a panoptic, uninterrupted fourth-dimensional cognition. Flat spacetime and curved spacetime become our two Horus Eyes, the Elder and Young Christ.

Through these two cosmic eyes, we can see our physical world afresh, as a playing field of *both* flat spacetime (the "unfallen" Light) and curved spacetime (the "fallen" Light), Spirit and matter, eternity and time, Word and flesh. Here's the exciting bit: With these spacetime double-Horus eyes, we see the Kingdom of Heaven is on Earth, through the Earth's fourth-dimensional visionary geography. We are—we have *always* been—living in its midst, in this terrestrial spacetime matrix.

Here's another way of putting it. Steiner said we'd be gradually experiencing a natural etheric clairvoyance as the centuries, starting with the twentieth, progressed. This etheric clairvoyance would facilitate a planetary level of perception akin to what near-death experiencers consistently report as a time tableau of all their life events spread out in space around them. This is a fourth-dimensional perception, and we can expect the same as our natural etheric clairvoyance blossoms—seeing Earth's time tableau of life events.

It will be like suddenly discovering and illuminating a fourth-dimensional hologram packed with information and embedded in our three-dimensional reality. Using a holography model from physics, we can say all the information describing the fourth-dimensional reality of Earth's visionary geography is recorded and embedded in the surface and boundary area of our physical world.

As one scientist puts it, "If the physics of our universe is holographic, there would be an alternative set of physical laws, operating on a 3-D boundary of spacetime somewhere, that would be equivalent to our known 4-D physics."[37] Just substitute "sacred sites" for "physical laws" and "visionary geography" for "known 4-D physics" and you see the application of the analogy. The Earth's sacred sites and Marian apparitional centers are that 3D boundary with 4D.

Let's summarize: The purpose of the Marian apparitions on Earth is to prime the planet and the human collective psyche to ascend to an etheric clairvoyance. I mentioned earlier that the residue of Marian apparitions creates an effect I described as a global Net of Mothers of Christ, thousands of Marys standing like pedestals on the Earth's surface, their hands upraised, holding a net.

Picture a thousand living statues of the Virgin Mary like holographic pedestals standing on numinous physical sites around the planet, as outlined in chapter 2. These are the Marian apparition sites, both well-known and obscure, where she has touched down on Earth in the past two thousand years. The arms of each living statue are upraised, making a Maidenwell of clairvoyant nurturance between her crown and upraised arms, and she's holding something—the 4D spacetime Net. Into or out of this Net is born in us the Christ Child, in one place or ten thousand places—it's all the same place in this fourth-dimensional reality.

So the Net of the Mothers supports the newborn Christ Child, our natural etheric clairvoyance finally extrapolated, born out of us and Earth. But the Net is also the 4D fabric of flat and curved spacetime, of the physics *and* spirituality of light and matter, consciousness and incarnation, Word and Flesh.

The Net is the means of our enhanced clairvoyant perception of it, in it, and through it, of ourselves and our transfigured world. The Marian presence at physical planetary sites is a womb we pass through and get incubated in, to arrive, newborn, out on the Net above her.

The three elements together—sacralized physical site, Marian apparitional presence and residue ("living statue"), and the upheld Net of Mothers underlying 4D spacetime—are one initiatory invitation, one marvelous sign on the Earth written for us by the spiritual hierarchies above.

Once we birth ourselves anew and arrive fresh-eyed in the spacetime Net, we have access to all that is there—Earth's visionary geography and its original model, the cosmic template. This is where Steiner's "natural etheric clairvoyance" will operate, our new four-dimensional world, space through time.

The "Imitation of Christ" on a Global Geomantic Scale

The Christ Event had five major publicly executed stages, each of which corresponded to formerly interior spiritual experiences. These were the birth in Bethlehem, baptism in the River Jordan, transfiguration on Mount Tabor, crucifixion on Golgotha, and ascension from the Mount of Olives. Not only did Ray Master Jesus, bearing the Christ, demonstrate the five stages of the Mystery initiations, but they took place on a geomantic stage. The practical application of this discovery is that, if we wish, we can copy or mimic these stages in the geomantically templated site for our own transformation.

Essentially, Jerusalem and its vicinity was the prime geomantic stage for the performance of the five stages of the Christ Event, from birth to ascension. Each stage took place at a particular type of geomantic site, but these types exist in multiple locations around the Earth, enabling us to interact with them and potentially to have the Mystery initiations publicly demonstrated by the Christ during his unique Earth incarnation without having to use the Jerusalem temple.

The appearance of the Virgin Mary at many seemingly unlikely sites tells us that the Christ Event can be copied virtually anywhere on Earth by an unlimited number of individual men and women. Think of the initiations as on a spiral; you go through them once, perhaps over a period of years; then perhaps again, but at a higher, more refined, or just deeper level.

BIRTH AT BETHLEHEM. Jesus was born at Bethlehem, a town five miles south of Jerusalem. The Magi were guided to his birthplace by a bright celestial light subsequently known as the Star of Bethlehem. This is the outer story.

The inner story is that Bethlehem is part of a landscape zodiac centered on Jerusalem and that within this star template it is the navel of Canis Major, or Greater Dog. The Jerusalem zodiac, one of 432 on the Earth, measures about 18.5 miles across (consisting of two partially intersecting equal-sized circles), and is energized by an even larger domed canopy extending across 41 miles. Thus Bethlehem, five miles distant from Jerusalem, is part of this zodiac feature, yet, appropriately, is not in the center of it all, just as the constellation Canis Major is outside the ecliptic of the 12 zodiacal signs.

The Star of Bethlehem was both external and internal. As an external sign, it was a rare physical manifestation of the Ofanim as a single blazing point of light. As an internal sign, it is the mark of their presence on behalf of the birth of the Christ. As the Ofanim told me years ago, they are the guides and the way to the Christ, just as in their Hindu guise as Garuda, Vishnu's bird mount, they were the foundation for the Hindu Christ to move about the created world.

Further, the Ofanim work with candidates in the Christed initiation through the navel point of the landscape dog, just as in our body the Ofanim as Blazing Star is concentrated just above the belly button. Obviously, to say "landscape dog" is to speak by way of analogy; it's a dog because the ancient psychics who formulated the myths and attributions found a suitable correspondence between the qualities we as humans perceive in dogs and the cosmic function of Canis Major and its major star, Sirius, in the galaxy.

I was introduced to this first feature of the Christed initiation at a tiny hamlet in Somerset called Wick, near Langport and Glastonbury in England. Like Bethlehem, it is situated at the navel or star-point of the geomantic dog in the landscape zodiac surrounding Glastonbury. While I lived there, the Ofanim concentrated their attentions and energies on Wick, me, and my housemates for the purposes of introducing us experientially to this first stage of the five.

The essential point here is that there are 432 zodiacal landscape dogs and navel star-points just like Wick and Bethlehem around the Earth that can facilitate this same experience in anyone wishing to devote time and meditation there.[38]

BAPTISM IN THE RIVER JORDAN. In this second stage of the Christ Event, John the Baptist baptized Master Jesus in the River Jordan at Bethany near Jerusalem. Biblical accounts say the heavens opened up, God announced that Jesus was His Son, and the Holy Dove or Spirit descended upon Jesus. This mark of recognition was the beginning of Jesus' public ministry.

Here the geomantic feature is a Cosmic Egg, around which flows the Great Stream or what the Greeks called Oceanos. Let's decode the Great Stream first.

Oceanos was said to be an ancient god in the form of a cosmic river that flowed around the periphery of the Earth; however, by Earth, the Greeks meant the cosmos, not our planet. Oceanos was the unbroken flow of primordial consciousness before any differentiation into themes, streams, or stars; Oceanos is before the cosmos. He had three thousand daughters called Oceanids, and each was an aspect or theme in the totality or sea of consciousness that he bounded or was in essence. His daughters flowed like arteries through the vastness of cosmic space.

The Oceanids had their physical, geomantic equivalents in Earth's original rivers, including the Jordan, each of which represented a stream of consciousness and was the gateway to its original source. In the myths of various cultures, notably the Greek and Celtic, the terrestrial Oceanids became known as River-gods and goddesses. However, at 48 sites on Earth, the cosmic setup of Oceanos encircling the cosmos (Earth) is replicated. Such sites are called Cosmic Eggs. A Cosmic Egg, a concept well articulated in Hindu, Egyptian, Greek, and other myths, contains all of creation, Heaven and Earth, in one undifferentiated original mass.

I first experienced this geomantic setup at a site near Glastonbury in Somerset, England. As mentioned, Glastonbury has a landscape zodiac, and some dozen or so miles from Glastonbury are Copley Wood and Worley Hill. Coexistent in the supersensible realm with Worley Hill is a Cosmic Egg, and coincident with a tiny stream through Copley Wood is a version of Oceanos. Geomantically, the egg sits in a ring of Oceanos, or we might say Oceanos is the egg albumen and the Cosmic Egg is its rich yolk. (See table 3-3 for selected locations of Cosmic Eggs.)

Table 3-3. Selected Locations of Cosmic Eggs

Uffington Castle, Dragon Hill, Wiltshire, England

Worley Hill, Kingweston, Somerset, England

Mount Sinai, Egypt

Mount Damavand, Iran

Mount Pisgah, Westhampton, Massachusetts, U.S.

Mormon Temple Square, Salt Lake City, Utah, U.S.

Banaras, India (at the Durga Kund)

Heliopolis, near today's Cairo, Egypt

Idaean Cave, Mount Ida, Crete, Greece

Bethany, at the River Jordan, Israel

Here's what you do with the setup: You sit close to the physical stream and allow its etheric counterpart to flow through your heart chakra. You visualize a golden Grail chalice as occupying the space of your heart chakra and allow the Great Stream to flow through it until something happens. It's not water flowing through you or even its etheric counterpart. It's a continuum of deep consciousness, of awareness before time and space, before incarnation.

You find that at the center of this visualized chalice is a seed of light. The Great Stream flowing over it after a while kindles this seed of the immutable flame of love, as the Ofanim have described it. It's like a white pearl that suddenly bursts into flame. Presumably the seed has always been present in the human but you need the baptismal energies of the Great Stream to ignite it.

Then you sit within the landscape confines of the Cosmic Egg and allow your blazing heart seed to expand until it forms a membrane of fire or eggshell of light around your body. Then you wait for the sword stroke: It comes by a hand wielding a mighty sword that penetrates your heart seed to quicken it. Whose hand? Presumably the Supreme Being's, the Great Handless One.[39]

TRANSFIGURATION ON MOUNT TABOR. The third stage of

the Christ Event was the Transfiguration. The Gospels of Matthew, Mark, and Luke tell nearly the same story about this: Jesus took Peter, James, and John with him to a "high mountain" where he was transfigured before them. His face shone like the sun, or the aspect of his face changed, his clothes became as white as the light or as brilliant as lightning, and his three disciples witnessed his glory. Jesus was joined by the spiritual presences of Moses and Elijah; then God spoke from a bright cloud overhead that Jesus was His beloved son and enjoyed His favor.

The geomantic feature that facilitates a transfiguration experience (and which describes the actual Mount Tabor in Israel) is called an Emerald. This is a complex subject, but in brief, the Emerald is an expression of the Heart within the heart chakra, the space between the outer and inner heart chakra in the human. It also represents what metaphysicians have called the Cube of Space, which refers to all of universal space being originally bounded by a cube. The cube tilts 45 degrees, and seen through the intersection of its six vertices is the Emerald.[40]

Geometrically, the Emerald, or Cube of Space, is the first shape to define and fill the cosmic space threaded by the three thousand Oceanids, or consciousness streams. Inside the Emerald is Light, so bright and intense as to remove one from the normal continuity of spacetime, identity, and physical context. Opening the Emerald, then, is a profoundly transfiguring experience, as the matter-based personality is subsumed by the Light of its own Higher Self, and beyond.

In the gospel account, Jesus was said to hear God speak to him from on high; interacting with the Emerald potentially enables anyone to have a direct, sustained, and unmediated encounter with the Supreme Being. But it's more than that; many people can have communication with God "above," but the Emerald transfiguration site provides an encounter that is deeper, more of a vista of the infinity of knowledge and awareness that is the Supreme Being.

Around the Earth, there are 445 Emerald locations. There is one for each landscape zodiac (432), one for each major geometric subdivision of the Earth's visionary geography (called Albion Plates: 12), and one for the entire planet.

It's easier to give some locations for the second and third types: You will find regional Emeralds at the Hill Cumorah in Palmyra, New York; the Hill of Tara, near Dublin, Ireland; White-Leaved Oak, near Ledbury, England; Mount Tabor, in northern Israel; Crnica Hill-Krizevach Hill, in Medjugorje, Bosnia; and, for the planet's prime Emerald, the churchyard of El Templo del Santa Maria near Oaxaca, Mexico, with its famous two-thousand-year-old El Tule tree, which was the focus and "ground zero" of the worldwide Harmonic Convergence in August 1987. You may also precipitate this transfiguration experience by spending some meditative time at Avebury in Wiltshire, England, a 28.5-acre stone circle 30 miles north of Stonehenge.

Undergoing the transfiguration in the Emerald experience may take a while and involve a series of encounters and immersions in the energies. You may at one point see your "body" explode into light, or more precisely, turn into a rectangular block of flaming white stone about three times bigger than you. Of course, it won't be your physical body; more likely your astral form or double.

CRUCIFIXION ON GOLGOTHA. This sounds grim, of course, and we immediately think of the gruesome, torturous physical death Master Jesus underwent crucified on a cross on Mount Calvary, earlier known as Golgotha. The name Golgotha, "the place or hill of the skull," is from the Hebrew *golgos*, meaning "skull" (or from the Aramaic *gulgulta*, which means the same; then later *locus calvariae*, "place of the skull" in Latin), and most historians presume the hill was so called from the abundance of dried human skulls remaining from decades of crucifixions performed there. There's another reason.

The site called Golgotha in Jerusalem is one of 12 sites around the planet called a Crown of the Ancient of Days. This term derives from Judaic mysticism and refers to a mystic perception of the Supreme Being as a White Head turned in profile, a vast countenance of incalculable age—hence "Ancient of Days." The Hindus had a similar concept for the extreme antiquity of their creator god Brahma, whose infinite life was reckoned in Days of enormous extent, each of which is 4.3 billion human (or solar) years. Golgotha is His skull or White Head on the Earth.

Psychic perception at such a site will likely register an energetic feature something like a vast white head or godly countenance turned sideways. In Homer's *Iliad,* the great chief of the gods, Zeus, observed, commented on, and manipulated the Trojan War on the plain before Troy from his seat at Mount Ida. The Olympian gods would fly there from Mount Olympus for meetings, and the mortals down below would tremble when Zeus rumbled the sky with thunder.

This is perhaps a more accessible description of the Crucifixion feature, of which there are 12 major forms and 60 minor, equally distributed on the Earth (see table 3-4 for selected locations). Major and minor as descriptive terms mostly relate to apparent size and experienced intensity of this feature.

Any of these 72 sites offers one the possibility of an even deeper encounter with the Supreme Being than does an Emerald transfiguration node. Our use of such a site would not be to copy Master Jesus' physical death, but to experience what this outward, physical demonstration actually signified: the absolute surrendering of the human I-consciousness to the Father. Christ again becomes one with the Father; certainly, that is a momentous death of identity, yet also a joyous rebirth. This presupposes that the site is functional.[41]

Table 3-4. Selected Locations of the Crown of the Ancient of Days

The Crucifixion at Golgotha

Major Crowns:	*Minor Crowns:*
Golgotha, Jerusalem, Israel	Rotunda, The Lawn, University of Virginia, Charlottesville, Virginia, U.S.
Shadwell, Hansen's Mountain, Charlottesville, Virginia, U.S.	
Gwynfryn, The White Mount, Primrose Hill, London, England	Troy, Turkey
Banaras, India	Forradh, Hill of Tara (near Dublin), Ireland
Abydos, Egypt	Harlech, Wales
Sacsaywaman, Cusco, Peru	
Sodorp Church, Vinstra, Norway	Dunkery Beacon, Somerset, England
Mount Ida, Turkey	
Vatican Hill, Vatican City, Rome, Italy	

ASCENSION AT THE MOUNT OF OLIVES. The Acts of the Apostles in the New Testament implies that Jesus' Ascension took place from the Mount of Olives, though it is very brief in its description of what it looked like. Jesus was "lifted up while they [the "group of apostles"] looked on, and a cloud took him from their sight." From my own contacts, I have heard that 1,080 Seraphim, a family of angels, accompanied the Christ not only during his Ascension, but throughout his Earth ministry after he merged with Master Jesus in the body.

Our concern here, however, is where can we go to copy this experience? But even to answer this, I must redefine the experience of ascension a little. It does neither you nor the planet any good if you ascend right out of matter. Rather, it benefits both if you ascend while remaining physically incarnate.

There are three places on the Earth where this on-Earth ascension is possible. These are called Seats of the Christ Consciousness, or as the Ofanim prefer, Seats of the Son of the Father. In the Crucifixion experience, you potentially visit the Throne Room of the Supreme Being, what the Norse called Odin's *Hlidskjalf,* his universal seat from which he administers all of reality. The Christ Seat is the inverse of this, and it's where the fulfilled Christ essence is grounded on the Earth for human interaction and eventual assimilation.

The three places are Beckery in Glastonbury, England; Lom, Norway; and the Church of the Holy Sepulchre in Jerusalem. At this latter site, Jesus Christ is said to have been buried and resurrected, then ascended to heaven, although, as mentioned, the Mount of Olives also claims this third event. The Church of the Holy Sepulchre and its environs may have the numinous imprint of the actual ascension, but the other two Seats deliver the equivalent spiritual impact.

The Seat may appear to psychic vision as a vast empty chair made of precious pearl, in fact, what Jesus referred to in a parable as the "pearl of great price." The Christ Seat or Throne revolves slowly, irradiating each degree in the full circle around it. It's empty because you are to sit on it to absorb the achieved Christ consciousness. It's a tall order, and it may take a lifetime, maybe ten, to accomplish this osmosis. But think about it: what do you ascend to?

To greater perception of the subtle worlds around you, the fourth through ninth dimensions, which lie unsuspected like layers of an onion about our third-dimension consensus reality.[42] Didn't Jesus say the Kingdom of my Father is spread out all around you and nobody sees it? In ascension, you see it all. It's as if the hologram of higher cosmic reality that is embedded in the Earth's material appearance suddenly rises up before you and you see it all—in fact, you see it through matter, like its hidden essence, Word made flesh and flesh made Word.

Through ascension, you upgrade your cognition to encompass this vaster field of spiritual activity, like a multitiered coliseum suddenly revealed to you, each of its many levels teeming with activity, hosts of angels, posthumans, Ray Masters and their legion of the Great White Brotherhood. It's both on Earth and beyond Earth at the same time, as Heaven is no longer separate from Earth.

The Christed Initiation and Walking in Albion

The preceding five stages of the Christ Event are part of what the Ofanim and their hierarchical colleagues call the Christed Initiation in the Buddha Body. This is a new, and from their viewpoint, preferred way—admittedly an unusual blending of terms and frames of reference—of going through the stages of bringing humans into the sphere of Christ, in the etheric or fourth dimension.

It's a way of bringing forward into present time, and beyond, the unique planetary impulse set in motion by the Mystery of Golgotha. As the Ofanim note, "We are instruments of the Archangel Michael in this activity. He brings the Christ Spirit from the final event at Golgotha. He prepares the Christed Initiation now for the coming of Maitreya, the event of your future."

This is truly long-range planning, for the "coming of Maitreya" is a reference to the prophesied Maitreya Buddha, presumably the last in a series of incarnations in the history of humanity; the Hindus similarly forecast an ultimate incarnation of Vishnu, as the Kalki Avatar. Both (more likely, they are the same being seen through different filters) are expected to manifest as harbingers of apocalypse, around the time of the "end" of the world. However, the similarly prophesied

End Time may well be a time not of death, annihilation, and termination, but rather of a wonderful human and planetary transfiguration.[43]

Let's return for a moment to the composite image presented above of the living holographic statues of the Virgin Mary standing on Earth's sacred sites and creating a global Net of the Mothers into which the Christ Child is born.

I suggested this Net of the Mothers could be seen as our entry into the spacetime fabric, our ascension into Steiner's predicted natural etheric clairvoyance finally blossoming in humans. The spacetime fabric is but the foundation for further subtle extrapolations of contexts for consciousness, for what we commonly label "higher dimensions," such as the fifth through ninth.

Similarly, physicists state that while 4D reality may be recorded in the surface boundary of our 3D reality, 5D reality is similarly embedded holographically in the boundary of 4D. So once we make it, cognitively, into the fourth dimension, we have potential access to the next subtle layer, the fifth dimension, and a revelation of its visionary geography and levels beyond.

All of this is to introduce the idea that there is something to note in the extended higher dimensions of spacetime and the Earth's visionary geography, something in fact that encompasses the spectrum of the fourth through ninth dimensions or layers of reality. We need to remember that the Earth's visionary geography, which consists of three physical and six nonphysical layers, is a replica of the cosmic visionary terrain, the extended dimensionality of spacetime.

I say "extended" because even though I simplified the concept of spacetime curvature with respect to individually described masses, spacetime *really* involves billions of spacetime warpers (spherical, symmetrical bodies of mass and/or energy) distributed not like points on a straight line but as scintillations within a sphere.[44] That means spacetime curvature is multilayered, and one way to conceive intellectually of how this works is to picture it as a layering of dimensions perhaps in accordance with the holographic model.

In experiential, cognitive terms, this means when we're psychically walking—perceiving—on the surface of spacetime, this is only the first of many levels we could potentially see and interact with.[45] If all the extended dimensions of spacetime are thought of as a cosmic giant, then in this first layer of spacetime we are but walking on its skin. There are still more skin layers and all the internal organs and the skeletal structure to visit before we have thoroughly explored "him."

Appropriately, several myths and Judaic mysticism describe such a giant. Judaic mysticism uses the term Adam Kadmon, while Chinese myth calls it P'an Ku, Norse myth Ymir, Persian myth Gayomart, and the Gnostics Anthropos. All present the same idea: all of creation expressed as a vast, spherical human form—a *rotundum.* Some of the myths say all of creation came out of this being when "he" offered his cosmic body in sacrifice for the proliferation of creation and its forms. Others imply that, mystically, all of the created forms are subsumed or culminate in him.

This cosmic being exists above us and within the Earth, so to keep the levels straight, let's call the upper, original, cosmic one Adam Kadmon, and the lower one that envelops the Earth, Albion, using the name favored by the early nineteenth-century English mystical poet William Blake in two of his major poems.[46] Adam Kadmon above has at least nine layers or dimensions, and so does Albion below, which is to say, around us. Albion is the colossal single figure that all the holograms embedded in the Earth's 3D reality generate when illuminated. In other words, if you could decode and spotlight the compacted, recorded holograms in each of the subtle dimensions, fourth through ninth, you'd get Albion.

This means all of the 92-plus distinct features and their multiple copies within the Earth's visionary geography are organs, bones, capillaries, cells, and atoms in this giant body of light. His name even acronymically encapsulates this—Albion: *A Light Being In Our Neighborhood,* our neighborhood being the six subtler dimensions surrounding us and our planet into which Earth's numerous sacred sites open like doorways and upon which Mary pedestals sit.

So we have this marvelous prospect of walking around *inside Albion,* this star-filled higher-dimensional cosmic being enveloping our physical Earth. It turns out that when we can walk in Albion, we are simultaneously taking or embodying the Christed Initiation in the Buddha Body, according to the Ofanim.

But that makes sense after all: Christed cognition enables us to perceive the subtler dimensions, all the mysteries and epiphanies of higher spacetime.[47]

But what is this mouthful, this conflation of Christian and Buddhist terms? Let me preface my comments by noting that Steiner also foresaw that Pauline Christianity and Shambhalic Buddhism would merge or find complementary ways of working together. He predicted that the Christ one day would lead humans into Shambhala, which for Buddhists is akin to the Seventh Heaven. In the vocabulary of visionary geography, it is one of the eight celestial cities of Mount Meru accessible through 1,080 different sacred sites around the Earth.

Shambhala, as Steiner described it, is the place from which initiates have always brought strength and wisdom for their missions among humanity. Increasingly, over the next 2,500 years, humans will glimpse this realm—"light-woven, light-gleaming Shambhala, abounding in infinite fullness of life and filling our hearts with wisdom"—coincident with perceiving the etheric form of the Christ, Steiner said.[48] Shambhala is the "deep fount into which clairvoyant vision once reached," and the Christ will lead us there, when we're ready. This will be a momentous turning point for us, Steiner said, through which our "understanding of the Christ Impulse will be enhanced and intensified."[49]

So what is the Christed Initiation in the Buddha Body? It's a series of initiation experiences, set in geomantic contexts (sacred sites) that include the five stages of the Christ Event described previously, only elaborated into ten stages. The Christed part involves an infiltration of consciousness by the living energy of the Christ, while the Buddha Body part refers to a certain transformation of the "body" of consciousness into something described that way in Buddhism.[50]

The Ofanim note that we're in the very early days of this initiation, and should not expect the Virgin Mary apparitions, despite whatever the Marian seers claim she says about the culmination of her appearances, to end soon. "When the possibility of the Christed Initiation in the Buddha Body is more generally accepted as a means through which to integrate the experience which goes beyond the reflection of self to the Christ within, then those apparitions will diminish," the Ofanim say. For the meantime, they are still required as initiation inducements.[51]

Cloud of Smoke: UFO and ET Visitations—An Irruption of the Galaxy into the World around Us

4 | Cosmopolitan Earth—The Implicit Planetary Reality of Extraterrestrials

Since the late 1940s, people around the world have increasingly been reporting sightings of UFOs and encounters with alien beings or extraterrestrials, commonly abbreviated as ETs. At the same time, governments have ignored, denied, ridiculed, or facilely explained away these empirical reports. This has left Western culture with a disturbing cognitive gap between actual experience—empirical, body-based evidence—and official consensus-reality denial. We experienced something alien, but the authorities say we didn't, or that what we experienced wasn't nonplanetary in origin, but something mundane, such as a military aircraft, swamp gas, or earthquake fault emissions.

I find this tedious, don't you? Metaphysically parochial. Limiting.

The simple fact is that knowledge of the Earth's vast geomythic body—its multileveled auric field—demonstrates convincingly that the Earth is a galactically cosmopolitan planet. There are, and always have been, ETs all over the place, all around us, and, legitimately so, within the Earth's subtle body.

Just as UFOs often cloak themselves in complex clouds and smoky shapes, so the issue of UFOs and ETs sits under a smokescreen of confusion, disinformation, invalidation, and disbelief.

To ask if intelligent life forms exist elsewhere in the universe is a moot, even silly, question when you probe even the surface description of the Earth's visionary geography. You find that "aliens" have been living in our midst ever since "we" got here; in fact, they've been here long before the advent of humanity on Earth. Their being here actually made our being here possible. The makeup of our ecosphere, noosphere, our inner and outer environments, is due to the abiding and implicit presence of numerous types of ETs in our midst.

Certainly, as an outward cultural phenomenon, ETs are prevalent. You see them in movies, TV shows, books, magazines, cartoons, product commercials. It's all out there in front of us almost daily, yet still "they" officially do not exist.

My intent in this chapter is not to prove the truth of UFO sightings and alien encounters. I take that as a given, amply demonstrated by empirical facts.

My interest is in deciphering what this second sign on the Earth might be saying. Some areas, such as the so-called Mysterious Valley in Colorado, the Hudson River Valley in New York State, Topanga Canyon in California, and Hessdalen, Norway, seem to attract ET activities. Perhaps there are geomantic features in these and other sites that support ET-human interactions. Perhaps these are "message boards" on which we may decode these newest signs on the Earth.

Public Opinion Challenges Official Consensus Reality

It's instructive to look at the results of various public opinion polls on UFO beliefs to see how strong is the empirical belief in their reality despite official denial. John F. Schuessler, writing for the

Mutual UFO Network in an excellent tabulation of 50 years of public opinion sampling on UFO belief and experience, remarks, "While the numbers have fluctuated from time to time, the general results of these surveys showed the public to be very aware of UFO sightings, interested in what may be causing them, and concerned that the government was not doing enough to resolve the mystery."[1]

In August 1947, more or less the year in which modern ufology began, a Gallup poll revealed that 90 percent of Americans asked said they had "heard" of "flying saucers," but that 33 percent didn't know what they were, 29 percent thought they were mirages, optical illusions, or products of imagination, 15 percent regarded them as a U.S. secret weapon, and 10 percent thought them hoaxes. In 1957, a Trendex poll reported that 25 percent believed there is some possibility the saucers came from outer space, though 52 percent said no. Curiously, a large number of those who answered no added that they thought flying saucers originated on Earth.

A 1966 poll showed that 96 percent had heard or read about saucers; 5 percent thought they might have seen one; 46 percent contended saucers were real; 34 percent that humanoid creatures are living on other planets. In 1971, Gallup polled leaders in the fields of medicine, science, education, politics, and business in 72 nations, and found that 53 percent expressed a belief in extraplanetary life. As early as 1971, in a poll of 90,000 readers, 76 percent stated that the government had not revealed all it knows about UFOs; 54 percent believed UFOs probably exist; 32 percent that UFOs come from outer space; and 36 percent knew somebody who had claimed a UFO encounter.

In 1982, Gallup revealed that 50 percent of those asked believed in life on other planets, while a 1984 *Psychology Today* poll of readers reported 50 percent believed in UFOs. A 1987 Gallup telephone poll of 527 Americans age 18 and older showed that 50 percent believed there are intelligent, possibly humanlike, beings on other planets, that 49 percent believed UFOs are real, compared with 34 percent who were skeptical and 16 percent who were unsure, and that 9 percent had sighted a UFO. Belief in ETs was substantially higher among college-educated people and males expressed a stronger belief (62 percent polled) than women (40 percent) in ET existence.[2]

A poll in June 1996 of 1,006 adults revealed that 19 percent thought it very likely and 31 percent likely that UFOs are real and the government suppresses the truth.[3]

A Gallup poll of one thousand American adults conducted in 1996 showed that belief in UFOs overall was steady, at 48 percent, about the same as for the previous two decades (1990: 47 percent; 1978: 57 percent). At the time of polling, 72 percent were convinced there is life elsewhere in the universe, although only 38 percent thought it would be humanoid in appearance. The poll showed that 71 percent believe the U.S. government is withholding information about UFOs from the public; 12 percent had seen something they thought was a UFO; 45 percent believed UFOs had visited Earth.[4]

A *Newsweek* poll that year reported 48 percent of respondents stating UFOs are real and 49 percent that the government is keeping back information. A Yankelovich 1997 survey showed that 79 to 82 percent of those polled believed the government was hiding evidence of ETs, 64 percent that intelligent life exists on other planets, and 42 percent that aliens had visited Earth. In Britain, a 1999 survey reported that between 43 percent and 65 percent believed intelligent life exists somewhere in the universe; the variance was due to geographic location of those polled.[5]

Lest we think it's just Americans who are running point on ufology, a Canadian poll published in October 1987 showed that three million Canadians, or about 9.6 percent of the population, said they'd seen a UFO. The study also reported that 78 percent believed in extraterrestrial life, 52 percent that UFOs are alien spacecraft, and 57 percent that there was a government or military cover-up about them.[6]

The copious data of public opinion makes one thing incontrovertible: there is a lot of smoke around the UFO/ET issue, highly suggestive of fire—ET presence and activity on Earth. Belief in ETs and actual experience of them or their craft have been steadily growing over the past 60-plus years. The key data pertains to belief in Earth visitation by ET races. That belief too has been essentially holding steady: 63 percent in 1987 (per a metaphysical society[7]), 27 percent in 1990, 58 percent also in 1990 (*National Enquirer* readers), 33 percent in 1994, 26 to 42 percent in 1997 (depending on whether those polled watched *The X-Files* regularly[8]), and 30.3 percent in another study in 1997.[9]

Even more interesting are data recording the public's probable reaction should the ET reality and Earth-presence be convincingly demonstrated. In June 1999, a Roper Organization nationwide survey of 1,971 people reported that 90 percent of "influential Americans" thought if undeniable proof of ETs were revealed, the U.S. government would classify or suppress the evidence while 25 percent believed that most Americans would "totally freak out and panic." If the aliens looked very different from humans, 34 percent would be open and receptive to interaction while 58 percent would be cautious about interaction until more was known.

However, 32 percent said they regarded themselves as psychologically "fully prepared to handle" the ET revelation, and 17 percent said they would use the confirmation as a catalyst to rethink their human place in the universe. The poll showed that 71 percent would not change their religious beliefs even in the face of a highly publicized ET landing; 64 percent said they would be ready and willing to learn how to communicate telepathically with the aliens; 42 percent said the announcement of an imminent ET arrival would only change their lifestyle to a small degree; and 69 percent believed governments would "pretend" to handle the ETs, "but not really be able to."[10]

The data from these various public opinion polls conducted since the late 1940s show a steady increase in the widespread acceptance of the probable reality of ETs and UFO visitations to Earth and the inevitability of contact. Thus despite official denial and invalidation of ET reality, the public largely believes otherwise and is gradually preparing itself for the impact of undeniable proof.

Where the ETs Already Are in the Earth's Visionary Geography

The aliens are already here on the Earth and among us, and have been essentially since the creation of the planet. We just haven't been looking *there*.

Where they already are is in the Earth's visionary geography, the planetwide domain of sacred sites and their fourth-dimensional energy structures. As I established in my two previous books (*The Galaxy on Earth*, 2002; *The Emerald Modem*, 2004), the Earth is a designer planet. From a geomantic perspective, its design was deliberate, purposeful, and ultimately benign with respect to the possible evolution of human consciousness within biological bodies. The design was implemented with the commissioned involvement of numerous ET families.

The goal was to make it possible for embodied humans to experience the highest states of consciousness while alive—in effect, to remember and embody Heaven on Earth. The means was to design a living planet with multiple copies of celestial and spiritual world structures, temples, residences, and processes. These structures were subtle, recessed from physical reality as we ordinarily experience it, yet easily accessed through outwardly marked sacred sites. Marked means various physical structures, often of stone, were placed there, from stone circles originally to cathedrals and other temples later. All this was done in accordance with the amended Hermetic axiom, "As above, so below, and in the middle too."

The *above* is the original structure of Heaven, or the spiritual worlds, and the galaxy; the *below* is the human, understood in the perennial wisdom tradition as the microcosmic embodiment of everything in the above; the *middle* is the forgotten Earth, usually (wrongly) left out of this equation, equipped with an equivalent microcosmic array of the *above* features. The key concept here is that the *below* (humanity) and the *middle* (planet Earth) have been "stamped" with the identical celestial template, though in a way appropriate to the obvious differences in form between a human being and a planet.

My research over the past 20 years suggests that both the human and Earth exist within the same hologram of the galaxy and spiritual worlds and that this galactic hologram is full of ETs. We could with some justification and a lively sense of paradox more accurately call them intraterrestrial, or ITs. They are, ultimately, *from* planets and star systems other than Earth, yet they live legitimately *in* our midst within the Earth's visionary geography—as it were, in *both* places at once due to the holographic nature of the Earth's visionary terrain.

There are four major ways cosmopolitan Earth is made possible through its visionary geography or the galactic hologram.

First, there is the landscape zodiac, the interactive energy feature I have previously discussed. Picture an edited version of the galaxy, emphasizing the major constellations and the traditional signs (constellations) of the zodiac (on the ecliptic) and about two thousand stars, represented in a hologram set upon a portion of the landscape, varying in diameter from one-half to one hundred miles. You could conceivably find the landscape touchdown point for the Pleiades, even specific stars in it, and even more conceivably, you could interact with Pleiadians through that conduit. Most probably the interaction would be subtle, on a visionary or psychic level. There are 432 of these interactive landscape zodiacs across the planet.

Second, there are 1,746 energy canopies called domes settled over many of the planet's major mountain and volcanoes. The domes, though not physically present or visible, are what make most sacred sites sacred. They give them a numinous quality that lifts consciousness. Each dome also corresponds to a specific star, not by archeoastronomical alignment, but again, by holographic copresence. Mount Palomar in Southern California, for example, is the dome-star for Alnilam, the middle star in Orion's Belt. This means that there you could psychically contact the energies, maybe even the presence, of beings from the Orion system, and there they could contact you, and the planet as well.

The Earth's domes each can generate up to 48 smaller dome caps, or subsidiary energy canopies, and these are arrayed around the "mother" dome so that if you viewed it from a considerable height, it would resemble a sunflower head in full bloom. The dome caps represent (and holographically present) minor stars and planets associated with them from throughout the galaxy. That means you could potentially see another planet and its form of sentient life through a dome cap. That also means that on at least a subtle level that same planet has access to our realm through the geomantic nodes.

Third, there is an even more direct, real-time connection with stars, planets, and the homeland of God knows how many "alien" civilizations. I call them stargates, even though the term has been used often and usually to mean something else. There are many places on the Earth where actual transportation between Earth and other stars may be achieved. There are, in fact, over two million such transportation portals across the Earth, going to planets in association with either major stars or constellations. I have heard of people and even objects being moved through these stargates in the deep past; the stargates are still among us, though very subtle, and are twice removed from the third dimension.

Fourth, a galactic consortium known as the Pleiadian Council of Light has 60,600 apertures across the surface of the Earth allowing us access to them. They're called Interdimensional Portals (I've been through a few of them) and they conduct you across dimensions to at least the outer foyer of the Council headquarters. It's a bit like tunneling from one end of New York City straight into the United Nations building, though you probably won't make it into the Security Council chambers on your first go.[11]

The Council has 26,000,000,000 members from across the galaxy. This Council and its many agencies disseminate the transmission of Light (consciousness) across dimensions. It is based at several of the planets within the Pleiadian systems, and its members come originally from the Pleiadian planets whose populations then expanded into their quadrants of the system related to the Pleiades. Even more interesting is the fact that, according to the Ofanim, 14 Council members are from Earth. Given the existence of the Council, the portals, and the Earth members, we shouldn't be (though no doubt we are) surprised that the Pleiadian presence on Earth is big.

These four features were part of the planet's original design, as implicit in its structure as a nose, elbow, and knee are for the human body. Earth was meant to be galactically cosmopolitan from its inception, and it has never stopped.

Here's how this might work on a practical, experiential level. Let's take the case of the Grays, today's most widely recognized alien, with their short gray forms and black almond-shaped eyes. These are the ETs most often associated with abductions of humans and presumed collusion with secret organizations within national governments. Various speculations have been forwarded as to their point of origin; one favorite source is the star Vega in the constellation Lyra.[12] Let's accept this for the moment and note the geomantic ramifications.

First, the constellation Lyra will have 432 landscape apertures on the Earth by way of its legitimate placement within the landscape zodiacs. Second, the dome on the planet that is the Vega dome is Brown's Hill, opposite Monticello in Charlottesville, Virginia. Third, multiple stargates provide transportation to both a planet near Vega and other destinations within the Lyra constellation. They also provide transportation from those locations to Earth stargates. Let's remember, all this is a two-way setup.

This means there are three categories of geomantic features where the Grays, if they actually come from Vega, can enter Earth's visionary geography as legitimately as vitamin D being absorbed by human skin through exposure to sunlight—no ships needed. In other words, no collusion with secret government organizations is required for this elementary level of penetration of Earth reality. The Grays can come and go as they wish from their dimension of reality to ours and can, if they wish, impart a sustained psychic influence on human consciousness through their legitimate holographic residences at multiple Earth sites.

All this is in addition to whatever interactions they propose by mobile "ships" in which their encounters with us are not tied down to specific geomantic nodes or where they occur through extradimensional or dream contact more or less on the Earth plane, and as popularized vividly in the works of Whitley Strieber (notably, *Communion: A True Story,* 1987), among others. Typically, these encounters are involuntary, forcible, somewhere between unpleasant and horrific, and often forgotten (suppressed) for decades by the experiencer.

I have seen Grays at the Lyra nodes in selected landscape zodiacs, and in the zodiacal correlates for Zeta Reticuli, a star in Reticulum. But I have also seen them on several occasions outside of either "official" context, such as in Island Pond, Vermont; Santa Fe, New Mexico; and Rondablikk, Norway. On some of these occasions, they were trying to interfere with spiritual work I was participating in with the angelic realm; on other occasions, they tried (and failed) to take "me" against my will, but in some cases they succeeded in abducting me, at least astrally.[13]

I put "me" in quote marks because often it is not exactly one's daytime, waking sense of self that seems to be taken elsewhere, and certainly in most cases, this daytime self has no conscious recall of the interaction. Even more intriguingly, when memories start to filter through from this other dimensional self that underwent the abduction or forcible interaction, it exists as an incongruent time track bizarrely parallel but not intersecting one's own sense of time continuity and experienced events.[14]

There are at least three further observations to put forward in support of the presence of "aliens" in our midst, even before humanity arrived on Earth.

First, the design, installation, and maintenance of the Earth and its visionary geography are credited to representatives from eight star families acting under commission from the highest spiritual authorities, presumably, the Supreme Being. These include stars and constellations. According to the Ofanim, these "beings" are from Sirius (Canis Major), the Pleiades, Orion, Cepheus, Cygnus, Ursa Major, Arcturus (in Boötes), and Canopus (in Argo Navis). These star families have maintained a cadre of planet supervisors ever since the Earth's inception, working through their appropriate and multiple landscape nodes.

Second, there is, of course, the widely disseminated idea that ETs created, cocreated, or genetically engineered humanity, and possibly still do. This subject is well covered elsewhere, so I will not delve into it, other than to recommend an excellent overview of the possibilities of this view by Paul von Ward, titled *Gods, Genes, and Consciousness: Nonhuman Intervention in Human History* (Hampton Roads, 2004). If certain ET families are biological parents to humanity, then it shouldn't surprise us if our parents want to have a peek periodically at how we're doing.[15]

Third, humans are not native to planet Earth, at least on a soul level.

After all, where did we all come from? As far as I can tell, none of us came from *here*. We are all foreigners, emigrants—aliens and extraterrestrials. We all came from *there*. According to my friends in high places, there is a greater diversity of souls and soul origins on this planet than nearly anywhere else in the known multiuniverse, which comprises more than 18 billion galaxies. In this galactic array there is a greater diversity of souls at different stages of development and a greater diversity of their point of origin.[16]

Mind you, we are not recent arrivals. This all happened long ago, many millions of years before now. The business of point of origin is what you may dredge up out of your own unconsciousness during regression or insight. What kinds of places might you find? The Pleiades is a popular point of origin. This is a star cluster of seven more or less visible stars and another estimated three hundred in the throat of the constellation Taurus. Of course, nobody comes from a star or sun, but I'm told the Pleiadian stars have a fair number of inhabited planets under their supervision.

The list of points of origin for human souls on Earth is extensive, but I think you get the idea. Maybe a memory of a strange and different place may surface in your thoughts one day, a planet you once lived on perhaps? (My angelic informants also note that before "we" started settling on Earth from elsewhere amidst the vast congeries of other stars and planets, humanity—or the idea for it or our deep ancestors or maybe yourself 100,000 lives ago—came from another galaxy altogether: Andromeda. The Andromeda galaxy is one of 35 galaxies in what astronomers call the Local Group, our Milky Way galaxy's local environment. Of the 35 described galaxies in the Local Group, the Andromeda galaxy, or M31, is the brightest in what astronomers dub "a remarkably dull corner of the Universe."[17])

So behind the fact that we, as souls, are not from Earth but truly ET in origin ourselves (deriving mostly from elsewhere in the Milky Way galaxy), before that, we were still ETs, hailing from another galaxy altogether. At this level of analysis, we can't get away from the conclusion that we are all one-hundred-percent alien.

Alien Lives, Missing Time, Enforced Amnesia, and Real Dreams

One clear benefit of ET contact, though in the short term packaged in some distress or trauma, is a rearrangement of our sense of reality.

Some people are starting to remember their galactic origin and lives on other planets, even though such a possibility seems very remote from daytime consensus reality. Dolores Cannon, author of numerous books on ET issues and a skilled past-life researcher, has helped many people remember suspected ET experiences through the technique of regression hypnosis.

For example, a woman was driving along a two-lane road in Maui in 1994 when she saw a small housing development of modular homes; it seemed familiar, yet she knew of no place like it on the island. Hypnosis revealed she had been transported to her home planet, which she called "the repository planet of knowledge," where during her missing time she gave a report on Earth conditions to a round-table colloquy of her fellow extraplanetary beings. The beings she encountered told her she was one of them. "But I have gone out from this place as an investigator to gather information," she said, and she was gone for a *very* long time. "I never thought I'd see this again . . . It's like I'm coming home."[18]

The "modular homes" were a provisional compromise image her human mind created to account for her translocation to another planet without fully admitting it had happened. Previously, she had had no clue as to her possible non-Earth soul origin and life mission.

In another prolonged hypnotic past-life regression, Cannon discovered that her subject, named Phil D., had never had a human life on Earth before. According to his subconscious testimony, all his past lives were on alien worlds and in other dimensions of reality, and even in his current life he was in continuous contact with his alien mentors and colleagues, although his self-knowledge of this was protectively hidden from him by his subconscious.[19]

Those who know they have sustained ET encounters, even if they have not retrieved the full memory, almost uniformly attest that their lives were profoundly changed. Their entire sense of physical reality was altered. Abduction researcher John Mack, M.D., points out that abductees are "ontological pioneers who . . . are helping us to break out of the bubble of a constricting world view."[20] Dr. Mack writes of the "ontological shift" most abductees experience as they are suddenly exposed to undeniable other (multiple) levels of reality, and aberrations in their sense of time continuity, commonly called "missing time."

A person cannot account for ten minutes or several hours, yet they strongly suspect something happened to them during that missing time—usually of an ET nature. An associated phenomenon is called "screen memory." In the cited example from Dolores Cannon, the woman interviewed "remembered" seeing modular homes in a new housing development on Maui; on reflection, she could think of no such place on the island. Her mind—or perhaps the ETs themselves—created a plausible cover or screen memory to account for the otherwise unaccountable lapse in the continuity of experience.

Our materialist paradigm says such experiences are impossible. But what if we have such an experience anyway? Then we need a story to smooth over the gap in time and lived experience. If we're fortunate, and courageous, we may see through the screen. Abductees realize that reality must be redefined in the light of such experiences.[21] For some contactees, that redefinition is unavoidable. "The very foundation of my sense of self, personal autonomy, and free will was undermined."[22]

Dr. Mack says that ET encounters are hyperreal, "strange hybrids of mind and matter" that seem to happen both inside and outside us, in a time frame incompatible with our conventional sense of passing time. Such experiences shatter our psychically comfortable understanding of space, time, dimensionality, reality, and matter—all the psychic structures in which we live. Dr. Mack's interviewees used terms such as fractured, deep shock, or a sledgehammer to describe their experiences; abductions are the "fast track" to personal change, one woman commented.[23] It's as if the alien encounters take place in a dimension outside our normal three-dimensional framework, one in which space, time, consciousness, matter, and experience work together *differently*.[24]

Alien encounters shake up our belief systems. We realize we don't know reality at all or understand the range of consciousness. Supposedly fixed parameters of space, time, and matter are mere mental constructs, arbitrary boundaries that can be moved, and abruptly. Consciousness and matter are no longer separate. We can have memories of experiences seemingly had in our body that are incongruent with our sense of time continuity. We can live for years consciously unaware of alien encounters, even though our body subliminally remembers the events.

Many abductees cannot figure out *where* and *when* their encounters happened, or in which body they experienced them—dream body or daytime physical body. They can remember, at least partly, terribly odd experiences, but these do not mesh with their ordinary flow of awareness and continuity of impressions. It's as if they run parallel, in another life or frame of reference or in a strange hyper-dream state that seemingly has no points of connection with daytime consensus reality. The otherworldly experiences work themselves out in the person's body and mind, but that person cannot logically account for them.[25]

ET interactions especially shake up our sense of reality when we have not remembered them. Often a screen memory is never penetrated. Our body and perhaps a part of our deep subconscious know that something deeply unsettling happened, but we in our daytime awareness do not know.

UFO abduction researcher Budd Hopkins discovered, as he reported in his now classic account *Missing Time* (1981), that most people he hypnotized to recover missing time experiences and UFO encounters "had absolutely no conscious memory of a UFO sighting." He realized that anyone in the general population could have been abducted yet have no conscious recall of it. People, he concluded, are being "picked up, 'examined'—sometimes marked for life—and released, their memories conveniently blocked."[26]

Hopkins uses the term "enforced amnesia" to indicate the process of efficiently erasing from conscious memory "all but the very slightest" recollections of anomalous experiences. Typical of abduction experiences is the merging in memory of its beginning and end, "a joining so seamless as to leave the abductee with no *feeling* that he or she has actually lost any time," despite what their clocks say. You remember sitting in your car observing a UFO, then you remember driving down the street with no UFO in sight. What happened in between is totally lost to conscious memory, and even suspicion.[27]

Early in her adult life, Angela Thompson Smith, Ph.D., began to suspect that she had missing time that needed to be filled with remembered content. A scientist and a psychic, Dr. Smith began to suspect she was living a double life, but only remembering one. She kept a meticulous journal for 13 years, a self-inquiry process of recording dreams, events, suspicions, and recalled fragments of a strange body of experience involving aliens. What was most strange was this other life seemed to run parallel to her bodily one, but on a separate time track or in a different sense of time duration or in some crack between the worlds. All this left Dr. Smith with an unsettling cognitive anomaly: *When* did it all happen?

Dr. Smith developed the term "real dreams" to account for the baffling aspects of the memory fragments. In real dreams, "events that seem to have happened in what Carlos Castaneda called the 'second attention,' are recalled during sleep and remembered as dreams."[28] So what she remembered as a dream was in actuality the memory of a real alien interaction, presumably involving her in some bodily way, seeping into the subconscious at night. The *when* of Dr. Smith's 13 years of ET experiences was outside our normal time framework, in a time flow in which time passed radically differently.

A Silent Invasion or by Invitation Only?
Aliens among Us on Earth

In case you think all this talk about ETs officially invited into the Earth's subtle geography, and bizarre human-alien interactions set in mysterious time and identity discontinuities, is remote from your daily affairs, think again. The aliens (primarily the Grays) have come "secretly and silently," and it's not for our own good, notes one researcher. "The aliens are deliberately confusing things to ensure we have no clear picture of what is occurring."[29]

Increasingly, psychics who "read" the auric layers and chakras of clients are finding evidences of alien intrusion right in the energy field of individual clients. Researchers have documented the finding of strange metallic physical implants in various parts of human bodies, but I am referring to something energetic.

Clinical hypnotherapy patients under hypnosis by trained medical professionals have reported an array of strange energy devices in their own auric field, of which they had been oblivious before hypnosis. These include (according to one practitioner) visual descriptions offered by the patients of displacement devices, devices resembling a radio receiver, focusing dishes, wave machines, black energy absorbers, silver rods, dark triangular shapes, black umbrellas over the head, and command, observation, and communication centers.[30]

So-called alien scientists can, according to another hypnotherapist, implant "physical and nonphysical probes and various devices into humans for the purpose of location, control, communication, monitoring, and gathering information." These devices, according to empirical observations of hypnotized subjects, "control aspects of emotion and behavior; in some cases, the anger and fear function is increased." In some cases, patients become aware of the physical repercussions (such as chronic pain or dysfunction) of implanted or emplaced alien devices such as, in one case, two mechanical clamps on a woman's head.[31]

Trained psychics who read or diagnose the energetic conditions of patients' auras report an even greater alien infiltration. Often alien energy (in a generic sense, indicating that kind which is unwholesome to humans) appears as a silver color. It may be in spots, streaks, or broad swathes throughout the seven layers or seven chakras of the person psychically viewed. There may be energy devices, such as a silver cowl over the crown chakra, or what resemble laser rays anchoring into different parts of the body.[32] These rays may be psychically traced upward (into the next dimension) into alien "ships" where they emanate from beam emitters of various types.[33]

Psychics further report that many people have their cognitive options and incarnational freedom curtailed by way of alien "report stations." The theory behind these stations is that in between lives, especially those lived on other planets or in other galaxies, the human soul is stripped of information gathered in those non-Earth experiences so that they cannot bring it forward (and eventually remember it) into their next human-Earth incarnation.

The report station is a kind of cosmic customs office and passport control. The restrictions imposed there (and the inaccessibility of one's spiritual information) may be undone during a human lifetime by a skilled psychic healer. You may have perhaps two dozen or more alien report station connections in your auric field; unless you have a skilled psychic reading or undertake a psychic training program, you may never become aware of them even though they are influencing you daily.[34]

In comparison with alien abductions as commonly described, the alien influences and devices I just outlined exert a kind of chronic passive influence. You may never remember an unpleasant alien encounter, yet you may possibly have various alien control devices in your energy field. What can they do? They can produce physical discomfort, headaches, illness, strange mental states, forgetfulness, oblivion of psychic experiences, fear, a disembodied state, and/or an inability to recall consciously any kind of extradimensional ET contact.

The matter of the relationship of Grays to humans is complex. The Ofanim note that humans can have radically different perceptions of the Grays, depending on their past karma with this race. In practical terms, some find the Grays to be an interference; others find them congenial.

Clairvoyants I have polled suggest that in most cases, Grays interact with humans on the basis of long-standing agreements, "contracts" that might have been formed long ago by the soul behind the present personality. To account for human-Gray interactions, you must entertain a multiple lives perspective. In one life, you might make an agreement with the Grays to provide information to you, or to help you with an energetic problem; in subsequent lives, you may have no interest in this or are oblivious to the outstanding agreement, but since the contract has not been nullified, you are subject to Gray incursions into your auric field, chakras, consciousness, and life. And in the present lifetime, you may regard these incursions as unwanted.

In some cases, the Grays want information that certain humans are able to collect from the Akashic Records (a kind of universal library) from which the Grays have been excluded for past inappropriate actions. In other cases, the Grays may imitate benevolent spirit guides or even the classical Muses to pose as a source of higher inspiration for people unable to discriminate finely enough. You think you are sensitively contacting higher benign beings with valuable information, but it's actually the Grays in disguise, using the deception to enter your space and have their way.

I have observed dimensional doorways or tunnels into our reality by which the Grays can pop into neighborhoods and observe, interact, or befuddle human residents. These tunnels do not seem to be extensions of ships, but rather conduits into the intricate energy configuration of the Earth's visionary geography; small groups of Grays can come and go through these.[35]

Alerting Us to the Long-Standing, Ambivalent ET Presence on the Earth

Perhaps you are sensing now that the alien-ET sign on the Earth is at best an ambivalent wake-up call. It can have both nightmarish and epiphanous aspects depending on the type of encounter and our reaction to it.[36] A prudent criterion for evaluating a budding awareness of the alien presence on Earth and your own possible or dimly suspected past encounters is freedom. Do the ETs respect and support your human freedom or seek to limit and control it?

The situation is similar to the biblical book of Job. God commissioned Satan to tempt, even harass, Job to see if Job still respected God when his life was ruined. The story shows how the Supreme Being can use an agency seemingly inimical to human freedom and well-being to provoke a potential spiritual upgrade. Similarly, the Supreme Being, in conjunction with the various levels of the galactic spiritual hierarchy, regulates ET infiltration of the Earth; following the Job analogy, a certain amount of seemingly inimical, unsavory alien presences are allowed (or not prevented from being here—the subtle difference may be important) as a prod for humanity's privilege of wakeful choosing.

Choosing what? Freedom over subservience. Wakefulness over unconsciousness. Seniority over being controlled by outside influences.

The Supreme Being, upon granting humans free will, also allows us to make agreements with various types of aliens, ultimately as a salutary learning experience. Of course, the short-term experience may seem like a nightmare.

In *The Galaxy on Earth,* I described briefly how a strange alien family, Lizard beings, had infiltrated a geomantic node and sickened the landscape. Here the incursion was long term, quite similar to the way opportunistic pathogenic bacteria can take advantage of weakened biological conditions to flourish. On a visit I made in 2001 to a site in Tennessee called Clingman's Dome, I saw that many hundreds of six-foot-tall astral Lizards had infested the astral space at the top of this mountain. Geomantically, this peak had a dome and was an important chakra point in a regional geomantic configuration that encompassed the North American East Coast, from Nova Scotia to North Carolina to Arkansas.

Here the alien-geomantic node interaction was negatively reciprocal. The dome (an etheric energy canopy many miles wide) over the mountain was energetically broken; the Lizards had gained entry to this geomantically compromised energy field, and pushed the disorganization further to suit their conditions. The trees around the peak were all sickened, and there was an irritated, almost baleful, psychic atmosphere at the mountaintop, which was visited by many thousands of tourists every year. Since every visitor was exposed to this noxious psychic atmosphere, they were also potentially vulnerable to influences and even attachments from the Lizard beings. Thus unwholesome aliens at one geomantic node can influence a much greater area.

Sometimes inimical aliens take advantage of one-time acutely traumatic situations on Earth, the way bacteria rubbed into a skin wound accelerate infection. On September 11, 2001, I was part of a clairvoyant group that looked at the psychic aspects of the terrorist attacks in New York and Washington, D.C., just hours after they had finished. Not surprisingly, the inner view we attained was markedly different from the external, media-driven perspective—not to mention the official U.S. government statements, which weren't much different from the media's.

Our group impression was that at a subtle level the United States had been attacked by alien ships. Specifically, Washington, D.C., and the White House were under the influence of multiple beams from up to 24 alien ships overhead. One massive ship had descended over the capital city and enveloped it, interpenetrating the city's physical space with its alien presence. Aliens of various descriptions were visible throughout Washington, including in the White House, as if overshadowing or even possessing senior officials.

The city resembled a portion of human skin exposed and made ready for surgery while the rest of the body (the continental United States) was covered in protective wrappings. This surgical space was highlighted or illuminated, as if held in a *Star Trek* type of tractor beam. The source of the "tractor beam" seemed to be a planet in another galaxy, and its intent was to hold open the connection between dimensions, theirs and the Earth's.

The beam resembled a light corridor, but it was a sickly, dirty pale-blue light. Aliens—not Grays—had facilitated (or encouraged) the outward terrorist attacks because they knew the mass fear created by it would rip a hole in the Earth's etheric aura sufficient to allow the extragalactic aliens opportunistic egress into the Earth sphere. It would rip holes in human auras and crank the root chakra wide open in a state of chronic fear, making the mass of people highly susceptible to influence, be it governmental or alien.[37]

The effect was to put Washington, D.C., and to some extent the upper East Coast, into an altered reality for a while as alien cognitive input was downloaded into this psychically opened region and from there infiltrated through the collective psyche of those living on the American landmass. During the day, the angelic realm was busy trying to narrow this beam and sew up the spacetime rip, but the alien "blood," so to speak, had already been transfused into the American psyche and to an extent, the global one as well.[38]

No doubt other mass events in recent experience could be similarly read clairvoyantly to reveal shocking ET contributions or manipulations of our reality.

The ET-alien sign on the Earth is hardly new; today it alerts us to a preexistent alien-ET presence in the Earth's geomantic terrain and human psyche. Since the ET reality has been denied, repressed, ridiculed, and marginalized for so long, the overabundance of evidence of ET-alien interaction with the Earth and us is sufficient to crack that wall of denial and put the matter in our faces.

One initial conclusion can be offered thus far: The Marian apparitions unquestionably *add something* to the geomantically prepared nodes at which they occur. They imbue these already heightened sites with an added spirituality. The UFO sightings and ET encounters at geomantic nodes do not add anything to them. They do not spiritually enrich such sites, but rather seem more to take advantage of the rich geomantic energies present or to manifest through them because such sites make physical or quasi-physical manifestations easier.[39]

Further, these phenomena seem to signify the releasing of something from the Earth, the sign emerging from within the planet's subtle terrain, namely, that ETs are inherently and always have been part of the Earth's psychic fabric. In this view, the geomantic nodes themselves release the signs on the Earth, testifying to the ET reality and its interpenetration with human life.

As such, UFO phenomena consistently associated with geomantic nodes *showcase* some of the subtle, energetic aspects of these places and their higher physics. In the next chapter, we'll look in detail at sites with high UFO activity and outline certain geomantic aspects that seem to support or enhance it.

5 | *UFO Hotspots—Is There a Geomantic Basis for Alien Encounters?*

Given the Earth's vast array of geomantic nodes, is there a direct correlation between UFO sightings, ET encounters, other human-alien interactions, and the various visionary geography features in a hotspot locale? Do ETs of different star origins have legitimate functions on the Earth through these geomantic nodes?

The answer to the first question, as we'll see, is yes with respect to sightings but not so much with encounters[1] and abductions,[2] and yes with qualifications to the second, as it depends on the particular ET-star family. In this chapter, we'll look at the geomantic basis for activities of six ET families and consider how the visionary geographic features of particular sites—among them, Mount Shasta, Hessdalen in Norway, and the San Luis Valley of Colorado, all renowned for constant UFO activity—support human-ET interactions.

Examples of Mandated Aliens Present on the Earth

We've been considering some of the dark aspects of alien involvement with humans on the Earth. But there is a salutary aspect to it as well. Some alien families or species were actually invited to Earth and are doing some good here. It is possible to have interaction with aliens while in a wakeful state and without any of the traumas to body or mind that often go with such encounters.

I recently interviewed 15 species of aliens legitimately present on Earth; I conducted my interviews by way of clairvoyant viewing and listening. The results are intriguing and possibly liberating, as the information was imparted in a state of neutrality and (no doubt mutual) observation. Here are the results:

Reagis. This first group identifies itself as the Reagis. They take the form of large orange orbs of light and call themselves "energy." They often congregate like myriad bubbles around the rim of important Earth geomantic sites; some sites are more potent receptors for their energies. They modulate the currents, including atmospheric, solar, lunar, stellar, and planetary (planets other than Earth), as they enter the Earth environment.

They say they number in the millions and when in motion are often mistaken for ships though they are only partly physical and certainly not metal-based. Sometimes, when swollen with collected energies, they can be seen by humans. They were assigned to do this maintenance work for the planet. They collect, intercept, assimilate, and deposit the energies like pollen where needed.

Retmors. These are dark-blue elongated beings, like bare tree trunks, with thin sticklike arms, an inverted broom or comb for a head, and two eyes. The broom-head is like an upward-facing comb with long thin tines or vertical rays. The Retmors say they are sentinels for the air element or possibly the ether, so it can carry thoughts. They are like air filters and are often stationed on prominences such as hills and mountains. There they assemble in circles of 20 to 30, facing outward, their backs to the center of the circle, and move thoughts through the Earth's ethers—"whatever is thought."

Aaoloans. These are part Grays and part "other." They look somewhat like the classic short-statured gray aliens with black almond-shaped eyes, but their skin is much paler, like a bleached gray-white, and their heads larger, like small bulbous octopus craniums. They say they have ships but are here for observation and information. They travel in pencil-thin conveyances and plant these as observation posts in the landscape; they reside at the top in the "eraser-end" of the ships. They observe the interactions of humans, plants, and animals—in effect, the ecosystem. There are "hundreds of millions" of these observation posts around the Earth, they say, but they are rarely seen by humans. The Aaoloans are not allowed to interfere with human or ecosystem affairs.

Reptilian-Heads. This is my awkward name for a group that did not name itself, at least in any way I could discern. They look like brown humans with a lizard's head—actually more like Australian thorny devils, which are quite intimidating to view. The Reptilian-Heads stand erect at perhaps three to four feet high; they have very scaly, horny, thick skin, appearing almost as a natural armor. They are primitive and fierce in the face, which is exceptionally thick and horny.

They are on Earth to study aggression. Their own race is too aggressive and they are collecting an antidote for that from the less aggressive humans. These beings were brought to Earth long ago and left here. They extract the energy of aggression from the atmosphere and distill it as a medicine for their people, like a poison to antidote snakebite. They go to war zones and areas of conflict to extract the aggression energy. They are not allowed to interfere in human affairs and are primarily scavengers of released aggression energy.

Centaurus. This type of being initially resembles a very tall praying mantis insect, standing very gangly with many thin limbs at about ten feet tall. Their heads are bulbous, like that of an octopus. They come from the constellation Centaurus. Their task on Earth is to "obliterate obstructions to the flow of joy," as they put it. They are hard for humans to see as they exist in multiple dimensions; we end up seeing only a portion of their true form, like an elbow jutting into our reality. They add something useful to our planetary geomantic system by emitting little orbs of joy into specific areas. These appear as blue orbs with a turquoise octahedron (two four-sided pyramids pointing in opposite directions). They were asked by the Supreme Being to do this for this planet.

Snail Beings. Again, this is my provisional term. This species of alien looks like a brown snail standing upright without its shell; they have two stubby antennae on their heads. For those familiar with the movie version of *Dune,* they resemble the wormlike beings. This is not what they look like, they told me, but their true form won't collapse or condense itself into anything cognizable to our human frame of reference. Anyway, they are more of a process than a fixed form. A pod of 20 or more of them will form a blue sphere; they line up side by side, their backs to the center of the sphere; in this form, they monitor incoming solar radiation. They keep the "shipping lanes" open for ships from other stars. Certain radiation lines are better for Earth-reality entry, and these beings "open doorways on the sunbeams for visitors."

Saurus-type Pleiadians. These aliens have a human torso but a very large, wide, bulbous head that seems so filled (presumably with brains) that it is almost bursting. They stand about four feet tall and come from a distant planet in the Pleiades star group, one not named in our star lexicon. They look after our intents and the development of higher mind capabilities on Earth. They say they have small craft, but these are mostly mind-made and shaped, borrowing a few Earth elements for a quasi-physical and mostly ethereal ship.

This family of Pleiadians moves in and out of the Earth, visiting the small human population inside the Earth and the much larger one on its surface. Sometimes they send "helpful rays" or thoughts to groups; in such cases, 30 to 50 of them form a halo and send down to a group positive, helpful thoughts like a focused rain shower of light.

Yellow Beings. This group did not identify or name itself, though their "physical" appearance was vivid. They are tall, yellow beings, like a flaming yellow column; inside this is a vague humanlike yellow form. These beings come and go from Earth as they please, no ships required; they come originally from another galaxy. Here they study sex and polarized energies. They congregate inside the domes and around the outer edges of the projected energy fields of these geomantic features.

Sun Emissaries. This name is provisional. These are blue beings (a medium shade, approximately cobalt) with a body consisting of a circular halo of blue, inside of which is a blue head or focus of awareness. These beings line the blue dishes (special concave geomantic features added to a landscape site by humans through meditation; they look like pale-blue tea saucers hundreds of yards in diameter) and help with geomantic energy enhancements, especially at prepared sites such as stone circles, henges, and ditches as found in Celtic Europe (see *The Emerald Modem* for more on this). Their work makes it possible for such features to receive more cosmic energy, which is a kind of food for the Earth and one of the purposes of these megalithic structures. A group of Sun Emissaries will gather together in a tight circle and form an insulating band or electrical ground (it resembles aluminum) around the site to hold in the charge. They make themselves into an electrical socket, analogously, into which a cosmic energy is inserted like a plug. Or you could say they form a protective, containing fence around these sites; then they disperse the collected energy into the landscape.

Red-Flame Beings. These look like adult humans with intensely red skin, enveloped in red flames that do not burn them but are part of their energy. These beings, whose demeanor is feisty, almost pugilistic, say they come from Antares, the bright star in the constellation Scorpio. (In Chinese star lore, Antares was known as the "Fire Star," among Hindus as *Rohini,* meaning "Ruddy," and among Persians as *Gel,* "the Red.") The Red-Flame Beings regulate heat on the Earth, especially through volcanoes.

Transmitters. This alien species is adult human in size, but their skulls are silver, as if they wear a close-fitting silver skullcap or sheer helmet in the area where a human would have hair on the cranium. The silver skull facilitates transmission of information and coordinates, they say. They are linked to one another through their silver heads; the linkage creates a fibrous web of tendrils, so that from a planetary perspective, the Earth is enwebbed by thousands of these Transmitters with their silver head-projected tendrils. They look after their own interests and ground the energy of their source (star origin) in the Earth.

Dinosaur Beings. These are 15 to 20 feet tall, dark, fierce, primitive, blue-green and gray, and much like the standard depictions of physical dinosaurs—scary and big. Their heads have long thick tails that come out the back of their skulls and trail down their spines. They hold the energy residues of the extinct physical dinosaur species and the original thought-forms from which they were created.

They were brought here and have no ships of their own. They may be intimidating to contemplate, but their function is more benign. They supervise the plant and oil interests of Earth, the energies around the long-term conversion of compacted ancient plant matter into petroleum. They look after the long-term fate of the plant kingdom from the Earth's earliest days (some esotericists call this planetary epoch Polaria, the time of plants, or as the Ofanim quip, Planet Plant). They are psychically vulnerable and can be manipulated.

Streaming Crowns. Again, this is my name for them. This species appears as Native American *kachinas* (masked spirit forms) standing three to four feet tall. They have immense feather headdresses, such as Native Americans wear for ceremonial purposes. The feather headdress is part of their head, perhaps a crown chakra made of streamers of light. These streamers flow down to their feet behind them. I saw thousands of these creatures in a desert environment where they combined to form a giant monolithic expression of themselves, several hundred feet tall.

In totality, this creature resembles a Native American chief with elaborate headdress. He appears to summon rain and lightning by raising his arms, but he may also be communicating with his home world, which I understand is somewhere in the constellation Cetus, the Whale. It appears that this species focuses discharges from the atmosphere, under commission of the Supreme Being, to replenish the Earth. They collect the energies in their streaming crowns, then shake them off onto the land.

White Wheels. I named this group based on their appearance. They are like white wagon wheels, each with an eye for a hub. They fly, or wheel, around the sky at all angles, rotating rapidly like little whirlwinds. In this way, they help clear the air element of obstructions and toxicity. They have no interactions with humans as a rule, though sometimes they are seen by people. When rotating fast, they can appear as a white sphere, a whirlwind of eyes, seeing in all directions at once, like eyes in the sky. They were created here on Earth by another alien race from a different galaxy to be factotums.

Artilarians. This is the alien race that created the White Wheels. They came in motherships long ago and their form is humanlike. They look like Vikings, standing six feet tall, wearing skintight armor, including a close-fitting metallic skullcap, though not the same as that worn by the Transmitters. The Artilarian I saw was male, about 30 years in age (by human standards), probably weighed two hundred pounds, was highly muscular and physically fit, and exuded an air of civilization and development, despite the macho exterior. They are only partly physical, as we define the term; they phase in and out of our visible realm.

This group created the White Wheels to be their watchers, to collect information for them. The Artilarians study the collected information as a way of keeping tabs on some of their old projects on Earth.

These 15 different alien species are here by permission of the Supreme Being and the delegated powers that supervise the Earth and its humans. As you can see, none interferes with humans, most are neutral observers or pursuing their own interests, most are not ordinarily visible by humans, and a few contribute positively to our well-being, even though we are routinely oblivious of their presence.[3]

Now let's examine the nature and activities of other ET families that have a more active involvement with Earth and its developing humanity. Some of these are better known, even more trendy, than the 15 I just detailed. Let's see what the beings from the Pleiades, the stars Sirius and Canopus, and the constellations Orion and Cygnus are up to on Earth, starting with the Pleiadians, probably the star family most familiar to most of us, by name, reputation, or at least rumor.

Lawful Activities of the Pleiadians in Human Life and Experience

I use the word "lawful" to emphasize activities by alien species or families that have been mandated by the highest spiritual authorities overseeing Earth.

As many readers are aware, a great deal has been published on the postulated involvement of Pleiadians in human life: as the source of some UFO encounters and mostly benign alien visitations; and as humanity's spiritual mentors in our time of personal and collective transformation. Throughout various cultures and mythologies of the world, from Greek to Native American, they have been prominently recognized, described, and to an extent interacted with.

I will describe two different and compatible clairvoyant impressions of the lawful activities of the Pleiadians in the human and planetary sphere.

Let's start with the human sphere. Astrology claims that the constellation of Taurus (the Bull) rules the throat. The Pleiades, a star cluster of six bright stars and one less bright (together often known as the Seven Sisters) along with an estimated 300 more stars, is situated in the throat of Taurus.[4] Astrology, to be more precise, should say that the Pleiades rules the throat. But how could this be so?

I saw how during a dedicated psychic research reading with a friend on the role of the Pleiades in the human constitution.[5] Seven light streamers were attached to the front of my friend's throat chakra in a horizontal row. At the beginning point of each streamer was a goddess statue, but as I looked deeper, each was a living personified expression of a Pleiades "sister." The whole setup was a kind of holographic temple or energy necklace in the throat chakra. Each Pleiades sister, through her energy temple position in the necklace, affected an aspect of the overall throat chakra function; generally, psychics agree this pertains to creativity, expressivity, and communication in all aspects of life.

Each sister was represented by a color, in addition to the visual presentation as a goddess or celestial being. These colors included spring green, pink, pale blue, purple, cobalt blue, emerald green, and yellow. These colors do not correspond with the conventionally described physical aspects of the stars, which are also given in colors for their spectral emissions. It's more useful to think of these perceived colors as energy signatures or frequency identifiers.

The node on the far left of the throat necklace (as I look at the person; it is reversed if you look down at your own throat) is a pale crystalline blue and is the starkness of pure consciousness, like a clear blue sky at midday. In the second slot is Taygete, whose color is spring green. It is a kind of cosmic chi or primary life force, almost a form of cosmic plant food, providing vital nutrients for sacred speech that, when uttered, quickens human consciousness.

The rich grassy green one, to the immediate left of Alcyone in the third slot, is like a diva's wide-open operatic mouth, full throatedly expressing the Pleiadian creativity in our world. This is the star-being Electra, the energy of generation and the potency of the voice, almost to the extent of being histrionic. This Pleiadian holds information about grammar, the alphabet, the gene pool underlying world-generating sacred speech, and the differentiation into form.

The middle or fourth Pleiadian throat temple is that of Alcyone, the brightest star in the cluster, with a connection with the thyroid gland, one of the body's main endocrine-hormonal glands, responsible for body-heat regulation, metabolism, and many crucial system-wide functions. The thyroid gland itself has a chakra, and perhaps the Alcyone presence there is that temple, or at least the goddess resident in the temple (minor chakra).

This Pleiadian star spiritually energizes the thyroid gland and establishes the fundamental ground or baseline for the expression of the six other Pleiadian energies through the throat. The esoteric function here is mantric speech, world-generating sacred speech, the kinds of holy utterances that sanctify and empower, and in traditions of sacred language, such as Hebrew or Sanskrit, give birth to energy forms, shapes, and directions for reality. You could say this is the chakra underpinning for the use of the focused voice in magic, both white and black.

The fifth slot is purple, and this Pleiadian sister is a tutor and mentor for cosmic ideas as filtered through or maintained in the Pleiades. Here you can access a repository of ideas for creation; the experience is akin to time spent with a wise, loving grandmother. The sixth node is Merope, whose color is yellow. This energy acts as a womb to incubate the products of sacred speech. On the far right, the seventh node is pink and is equivalent to the breast, a nurturer for spiritual creation.[6]

No doubt this is an unusual perspective on the Pleiades and the human. It does give us a new way of understanding why astrology says

Taurus rules the throat, though I propose the verb "rule" is a bit misleading. It is more accurate to say Taurus, especially the Pleiades, influences, works through, and has its legitimate place within the human constitution through the throat chakra and is particularly involved with supporting and facilitating human creativity.

The second clairvoyant impression I'll relate here pertains to an activity I saw a group of Pleiadians conduct at Fajada Butte in Chaco Canyon in northwestern New Mexico. Fajada Butte (the Navajos call it *Tse Diyili*, "Holy Rock") is a prominence that rises 423 feet above the canyon floor, giving it a total elevation of 6,623 feet.

Fajada Butte is one of the Earth's 45 time portals. This recondite geomantic structure involves the nature and dynamics of time. Don't think of time as a straight line but as a sphere, giving it a vertical and horizontal dimension. Time is not so much an arrow as it is a liquid pool.

The time portal gives you access to time across dimensions and parallels; in this way, you can study, perhaps influence or manipulate, the ambi-dimensional ripples in time that any single event creates. Drop a stone in a pond and observe: The ripples spread out laterally, the stone plunges to the bottom, the splash interacts with the air around the pond. Any moment in time, any action committed in time, has potential ripples across many dimensions, up and down. So the time portal is a place of entry into a highly sophisticated time realm, and it was with this arcane geomantic feature I saw a group of Pleiadians working.

At first glance, it appeared they were inside Fajada Butte, but of course they were not. They were in the *same place* but one or two dimensions removed from the stone of the butte. The butte marked the spot. There were six Pleiadians: tall, robed, hairless, with enlarged craniums, and not speaking; they communicated telepathically as they stood around a large pale-blue crystalline basin situated inside what appeared as a turquoise igloo of shaped light. Inside the basin was a complex interconnected web of lines and points of light. From my technical perspective, it seemed to be a four-dimensional engineering grid of the Earth's living energy matrix. I say "four-dimensional" because it had the quality of movement, spinning, being seen from different or multiple angles.

The Pleiadians were inserting what seemed to be glowing marbles at certain intersections of lines in this complex web of light. I later understood that they were placing what I call time caves or time wombs in the light matrix. Since they were working at a holographic level involving many dimensions and parallel time tracks, the Pleiadians were generating these time caves both in the Earth's geomantic web and throughout the galaxy in other solar systems. Think of a time cave as a hollowed-out space filled with time, like blood—a galactic uterus, so to speak—in which life could evolve, be it a planet or solar system.

The tableau was paradoxical. The Pleiadians phased in and out of humanlike forms. One moment they were eight feet tall, highly mental and psychic neo-humans; the next, they were shimmering pillars of light, like in a rotunda. Technically, they probably were not even on the Earth, but somewhere in the Pleiades, yet their work was specifically focused through or deeply within Fajada Butte. Since the Pleiadians were working through one of Earth's 45 time portals, clearly there was relevance both to the portal at Chaco Canyon and to the Earth and its needs as well.

According to information provided by the Ofanim, during the period of Anasazi residence at Chaco Canyon,[7] there were points at which the time portal was opened and they had access to its ambidimensional matrix. To what end? Interaction with the time portal enables you to consolidate all your time bodies—the residues of previous lives lived in Earth time—into a wisdom body. It's a kind of distillation process, whereby you winnow elements of wisdom from the vast stretch of yourself spread out over past lives and consolidate them into one composite body of wisdom. In this work, the Pleiadians are our mentors.[8]

Repercussions of the Early Days of the Pleiadians on Earth

Less esoterically, the Pleiadian presence and presumed continuous interaction with humanity has clues out in the open once we recognize them. Take the House of Atreus at Mycenae, Greece, the focus of a fair amount of Greek myth, tragedy, and early history, including the Trojan War. You know some of the names: Agamemnon; his wife, Klytemnestra; his brother, Menelaus; his wife, Helen; Agamemnon's children, Orestes, Electra, and Iphigenia. Atreus's lineage is second-generation Pleiadian, and to discover this you need only consult the exoteric family tables in Greek literature. Aeschylus's *Oresteia* is a Pleiadian saga.[9]

We find another Pleiadian clue hiding in plain view with the classical Greek reference to Hyperboreans.[10] Scholars customarily interpret the term Hyperborean to mean "those living beyond the North Wind (Boreas)," but that is only geographically correct. The Hyperboreans were actually Pleiadians resident on Earth, fulfilling a geomantic commission from the Supreme Being to help set up the Earth's web of sacred sites and the planetwide matrix of visionary geography. The term more properly should be interpreted as "The Wandering Ones," in accordance with the Greek root for Pleiades, *plein*, which means "to sail," hence, "the Sailing Ones."

A certain cadre of Pleiadians more or less permanently wandered the galaxy, visiting planets, helping out where invited, staying for a while, then leaving. Other Pleiadians remained at home, so to speak, where even today, according to the Ofanim, on some of the planets within the Pleiades star system reside many of the teachers waiting to incarnate on Earth to assist in our planet's and humanity's transition to a more spiritually sophisticated view of the world.

Those Pleiadian teachers-in-training get regular updates on our progress, including telepathic briefs from the Ofanim, so they can access how humanity is being prepared for their forthcoming presence on the Earth—and the new level of information and experience they will impart. Generally speaking, the Pleiadians are able to bilocate and manifest their energy bodies, normally invisible to humans, in such a way that we can sometimes perceive their energy fields, though most often we mistake these fields for UFOs, ships, and spacecraft.

Greek drama and myth provide us another key clue about Pleiadians.

The House of Atreus, Greek tradition tells us, was cursed from bad deeds committed by its earliest members, Tantalus and then Pelops. Tantalus, a son of the high gods, was blamed for several malfeasances, most notably serving up his son Pelops as a dinner dish for the gods, who at first ate him unknowingly. When they realized the offense, they reconstituted Pelops, except for his shoulder, which was already consumed, so he got an artificial one. Tantalus was banished to Tartarus for his offense against the gods while Pelops had the whole of southern Greece named after him, Pelops' Island, later known as Peloponnese.

Pelops later offended the gods by drowning Myrtilus, another child of the gods, so he could win a chariot race. Just before he died, though, Myrtilus cursed Pelops and his descendants, the future House of Atreus. The curse had its most potent effect on the two sons of Pelops—Thyestes and Atreus—who feuded implacably. Atreus repeated the dinner trick of Tantalus, by serving up Thyestes' children for a meal, leading Thyestes to repeat the act of Myrtilus and curse the House of Atreus again.

How is all of this relevant to the subject of aliens on Earth? The cursing of the House of Atreus holds a secret pertinent to the origin of the Earth.

In simplest terms, there are good Pleiadians and bad Pleiadians, the moral line being drawn on the issue of supporting or hindering human freedom. The true history of the earliest days of the Earth and to an extent everything since is to some degree a saga of Pleiadian karma, of offense and retribution, impropriety and redress.

To start with, in the geomantically formative years of the Earth, when its visionary geography was slowly being implemented, the Pleiadians were major players on a team that comprised many representatives from different stars. (This arrangement is described in detail in *The Emerald Modem.*) One of the principal reasons the Pleiadians (and some of the other star families, including Sirius) were involved so intimately in Earth's geomantic extrapolation was that such work is apparently part of their galactic mission. Another reason was to pay off their bad karma.

Some Pleiadians had been involved in the solar system disaster that led to the destruction of the planet Maldek, between Mars and Jupiter, now an asteroid belt. They had interfered with the planet's orbit and sentient life evolutionary agenda, and basically tried to speed things up. The planet wobbled and exploded. Another planet needed to be readied and then supervised and maintained for the continuation of the conscious life evolution begun by those many souls on Maldek. Another place had to be found where the Maldek conditions could be simulated. Earth was that planet, so the Pleiadians, Sirians, and other star colleagues came on assignment here to accomplish that.

The Ofanim tell me that, paradoxical as it sounds, prominent among the specific stellar forces arrayed against their intent of facilitating the Earth to be a place of spiritual freedom and soul evolution into Christed initiation are Pleiadians. But prominent among their allies and cocreators are also Pleiadians. "There are many forces interested in the outworking of energy on this planet."

Emissaries from the Dog Star—
The Sirian Presence on the Earth

How about the star Sirius? This is our galaxy's brightest star, 8.4 light-years distant from Earth, located in the throat of the constellation Canis Major, the Great Dog. Hence Sirius is often called the Dog Star. Most myths say of the Dog that it is the Guardian of the House of Stars, or our Milky Way galaxy.

Sirius is connected to our planet in a very intimate geomantic way. First, the Earth's umbilicus, grounded at Avebury stone circle in Wiltshire, England, consists of two energy strands: a silver strand from the star Canopus (the rudder of Argo Navis, our galaxy's second brightest star) and a gold strand from Sirius. (Energetically, the Earth is fundamentally extraterrestrial in origin and nurturance.) Second, Sirius is "wired" into the Earth by way of its dome at Karnac in Brittany, France. Third, each of Earth's 432 landscape zodiacs has a grounded star point for Sirius. Fourth, there are stargates on Earth for Sirius.

On these four counts alone, Sirius is already fundamentally part of Earth, and since the Earth's visionary geography creates and sustains all biological life and higher consciousness states in humans, we are already living and psychically immersed in a continuous Sirian (and Canopean) atmosphere.

But here are some clairvoyant impressions of aspects of the subtle connections between Sirius, the Earth, and humans, if we choose to participate. Whether we perceive the Sirians in ships or palpable bodies or light forms (along the quasi-physical lines by which we are culturally accustomed to perceiving the Grays, for example), this race of ETs is deeply involved in the maintenance of Earth and its evolution of higher consciousness through humans.

In addition to the four geomantic features (mentioned previously) that holographically interface with Sirius, an additional feature called an attunement bridge (or resonance bridge) facilitates human-Sirian exchange. These bridges are dedicated geomantic spaces found in Canada, California, the Southwest, and places west of the Mississippi River. They appear to resemble seven- or eight-pointed blue stars overlaid on the landscape, and they provide a bridge, or link, between human and Sirian universal consciousness. You might think of the attunement bridge as a consciousness oasis through which people can have the experience of connecting in vision with beings from Sirius.

What will you see? Here is one impression: A tunnel of light opens over your head and a series of cobalt-blue transparencies or blue films come down the tunnel. They are about the size of humans and seem sentient, but they have no thickness, no palpability, and seem like superconscious blue tablets.

An aspect of yourself arcs out of your head and spirals up the light tunnel as a golden-yellow ray. You travel rapidly and effortlessly through the galaxy until you see a wreath of beings surrounding a red planet. You approach and enter this, and it now appears as a transparent red sphere with multiple passageways leading into a central chamber.

It's made like the layers of an onion, and each layer has scripts, symbols, and hieroglyphs on its surface. You enter the central chamber and note that a tetrahedron also occupies that same space. You sit inside this and communicate telepathically with the Sirians, mostly with symbols.

It is a vast cathedralic inner space whose walls and ceiling are made of huge interlocking blue slabs, each 50 feet long and about half that in width. These slabs maintain the energy or consciousness vibration at a set level for the vast interior meeting space, which resembles a council chamber. I saw perhaps one hundred Sirians seated in council around a massive rectangular table. They looked much like the ancient Egyptian depictions of their gods' tapering headpieces two feet high.

If your focus is geomancy and Earth energies, you may become aware of our planet at this point, especially of the fact that it emits many different tones. In fact, at first hearing, it strikes you as a cacophony of tones and vibrations. Your task here is to help modulate and balance these disparate, possibly chaotic tones. The Earth emanates *many* tones: whale songs, coyote calls, human distress. Inside this red sphere, you are able to adjust the symbols, which in turn adjust the range of Earth tones. You do this to help relax the planet. You notice that inside the Earth is a spinning red sphere just like this one. A copy perhaps?

You observe the vibrations emanating from the Earth and, putting it simplistically, reset the dials by way of the symbols. It is a finely tuned feedback, like a finely strung 12-string guitar that periodically goes out of tune from neglect, unwholesome manipulation, misuse, entropy, growth spurts, even climatic changes. The job here—and this is a part of the Sirian responsibility for Earth—is to observe fluctuations in tones, study the cacophony of influences that continually seek to change the Earth's essential vibration, and restore things to harmony, using the symbols as dials, knobs, and gauges. Somehow the symbols activate pure tones and harmonics that are converted into (or modulate) the denser vibrations and tonal frequencies of the Earth.

Orion—The Galaxy's Spiritual Warrior and Immune Defense System

Let's look at the constellation Orion next. This is a huge star figure with many very high magnitude stars in its form, including the three belt stars. In myth, Orion is the Great Hunter; he was once the tallest and most beautiful of men, as Homer put it, and before he became a constellation, he claimed superiority over all Earth creatures. Orion is also credited with trying to carry off and marry one or all of the Pleiadian sisters. Orion's presumed boast of superiority may hold a key to its geomantic function.[11]

Here is a general clairvoyant impression of some aspects of Orion's galactic function with respect to Earth. Picture Orion as an androgynous, humanlike, multidimensional star being, which means he has many facets simultaneously expressed, though you may cognize only one at a time (as if you're circling a massive statue). Planet Earth sits inside this star being like an egg or a fetus, surrounded by a maroon amniotic fluid. The Earth is continuously bathed in this fluid, which seems gelatinous, like aloe vera gel.

Orion nurtures Earth through this amniotic fluid. It is one way Orion protects the Earth, acting as its galactic immunological shield. It is a shield for consciousness, for the foundational distinctions between self and not-self; but here the immunological function is more than biological. These distinctions pertain to self (Milky Way galaxy) and not-self (other galaxies). Orion's reputed warrior aspect is executed by the way it acts as a filter for extragalactic energies, alien viruses and DNA, and other destabilizing influences that seek to enter our galaxy. You could usefully construe Orion as an immune system, white blood cells, T cells, and macrophages, all maintaining the integrity (here expressed as consciousness and DNA parameters) of Earth.

The DNA aspect is also central to Orion's role. In clairvoyant visits or readings of Orion's role with respect to Earth, it was clear that in some way Orion regulates DNA expression, integrity, and experimentation in the galaxy. Orion claimed his "superiority" to indicate "he" was capable of protecting DNA evolutionary streams throughout the galaxy; you can only effectively protect something if you are superior (or senior) to all potential adversaries. So Orion shields our galaxy from unwholesome or "indigestible" extragalactic energies just as the human immune system filters out foreign proteins or antigens.

On a planet in the Alnilam system (one of the belt stars), there appears to be a council or standards committee that oversees DNA expressions throughout the Milky Way galaxy, including here on Earth. Picture a trade show with exhibits and lectures in a building that resembles the Sydney Opera House in Australia; an Orionian—their bodies are vaguely humanlike, comprised mostly of gas and little water or earth—stands on a stage with a hologram of DNA, giving a report on recent experiments. Above and around him, like a blue corona, levitates the five-member standards committee.

Apparently certain renegade, duplicitous, or simply disobedient ET families conduct their own unsanctioned DNA experiments on planets, including Earth; since the consciousness vibration on Earth is, relatively speaking, dense, it is easy for the ETs to hide or mask their intentions and experiments.

The trouble is that the secret introduction of alien viruses on Earth can, when the viruses are triggered, create inexplicable DNA mutations, shifting human biological and consciousness evolution away from its intended track. One aspect of Orion's work on the Earth, in cooperation with human geomancers, is to clean out these alien DNA experiments and disable the mutation triggers. This immunological work can be done through particular Earth geomantic nodes.

The Earth Activities of ETs from Canopus and the Great Bear

Canopus (Alpha Carinae) is our galaxy's second brightest star, located at the rudder or keel of the constellation Argo Navis, the Ship. Greek mythology tells us Argo Navis was the fabulous talking ship—it had a sentient effigy of the Olympian goddess Hera as its stern, dispensing guidance on the journey—on which Jason and his 50 Argonauts sailed, visiting the ancient Mystery temples.

Geomantically, Canopus is well represented on Earth. It is the source of the silver strand that interlinks in a double helix with Sirius to be grounded at Avebury as Earth's galactic umbilicus. The star dome for Canopus is at Iona, the sacred island off the western coast of Scotland; Canopus has stargates on Earth, and it is represented in the planet's 432 landscape zodiacs.

Clairvoyant research suggests that the Canopeans are a migratory race, traveling across the galaxies not in bodies but in consciousness, and inspiring, supporting, or benevolently influencing a host of civilizations on various worlds. They may partially incarnate on selected planets, such as in the Sirian or Pleiadian system, assuming for the most part the dominant physical form on each place, and maintaining varying amounts of their essential Canopean energy signature within those forms, as a kind of active soul essence memory, we might say.

On the Earth, their manifestations are highly subtle and very light. They do not assume palpable forms or even psychically perceivable forms, only outlines or insinuations of a shape. Picture a diaphanous ethereal being, in shades of blue with a bright white glow, in a form more or less vertical like a human. They move fluidly through the air in the airwaves or in moving water.

Here is one way Canopus can interact with humanity on Earth: Take a war-torn area, such as the Mideast. To psychic perception, such an area might appear like a gray hurricane, black swirls spinning around a dark center of negativity. One Canopean being touches the tip of her "finger" to the top of this dark vortex and transmits a harmonic of peace into the churning darkness. The swirling slows down a little, the dark clouds break up a little, and a few humans pop out of the darkness below on the surface of the Earth and rise into the light.

The Canopean harmonic enables these humans to shed some of the darkness in them so that they are no longer resonating with the war vibration. The Canopean touches the vortex a few more times, and each time, humans are able to ascend even higher, through layers of magenta, then garnet, then emerald light, shedding layers of ash from their spiritual bodies. Thus the single Canopean can transmit the vibration (and memory) of peace to those humans in the war vortex who can possibly respond to it and thereby shift—a little—the consciousness valence in that war vortex.

What if, say, four dozen Canopeans simultaneously touched the vortex and transmitted the pure vibration of peace? It would actually be apocalyptic. It would be too shattering to most people vibrating at the density of war, despite what they might think or say about desiring peace. Ironically and sadly, the pure vibration of peace would be energetically indigestible to them; it would be like a bolt of lightning, far too bright and potent to handle (or, possibly, survive). It would starkly illuminate everything, all the hidden pockets of the collective psyche, its shadow, and that of the individual's too, revealing far too much of the human self at once.

166

So it's too dangerous for humanity at its level of consciousness today to be exposed to more than a homeopathic finger-touch of active Canopean light. The four geomantic features that emphasize Canopus transmit a more passive form of Canopean light (and the vibration of peace), and to a large extent, humanity has become used to that level of input and can accommodate it.

The Great Bear, or Ursa Major, we met in the earlier chapters on the Marian apparitions. This constellation (known popularly as the Big Dipper) of seven bright stars (the Bear's pelvis and tail) is the home of the 14 Ray Masters, known in Hindu myth as the *rishis,* each assigned a star. These 14 Ray Masters—we might think of them as humanlike gods, like the Greek Olympians—administer 14 light and consciousness frequencies throughout the galaxy. These are the basic seven rainbow colors and their seven subtleties.

Geomantically, Ursa Major is amply represented on the Earth. The Ray Masters have a celestial city I call Mount Olympus with 108 entrances on Earth; individual Ray Masters have in present time 443 Ray Master Sanctuaries, but once they had 1,080; these are dedicated Mystery temples for the administration and human experience of their specific Ray frequency. Each of these Sanctuaries grounds that aspect of the Great Bear's energy in the Earth.

Further, the Great Bear's energies are represented in 12 Oroboros Lines; these are planet-encircling energy lines (very large ley lines), each grounded at a specific place on the Earth (at Delphi in Greece, for one). Each line originates at one of the seven stars in the Great Bear. The Bear is the galactic home or seat of the Great White Brotherhood, the home of King Arthur (not so much a mythical Celtic King as the ruler of the Great Bear and its Brotherhood), and the actual *Ananda-kanda,* or inner heart chakra at all levels, human, planetary, and galactic.

The latter means that at all levels in which the inner heart chakra is expressed, be it in the human, in landscape zodiacs, or in chakra hierarchies in the Earth's visionary terrain, the actual seat of this consciousness center is Ursa Major. I say "actual" to distinguish from virtual or holographic as it is in all expressions on Earth. Appropriately, in Hindu chakra iconography, the *Ananda-kanda* heart chakra is depicted with a jeweled altar; that is a code or symbol for the Great White Brotherhood, the variegated jewels of awakened and pure consciousness.

So Ursa Major is intimately and intensely involved in the Earth's visionary geography and our own extended energy field and layers of consciousness. We could, if we wished to, reinterpret much of world mythology, with its vivid descriptions of apparitions of the gods or the more human-flavored foibles of the Greek Olympians, as encounters with ETs from Ursa Major. But perhaps you can sense already how inherently foolish, even parochial, it would seem— might seem even now—to think of the Olympians as extraterrestrials, even if true.[12]

The Planet and Human Are Thoroughly Wired into the Galactic Body

Let's take a moment out from reviewing individual stars or constellations and their connections with humans and look at the big picture based on a vision.

We've seen how some stars or constellations, notably the Pleiades, have direct bodily connections—the throat in this case. Astrology postulates correlations between the 12 zodiacal constellations and particular body parts or regions, Pleiades being subsumed within Taurus at the neck. But let's expand this picture to include the 1,746 stars represented by domes.

Picture the human body and its seven-layered energy field (or aura) as the receptacle for many hundreds of differently colored cords of connection to stars. From the atlas vertebra in the neck, for example, a cord of light goes up to Arcturus, a high-magnitude star in the constellation Boötes and with a 25-million-mile diameter. When this connection is in place, then whatever Arcturus's function is in the galactic body, we get that same benefit in our human body.

So it goes with the rest of the 1,746 stars. Picture yourself with almost two thousand cords of light wiring you to these important stars in the Milky Way galaxy. You're like a pin cushion. What's the overall benefit of this galactic wiring? You have cosmic consciousness.

It's similar with the Earth. These 1,746 stars each have a representative dome somewhere on the planet. Arcturus's dome, for example, is at Chaco Canyon in northwestern New Mexico. During the time when the Anasazi lived at Chaco and their culture flourished, so did the Earth's connection with Arcturus. Gaia was wired to this massive star and participated in its galactic life as the Anasazi performed the acts of their spiritual (and clairvoyant) culture.

Arcturus, the Ofanim once told me, is the Lord of the Dance. Recently, I looked at this clairvoyantly. Picture Arcturus as a ruby-maroon human with a lariat that resembles a complex Möbius strip. It loops and twists throughout the galactic body, which seems bounded by a membrane, defining its limit. The broad flat strip passes through clusters of stars, combining them in different relationships from the soul families or groups represented by constellations. Arcturus "himself" is connected to something outside our galaxy; he has a dark vertical slit up his middle, and it's like a dimensional doorway to something beyond. Stars and starlight stream through this dark doorway into the strip.

As Arcturus jiggles the strip, the entire galaxy wriggles, colors jump up from all over the strip like a thousand aurora borealises, and a sound, almost a choral singing, accompanies this jiggling, wriggling, and curtaining of light. As he moves differently, gently yanking the strips like a lariat, so to speak, different harmonics sound forth from the strips. It is a chorale for two thousand star voices, the fabled Music of the Spheres, the vibrating, harmonic strings (or superstrings) that may underlie all physical creation.[13]

When Arcturus is grounded on Earth through its star dome through the spiritual work of an attuned community, Gaia gets the rich infusion of this flavor of galactic consciousness. You have the Arcturus original above, and the Arcturus hologram below, and an umbilical cord of light connecting the two.

Now expand this vision to a time when most or all of the 1,746 stars were similarly grounded and alive on Earth. Gaia, and her humanity, would be *cosmicized,* connected and grounded to all the stars and their vast life and realm of awareness, and the galactic body would be on Earth.

Just change the language slightly and you'll see the instant relevance to our UFO-ET subject. With all these star beings and their fields of influence (solar systems, planetary systems with sentient life) connected into the Earth through its geomantic network, vast numbers of extraterrestrials would be virtually walking upon the Earth, living amongst us, enriching us. Who would need ships?

A Christ Mystery Initiation Facilitated by the Constellation Cygnus

With the constellation Cygnus (the Swan) we come upon the intriguing border between presumed ET activity and mystical initiatory experience. These are two areas not usually associated with each other.

One of the myths about Cygnus is that it's the god form that Zeus assumed when he wanted to copulate with Leda, wife of the King of Sparta, in ancient Greece. Either way, they produced the immortal Helen, born of an egg, as well as Polydeuces, the immortal half of the Gemini Twins, born from the same egg. In some versions, Leda ends up being the mother hen, so to speak, hatching the egg and Helen.

Cygnus is represented geomantically on the Earth by way of several domes (e.g., Albireo, Beta Cygnus, is at Montserrat, Spain) and, of course, within its hologram in the landscape zodiacs. Possibly the typical Cygnus-human interaction may be very different from the usual ET-human exchanges, and the myth of the swan's egg may hold the secret to this interaction.

The energy of Cygnus, or let's say its effect on human consciousness, is one of floating and immersion in a purity of consciousness. There is a sense of being lifted out of the body and auric shell into a purified realm of awareness. Contact with the Cygnus energy seems almost instantly to detoxify a layer of astral pain, trauma, and karma. You return, at least for a while, to your original essence, and it is as if you are a swan floating rapturously on the waters.

The image of a graceful swan floating serenely on top of still lake waters is apt, for in some poetical or mystical visions the swan is construed as a celestial ship on which enlightened souls sail in perfect equipoise across the galaxy.[14]

Or upon the sea of consciousness. In Hindu myth, the swan is seen metaphorically as a ship and is associated with the celestial realm called Vaikuntha where objects are made of a sentient substance called *cintamani*, the consciousness gem. "The Vaikuntha *vimanas* [ships, airplanes, divine conveyances] are often compared with swans, or are said to be swanlike in shape, but they are not swans. They are flying structures that are made of *cintamani* and travel by the power of pure consciousness."[15]

How does the Swan—or, in effect, beings from the star group Cygnus—induce this rapturous floating experience? They hand you a pearl. In my interaction with intelligences from Cygnus, I was presented with a pearl, although it could easily be seen as an opalescent egg, which, mythologically, is the progeny of Zeus (the Supreme Being) and the star-being Cygnus.

Where the pearl sits in the human constitution is variable; it started out in my diaphragm, where it did some "housecleaning" of pain, alienation, and blockages, as if electrifying my body and auric field with a jolt of pure oxygen; then it migrated up into my brow chakra to sit in the middle of my head. There it is available for further exploration and serene floating in higher consciousness, as it can be for anyone who accesses Cygnus with this intention.

Here's how Cygnus—or beings from or the energy of this constellation—supports human mystical and initiatory experience on the Earth. In central Virginia, about 20 miles west of Charlottesville is a site known locally as Swannanoa. It is a hill-perched property near Waynesboro on the edge of the Blue Ridge Mountains, which was occupied for some time by the polymath artist-visionary Walter Russell.[16] Today, it is a privately owned estate with a huge and marvelous mansion, fronted with great amounts of marble and, sadly, all falling apart. Up until the late 1990s, it was the headquarters of Russell's University of Science and Philosophy, an educational initiative based on his scientific insights.

Swannanoa is topped by a dome that corresponds to a star (at present, unnamed and unnumbered) peripheral to Cygnus. Russell's name for his estate (and, in effect, the hill) came to him in a dream, and according to the Ofanim, it means "close to the swan." Again, in this context, the swan represents pure consciousness or omniscience, they add.

Here is a vision of a central aspect of this site's mystical function: The hill under the Cygnus dome appears crystalline and transparent,

171

like a glass mountain. More precisely, it appears as a broad vertical glassine shank that rises far above the hill. Inside and at the ground level of this shank is a circlet of several dozen golden angels; they are both site guardians and initiation chaperones. You pass through the angelic circlet to approach an altar with a swan of light on either end. You see a priestly figure offering an infant to this altar, and for some reason it reminds you of the Christ Child.

Then you realize *you* are the priestly figure and you are offering your own Christ Child—the expression of the *reborn Christed you* as the product of an extended spiritual training—to this swan altar. As you place your new self on the swan altar, you are whisked away to another site. You stand in the middle of a vast sports stadium filled with spiritual, celestial beings. You have gained access to the Hall of the Slain, known in Norse myth as Valhalla.

The slain, however, have been "slain" in the spiritual "battle" to transmute the ego into the reborn Christ Child; success at this gains you access to Valhalla, where you stand among the *Einherjar* (again, the Norse term), the spiritual warriors who perpetually participate in—the image given is usually of feasting and drinking—the Christ consciousness or, as the Ofanim said, omniscience, the swan's pure consciousness. Those who perpetually feast on the Christ (often depicted in Irish and Norse myth as a huge boar) are members of the Great White Brotherhood, the esoteric conclave of ascended posthumans.

The important point here, and what brings our attention back to the role of the ETs from Cygnus, is that this geomantic site, with its Cygnus-related dome, facilitates the demonstration of one's spiritual credentials, the presentation of the Christ Child. Swannanoa is the Mystery theater for the performance of the drama of the Christed Initiation in the Buddha Body, referred to earlier in this book. Again, this is a series of geomantically referenced mystical steps, performed in consciousness, that enable you to participate in a fresh, nondogmatic way in the Christ Mystery and in so doing, birth it within you as a living reality.

It's interesting to note that when the Russells were seeking a suitable East Coast location for their efforts, Lao Russell had a vision of Christ standing on a mountaintop. That place was Afton Mountain, and later Walter Russell executed a sculpture called Christ of the Blue Ridge. The Ofanim note that the Archangel Michael inspired Lao

Russell's vision: "The sentiment was of the Christ in the Buddha Body, but her filters presented the image to her in a way she could comprehend." In effect, she *saw* the Swannanoa Christ Mystery center.[17]

The setup with the ETs from Cygnus, I contend, is sublime. Are they even ETs? Do they have or need ships? It seems trivial to think in these terms.

Here we see how the energies and consciousness of a star family through a geomantic node are part of a mandated initiation experience involving the Christ and offered to all humans on Earth.[18]

So let's take the large view of all this now. What is the sign on the Earth that all the UFO phenomena point to or embody? That the Earth is galactic in composition, and so are we. That various groups of ETs have been mandated to have a permanent, inherent role in the Earth's visionary geography, to maintain certain energy features, processes, or connections, and to occasionally interact with humans in collegial ways. A smaller number of ETs, such as the Grays and other star families not discussed here, have missions of a more ambivalent nature, or perhaps have stretched the terms of their agreements, or more or less ignored them, hoping they could get away with things for a while.

The physical aspects of the UFO phenomena, the sightings, lights, orbs, ships, aerial anomalies, and the rest, as well as the more experiential interactions (the five official classifications of Close Encounters) that seem to be less physical and more psychic or astral in nature—all of this is a big sign that humans coexist with multiple ET species both on and off the planet. The proliferation of evidence suggesting this brings the fact undeniably before us.

With these preliminary observations in hand, let's move on to look at some specific geomantic features that are associated with UFO phenomena.

Is There Site Specificity for UFO Sightings and Encounters?

Involuntary abductions by aliens are not site specific or in any clear way referenced to the geomantic terrain of the planet. Evidence suggests people are taken from all manner of mundane locations. Some abduction or interaction sites may be geomantic nodes, but it's not always the case. Repeated ship sightings, by contrast, do seem to have some site specificity.

The UFO-watching community uses the descriptive term "UFO flap area" to indicate "a geographically defined location that produces a disproportionately large number of UFO reports."[19] Others use the term "UFO hotspots." One veteran UFO researcher (and contactee) contends that "there are concentrated landing areas where UFOs almost always can be found, but not everyone who goes to such locations sees UFOs."[20] An area with frequent UFO sightings, from the Hudson River near New York City eastward into Connecticut (discussion to follow), has been dubbed a "UFO corridor."

Still other terms that imply a geographical reference to UFO phenomena include UFO "window areas"[21] and "ufocals" (presumably meaning UFO locales).[22] All these terms are helpful to our examination here because they presume meaningful site specificity.[23]

As with the Marian apparition sites, in many cases a high incidence of UFO activity in a specific area may actually illuminate implicit geomantic features previously unsuspected or forgotten. And the presence of these geomantic aspects may further illuminate *why* UFO activity is focused specifically *there*.

A map of UFO hotspots in the United States shows the highest concentration of activity (between 90 to 2,900 sightings) in specific places, including southwestern and northeastern New Mexico, southern Colorado, southeastern Nevada, and selected areas in California, Oregon, Washington, Idaho, Montana, Utah, Wyoming, and Minnesota. Overall, the western states from New Mexico north to Montana and west to the Pacific have the highest number of sightings, though the entire continental United States shows evidence of sightings in the range of one to 89 episodes per area.[24] In Canada, UFO sightings are prevalent in British Columbia (almost 1,200 between 1989 and 2002) and Ontario (slightly more than 800).[25]

These numbers give us an idea of the general trend in recent years toward increased UFO and ET sightings across North America, with certain areas receiving a higher percentage of activity than others. But now let's look at a few specific sites where UFO-ET activity has been pronounced, starting with five: Frijoles Canyon-Bandelier National Monument, New Mexico; Devil's Tower, Wyoming; Hessdalen in Norway; Mount Balsam Cone, North Carolina; and Mount Shasta in northern California.

Frijoles Canyon, located near Los Alamos in northern New Mexico, is not known for its UFO sightings, but on a recent visit to this canyon, I had a vista of how it had once served as a meeting place for ETs, humans, and angels.

The canyon has at least six geomantic features, including a dome cap (an etheric energy canopy about two miles wide that uplifts consciousness in that area), a Mount Olympus (a celestial city to do with Ray Masters from the Great White Brotherhood and Ursa Major), and a sipapuni, the Native American term for an emergence point from the Hollow Earth. In addition, the canyon has a Three-Star Temple (facilitating a fusion of angelic, human, and elemental energies, presided over by an archangel), a lily (a geomantic expression of the achievement of enlightened consciousness in that terrain), and a landscape angel who maintains the purity of the geomantic "charge" for that canyon.

Frijoles Canyon is a geomantically well-prepared space for activities in "higher space," as one writer on human-ET interactions termed it.[26] In the clairvoyant vista I had of Bandelier in full operation, numerous Native Americans (members, presumably, of the Keres tribe who lived there) had assembled in the canyon; other humans from inside the Earth were also present,[27] as were an impressive angelic host, including the Ofanim, and a large number of elemental Nature spirits, notably gnomes and sylphs.[28] The stage for this assembly was the beautiful white lily, easily the width of the canyon or more (about a half-mile in diameter), overlit by the shimmering dome cap.

Then, with the geomantic stage set, a mothership appeared over the canyon, and the five realms—terrestrial humans, subterranean humans, elementals, angels, ETs—had a conclave or gathering in higher space. My impression was that this meeting or intermingling had elements of an agape, or love-feast, so unlike the charged, anxious, uncertain, and usually frightened quality that imbues most present day ET-human interactions. Rather, the appearance of the

ET mothership or manifestation sphere—sometimes they only seem to be "ships"—was a natural, exuberant, and appropriate activity for this location.

Devil's Tower is the flattened cone of a mountain in Wyoming that figured centrally in Steven Spielberg's *Close Encounters of the Third Kind* (1979). It has been rumored that during the filming, the movie crew were aware of ET activities and may have sighted a few UFOs in the vicinity, as if the subject and special effects of the movie evoked the presence of the real thing.

Devil's Tower, geomantically, is a stargate (a subtle device that transports people or objects to planets in the galaxy), probably to a destination in the Pleiades, which means ET craft have conceivably been using the stargate for near instant transportation across the galaxy to pop into our third-dimensional reality from the Pleiades. Five different Native American myths of the Tower have seven young women chased by a grizzly bear; they flee into *Mato Tipila* ("Grizzly Bear Lodge"—their name for Devil's Tower). It rises and grows radically upward until it reaches the Pleiades and the women are safe.

Hessdalen is an area in south-central Norway on the edge of the Rondane Mountains about 20 miles northwest of Roros with a strong reputation for UFOs and unusual light phenomena. These lights have usually appeared in the form of fast-moving, pulsating, yellow-colored spheres, and in the early 1980s, were observed almost daily. The fastest sphere was clocked at 8,500 mph. In fact, up to 20 sightings a week of alien craft were reported between 1981 and 1984, after which sightings tapered off to about 20 annually. The site and its UFO phenomena were deeply researched and documented, and Hessdalen remains a UFO hotspot.[29]

Hessdalen's geomancy helps explain the UFO phenomena. The hill is topped and illuminated by a dome cap several miles wide; on the side of the hill and essentially invisible to third-dimensional eyesight is the opening of a large sipapuni.[30] The human civilization within the Earth has its own fleet of "ships" and other UFO-type conveyances, and they come and go through the Hessdalen sipapuni or doorway a bit like bees swarming out of a hive, if only a few at a time, according to the Ofanim.

This is only an approximate description, but to some extent the interior Earth ships phase-shift as they emerge from the sipapuni; in other words, the sipapuni is not exactly a wide-open, very large garage door that you can simply fly through. At least in some cases, it seems more akin to a valve that opens as necessary. The dome cap overhead helps the sipapuni valve open, and were you to observe the area of the sipapuni, the spherical light (or ship) would suddenly appear outside the entrance and zoom away; you wouldn't see it actually emerging from the Earth—that's where the phase-shifting comes in.

There are many important geomantic features near Hessdalen in the Rondane Mountains, including prime planetary chakra points, assembly points for the Great White Brotherhood, a large landscape zodiac, eight celestial cities, the prime Garden of Eden template, and more. Presumably, the Hollow Earth humans found it necessary especially in the 1980s (and still do) to make repeated reconnaissance missions across the Rondanes, possibly to monitor the integrity of our topside geomantic features. Quite likely, ETs from outside the Earth sphere also visit the Hessdalen Valley and Rondane Mountains.

Geomantically, it works both ways. Not only does the preexistent geomantic setup in the Hessdalen area make it likely that UFO phenomena would occur, but to an extent the "UFOs" want to partake of those geomantic features, like bees attracted to especially lovely flowers. According to the Ofanim, "Many beings from many dimensions, both material and nonmaterial, are attracted to what is here. There are lifesaving benefits to what is here. They come for what is still a primary focus point from an original creation [the Garden of Eden template] fashioned by the Supreme Being."[31]

Mount Shasta in northern California enjoys a considerable reputation among mystics and UFO enthusiasts for ET and UFO activities. Claims of sightings of unusual aerial phenomena, lights, and ships have been coming out of the Mount Shasta community for decades. The 14,000-foot peak is also well noted for attracting the enigmatic, disk-shaped lenticular cloud formations (usually in stacked horizontal layers of thin disks) that many UFO commentators propose are almost literally smokescreens to hide ET ships.[32]

Mount Shasta's geomantic array is formidable, including at least 14 features. These include: dome; two stargates; sipapuni; Mount

Olympus; Valhalla (conclave of the Great White Brotherhood for Christ consciousness adoration); Og Min Cave Heaven (a conduit to beings from the Andromeda galaxy); minor dragon; Jewel of Michael (higher dimensional meeting place for humans with the Archangel Michael); a ring of six Interdimensional Portals around the mountain's base (for meeting with the Pleiadian Council of Light); parallel world intersection node (for slipping into an alternate reality); Palladium (minor Head or Crown of the Ancient of Days—a meeting place for humans with the Supreme Being); regional Albion chakra (an energy node in a geomantic being occupying one-twelfth of the Earth's surface); the root chakra at one level (of seven) for the Earth (one of the planet's 49 prime chakras); a functional "organ" in the planetary body expressed as Albion (Gaia's mate); and an Epiphany Focus (carrying a potent residue of Christ Consciousness from a previous [January 6, 1990] Christ focus there).

With such a rich and multilayered geomantic texture enveloping the physical peak, it shouldn't surprise us that ETs would find this highly desirable and tend to manifest and congregate within this numinous domain.

Balsam Cone, a 6,600-foot peak in the Black Mountains of North Carolina, is accessed off the Blue Ridge Parkway, a little less than 20 miles from Waynesville. This peak does not specifically have UFO-ET allegations, but my own experience there attests to it.

Admittedly, this description will sound quite strange. Over the physical mountain is a translucent half-sphere similar to one of the cups sometimes attached to the skin during acupuncture treatment. Inside this half-sphere are numerous white crystalline spikes; when examined more closely, they seem to be tall, clear crystalline vertical shafts rising hundreds of feet. In the center of this forest of crystalline spires is a red disk that when you stand on it (in vision), functions as an elevator, taking you deep into the Earth. The "elevator" emerges in a vast golden chamber or cavern in which all manner of ETs walk about. My first impression was I had arrived at a galactic United Nations headquarters.

A later, and I hope more clarified, impression was that this place is a subagency of the Pleiadian Council of Light, charged with specific tasks. Overall, the structure (cavern, elevator, crystalline spires, half-sphere) resembles a tent peg inserted into the Earth. The outer surface of the half-sphere continuously pulsed out light, energy, beams, or information, like a beacon. But this emission may also have been of benefit to the Earth atmosphere, both physical and geomantic. In a sense, the overall structure looks like an alien ship that inserted itself into the Earth; more precisely, an ET structure more subtle than physical matter inserted itself like a tent peg into the equally subtle visionary geography of Balsam Cone.

Just under the base of this "alien tent peg" is a sipapuni, and over its topmost half-sphere is a dome. Whether locals report UFO or aerial lights phenomena around Balsam Cone or not, there certainly are ETs resident there.

UFO-Human Interaction Zones—Regional Geomantic Hotspots: The Mysterious Valley

Now we turn to three larger areas, encompassing many hundreds of square miles, in which consistent UFO activity has been reported over the years.

One site with consistent UFO and ET-encounter reports is the so-called Mysterious Valley, the San Luis Valley of southwestern Colorado. The four-thousand-square-mile valley, shaped like a wishbone, sits at an elevation of 7,500 feet, is 120 miles long and 45 miles wide, and ringed by snow peaks, the San Juan and Sangre de Cristo ranges that merge at its northernmost point. The southern tip of the valley extends down into New Mexico to around Taos.

At least 12 different Native American tribes ritually knew this area as the Bloodless Valley, considered it sacred, used it for vision-quest purposes, and refrained from fighting and warfare in its midst. The New-Age community of Crestone, on the northeastern edge of the valley, tends to emphasize the area's numinous and sometimes bizarre and anomalous aspects.[33]

Since 1993, many dozens of sightings of strange aerial phenomena, lights, orbs, green fireballs, plasma streams, ships, glowing objects, silver spheres, inexplicable booms, and even a battleship-sized array of six glowing green objects in close crescent formation have been reported in the Mysterious Valley. Complicating matters are the widespread rumors of secret and/or underground U.S. military and possibly alien bases in the San Luis Valley area, as well as the documented fact of several actual or overt military establishments. I say "complicating" because the presence and activities of such installations are often credited, in part or full, with many of the UFO phenomena.[34]

Here is a clairvoyant impression of some aspects of the San Luis Valley: The peaks of the Sangre de Cristo and San Juan Mountains are enveloped with translucent dome caps and much of the valley is also cupped by dome caps. The originating domed mountains for the dome caps are Blanca Peak on the central-eastern flank, Wheeler Peak on the southern flank, about ten miles north of Taos, and Culebra Peak, on the eastern flank near New Mexico. Seen from above, the valley looks dotted by several dozen adjacent shimmering globes, perhaps one-half to one mile in diameter.

Running the length of the valley and up its center from south to north is a long runway and landing strip. Many ships, craft, and shuttles continuously land and depart. Obviously, this is not a military airbase, nor is it even physical. Underneath the valley floor, as if under its skin, are perhaps 50 large yellow-white spheres or bubbles, about the size of the dome caps on the valley floor. These look like so many carbonation bubbles trapped just under a membrane or like a blistering rash just about to pop out on human skin.

The simplest statement to make is this: The Mysterious Valley is a cosmic womb.

The array of closely packed yellowish-white subcutaneous bubbles is some form of sanctioned alien experiment. Or maybe it's an experimental seedbed. Inside the bubbles are numerous milky humanlike forms, more like spirit bodies for potential humans, or human-ET blends. I don't mean alien-human hybrids based on manipulation of tangible DNA strands of species. This is more subtle, like something prepared long in advance for the future and at present in a slow germination and ripening phase. The borderline between Colorado and New Mexico is distinct even at the energy level, and there are more bubbles north of the line in Colorado than south.

As I watch, a few bubbles rise to the surface and pop through the Earth's skin, then burst, releasing what I will call consciousness beads. These are like moisture droplets that seed the fabric of reality through the air element with something new and galactic, like a nutrient for human consciousness.

The valley also appears to be flooded with a layer of water perhaps one-quarter mile deep, except it's not water, but a layer of consciousness that acts as a *differential* between the galactic-subtle and human-physical realities copresent there. It is a blend, or result, of the differences (and the creative tension between them) between the two different consciousness layers; hence the differential. This is prime spiritual real estate for vision quests, which explains in part why Native Americans consistently used the valley for psychically attuned walking.

To a large extent, the flurry of UFO activity in the Mysterious Valley pertains to the other ET families *not invited* to participate in the experiment. You could think of them variously as observers, spies, interfering agents, or disturbers. Among these are the Grays, persistent gate-crashers as always.

There are at least four unusual geomantic features in the valley. First, in the vicinity of Blanca Peak is a structure that looks like a yellow kidney bean, though it could well be ten to 30 miles in length and several miles across. It is full of yellowish-white alien beings, vaguely humanoid, and they enter this subtle domain from the already subtle environment of the valley. My estimation is that this yellowish kidney-bean domain is two dimensions removed from the physical, and the aliens enter by passing through a dimensional sphincter.

Second, behind the town of Crestone, at about nine thousand feet, is a geomantic feature that resembles a black hole in both appearance and seeming function. It exerts what I would term, at least metaphorically, a strong magnetic attraction, just as a black hole sucks in all light around it due to its intense gravity and density; on the other side of the Crestone "black hole" is another world in another dimension.

A third feature, like a centerpiece set before the "black hole" feature, is a Prana Distributor. It looks like a spherical pockmarked crystal, a big clear glass marble around one hundred feet in diameter. It's like a huge negative ion generator, pumping out revivifying, invigorating, and uplifting negatively charged ions; the device emits energy and consciousness and invigorates the life force. The planet has only 288 of these features, which explains why with one placed above Crestone, the site could draw people almost irresistibly to the area.

The fourth aspect is in the northwestern section of the valley, roughly between Del Norte and Saguache. It looks like a yellow rectangle with stairs, like a very broad entrance to a subway. Many alien beings scurry down its steps into a massive interior yellowish space with many geometric structures—a city perhaps. This yellow rectangle is a dimensional doorway to another planet. Dome caps (and there is one over this site) correspond to and, in effect, are holograms of either minor magnitude stars or satellite planets of these stars. That means at a given dome cap you could possibly look through Earth's geomantic node and into the light body of a planet elsewhere in the galaxy.

Let's put all the parts together for the Mysterious Valley. First, you have its physical features, a four-thousand-square-mile valley, 120 miles long, 45 miles wide, flanked on both long sides by snow peaks, and bearing a reputation of former Native American reverence, frequent UFO activity, and high (if exciting) strangeness. Second, you have the geomantic features, at a minimum, three domes, many dozen dome caps (potentially 144), and a Prana Distributor. Third, you have a long-term alien enclave and experimental seedbed filling the entire valley, and a great deal of alien attention or interference from nonparticipating ETs.

So the frequently observed UFO activity and aerial anomalies are but clues and *secondary effects* of the real mystery in the San Luis Valley: the alien bubble seedbed and the two ET-dimensional doorways already mentioned. It's not exaggerating to say there is an entirely other world going on in the Mysterious Valley.

Decoding the Activity of UFOs over Topanga Canyon

Topanga Canyon, which lies to the west of Los Angeles in California, certainly qualifies as a UFO flap area, and in 1992, it experienced a UFO wave.

Topanga Canyon is sandwiched between Santa Monica (south)

and Malibu (north) and is situated in the center of the Santa Monica Mountains that edge Los Angeles in the southwest. The canyon itself is rural, sparsely settled, with mountains rising about three thousand feet on both sides; Highway 27, a two-lane road, passes through the canyon from the south (Pacific Ocean) to the north (Woodland Hills), and Topanga State Park is situated within this canyon.

Interestingly, Topanga Canyon is much like the Hudson River Valley in New York (discussed below): a rural area close to a large urban center, and according to UFO researcher Preston Dennett, a good hiding place for aliens if they want to lie low and undetected while studying or interfering with or abducting members of a large human population as is found in New York City or Los Angeles.[35]

Residents of Topanga Canyon had been witnessing UFO activity since the 1940s, but in mid-1992, the frequency of sightings and encounters intensified. In the space of a few months, 130 witnesses reported 82 different UFO encounters; Dennett reasons that on average only one to two percent of observers ever officially report their UFO sightings to authorities, so the real number of UFO sightings in general and in Topanga may be one hundred times higher than the 82 actually filed in 1992. Of the 82 events, the most common were anomalous lights, followed by sightings of metallic craft; also observed were light beams, strange physical effects in the landscape and in observers' bodies, and some telepathic communication with the aliens, mostly Grays.

The majority of the UFO encounters took place in the heart of Topanga Canyon, and, Dennett notes, the total amount of time logged in seeing UFOs was an astonishing 1,342 minutes, or more than 11 hours, with the average sighting lasting 23 minutes. The focal point of all the activity was clearly the Santa Monica Mountains. "For whatever reason, it is extremely attractive to UFOs," observes Dennett.[36]

My clairvoyant impression here is that it is actually Topanga Canyon that is of highest interest to the aliens, with the mountains providing geomantic packaging and geological isolation for a highly arcane ET experiment.

In the greater Los Angeles area are at least four domes, three in the San Gabriel Mountains to the northeast of Los Angeles and one in the Santa Monicas (probably over Castro Peak, the second highest point in that range). These domes proliferate up to 192 dome caps throughout the greater urban area including six in the Topanga Canyon area. In addition, there is a 30-mile-wide landscape zodiac (consisting of two contiguous halves or spheres, each 15 miles wide) occupying the central Los Angeles area, topped by a zodiac dome 66 miles in diameter. These intense geomantic features alone account for most of the area's high numinosity, cultural creativity, and anomalous phenomena.

But in Topanga Canyon something very secret and long-term is under way. It is similar, though not identical, to what we glimpsed in the San Luis Valley. Picture flying slowly, with psychic vision, over the canyon. In the same space as the canyon but in the next dimension is a long, clear crystalline ridge that runs the length of Highway 27 as it passes through the canyon. This ridge has several subridges and is highly geometric and see-through. It is topped regularly with broad dome caps, each about a half-mile wide. They are like spotlights that illuminate what's going on deep inside the ridge.

It is like looking through clear ice to see the strange cold-water fish below. The entrance appears to be at the southern end where Highway 27 enters the canyon, and from this perspective, the ridge is like a glass sliver wedged under Earth's skin. Inside this glass sliver is an alien colony in another dimension.

There are numerous ETs about. They are like a distant relation to the Grays. Of about the same stature and seeming weight, they are mostly yellow; their heads are large and diamond-shaped as are their eyes. They give the impression of being structurally related to the Grays but of a different spirit essence. And what they are doing in Topanga is more beneficial to Earth than what it generally seems the Grays are doing.

The Yellows—just a provisional name—are breeding light. But "breeding" in this context is more akin to, say, a breeder nuclear reactor than genetic breeding and hybridization, often attributed to the Grays. Inside this crystalline ridge or glass sliver in Topanga Canyon are dozens of bright yellow orbs or spheres the size of mansions or palaces. They resemble bright yellow suns, and their brilliance reflects off the crystalline roof and makes the entire interior sparkle and glitter with yellow light.

What are they breeding? These yellow orbs are breeding bulbs for four-dimensional reality, for a reality that's like living inside a time-lapse photograph. Eventually, these orbs will be hung out aboveground along the canyon like massive celestial street lamps to illuminate the multiple dimensions of reality that already lie just below the skin of our consensus reality, our 3D world. You'll sense the presence of these orbs as skin tingles, flashes of intuition, heightened coincidence, or, as C. G. Jung called it, synchronicity. It will be like having many eyes that take in all kinds of aspects and angles of what's going on around you.

To a large extent, the significant UFO activity in this area is in reference to this secret alien light-breeding program. You might think of it this way: Some ships are like security guards; others are like gate-crashers and saboteurs. In other words, to a large extent, the perceived and experienced UFO presence is secondary to the real event in Topanga Canyon. The gate-crashers and saboteurs mostly seek to interfere with the mandated progression of consciousness that will be implemented through the placement of these yellow orbs "topside" more or less in our physical reality, though they might, if seen, seem more like heat waves or colored glows without precise focal objects.

Topanga Canyon, then, is one of several alien test areas around the world, protected, underground, secluded, geomantically enhanced (or prepared). It's like a 4D park, like the fabled magical, hidden valleys in Tibet, like Shangri-La, where reality is marvelous, happiness rampant, death minimal, and insight maximal. One day you will be able to drive through this transformed Topanga Canyon and emerge at Woodland Hills on the edge of Los Angeles ontologically refreshed, irradiated in 4D reality, cosmicized.

Geomantic Aspects of the UFO Corridor of the Hudson River Valley

A third regional area that has attracted a fair amount of UFO activity and human speculation is the Hudson River Valley of New York State. Between 1982 and 1987, an estimated five thousand sightings were reported of triangular or boomerang-shaped UFOs over a

1,400-square-mile region, encompassing three New York and three Connecticut counties. Specifically, the region overflown stretched from White Plains (just north of New York City) north to Newburgh, and northeast to Brookfield and southeast to New Haven, both in Connecticut.

At least 16 towns or small cities in this region reported significant UFO sightings, although 85 percent of the sightings on one night in 1983 came from an area three miles wide by 12 miles long in just two counties. For good reason, this horizontal rectangular swath of New York and Connecticut countryside has been dubbed the UFO Corridor.

Nearly all sightings occurred at night, and the reports were highly consistent as to the type of UFO observed: as big as three football fields (900 feet long), or a 747 airliner, or like a flying city, shaped like a triangle or boomerang, moving very slowly or hovering only a few hundred to one or two thousand feet above ground, and emitting beams of light or numerous pulsing lights. One observer noted that the lights kept changing color "as if it [the ship] had a rotating prism within the lights." Another reporter noted a "faint, deep hum that sounded like a factory with a lot of machines operating in the distance."[37]

Evidently, only a few residents of the area were conscious during the time of the UFO sightings of any kind of human-alien interaction, which, of course, does not preclude a wider range of experiences registered in but not retrieved from the subconscious. One woman reported that at the time of the March 1983 sightings, as she lay in bed, a beam of light awakened her. She felt her insides probed as if by a doctor and saw "a being with claylike skin and a large head with large eyes" (a Gray) who told her not to worry, that he was "part of a team of explorers studying the people."[38]

Apparently UFO sightings and other paranormal, anomalous type experiences are common to that part of the Hudson River Valley. Documentation exists showing that sightings of similar UFO craft have been reported there in 1956, 1957, 1958, 1976, and 1978. Further, since the mid-1970s, residents of more than one hundred U.S. communities have reported seeing a triangular, diamond-shaped, or boomerang-shaped UFO overhead, with the same flight pattern of low altitude, slow flight speed, and usually no sound.[39] Further, during the 1990s, another two thousand sightings were reported in this area.[40]

The startling clairvoyant discovery about the Hudson River Valley UFO phenomena is that the physical data—the sightings, sounds, lights, and craft encounters—are only a fragment of the actual events, a mere hint and glimpse of grand activities involving the Earth and galaxy. In fact, to a large extent, as at some of the other sites, the UFO sightings are of secondary interest, evidence of other secret activities under way.

To investigate this diffuse geographical area—not one valley but many, as well as hills, towns, farmland, and a river—I took a tip from Virgil. In his *Aeneid*, when Aeneas arrives in Italy, he is greeted by the Tiber River-god, understood to be the sentient spirit of the river Tiber that flows through Rome. Tiber gives Aeneas the lay of the land, pointing out sites for future temples and even the site for Rome.[41] For those willing to take this anecdote seriously, it suggests that the spirit or landscape angel for a river may be a valuable source of information for events and geomantic hotspots within its domain. This proved true with the Hudson.

In my clairvoyant investigation of this area, I consulted the River-god of the Hudson. What did "he" look like? Let's say we settled on a provisional image of him as a water-drenched Poseidon, dripping some water grasses. More important is that he has knowledge of the environment of about 50 miles on either side of his river body, and the UFO Corridor. You could usefully picture the Hudson River— 350 miles long, it flows from the Adirondack Mountains to the Atlantic Ocean at New York City—as the physical expression of the energy body of the Hudson River god; this appears as a pale-yellow energy fissure or gigantic vulva. The UFO Corridor sits at about the figure's knees.

Along this fissure or energy spine of the River-god are nodules branching out from the main river root much like nodules do from plant roots. There are about two dozen such nodules ranged asymmetrically on either side of the river in the area between New York City and Albany. The nodules remind you of lymph nodes and how they cluster about certain areas of the human body.

The top of one nodule is like a manhole cover on a city street; open it up and you descend into the Earth into a hive of alien beings, primarily purple in hue. This place is packed with protohumans, like a host of homunculi in an alchemical retort. This is a vast hive, a congeries of possibilities for something being incubated, in the Earth but not for the Earth; it's for the galaxy.

This nodule is in the Pine Bush vicinity, in the 11 o'clock position from something much larger in the River-god's river body in the area triangulated between Newburgh, Fishkill, and Beacon, New York. Seen from overhead, it is like a huge spherical greenhouse of clear glass panes, about one-quarter mile in diameter. It is filled with light; it radiates light like a city of crystal sparkling in the midday sunlight, except the light originates in this crystalline cluster. Among other functions, this crystalline cluster or city is a spaceport; extraterrestrial and highly subtle ships are continuously coming and going from it, seemingly in a parallel dimension to ours, for most are not physically visible. A small number, perhaps ten percent, phase-shift into and out of our seeable dimension.

I call this feature a Reciprocal Maintenance Resonator. It's a complex piece of geomantic feedback hardware, and not a feature I describe in *The Emerald Modem*. There are 2,472 of these around the Earth, distributed equally per landmass (more specifically, 206 for each of the 12 Albion Plates, which are geometric divisions of the Earth's original surface). They have at least three functions.

First, the Resonators balance all the cosmic energies circulating through one of these Albion Plates, both among themselves as an Earth system and with their source in the galaxy. Second, they receive and transform energies from other Albion Plates (each Plate has different flavors of energy due to astrological influences) and balance them with their own energies. Third, they are time doorways, enabling energy from former and future times to feed into the Earth's visionary geography at any point in time. This third function seems germane to the cosmic womb-incubatory function of the Hudson River Valley.

Meanwhile, the nodule around Pine Bush exhibits pulsatory activity. It seems to swell up with energy or light, then release it into the psychic atmosphere—like spraying the area with otherworldly pollen. This is what attracts much of the seeable UFO activity; they are drawn to the delicious psychic pollen. The ET pollen pulses through and out this and other nodes like a structured heat wave or like an atomizer mister spraying a room with floral scent to freshen the air.

Here's an analogy for understanding this. In the healthy human body, toxins get pushed to the surface for release. Often this manifests as acne. Where the acne appears on the face is correlated with acupuncture energy channels and *nadis* (even subtler channels), and nodes or openings on both. Similarly, the Earth throws up energy through various nodes on its surface, except in this case, it is positive energy. The crystalline cluster and the two dozen nodules off the River-god's energy body are like the acne spots on the face, except that it is not toxics being discharged, but light and nourishment.

Gaia flushes the crystalline cluster and nodules with planetary "milk" or light, and this filters through the cluster and nodules, gains molecules of fragrance, and is misted into the psychic atmosphere, and that draws the UFOs.

The Hudson River god, in cooperation with Gaia, the landscape angel for the entire planet, is responsible for the midwifery of these ET nodules in its energy body. All of this activity, we must remember, is happening in a very different realm from our three-dimensional reality. Seeing this is like getting a glimpse into wholly unsuspected secret activities of our home planet. Shockingly, the incubation of these protohumans may have nothing to do with us at all.

It seems that these homunculi under incubation in the energy body of the Hudson River are meant for another star system elsewhere in the galaxy. These are star beings being grown inside an energy layer of Earth to be delivered when ripe to a leading spiral arm of the Milky Way galaxy. There they will embody a more advanced stage of consciousness evolution for the galaxy. In this case, then, Earth is a midwife commissioned to incubate, nurture, and birth star beings for life elsewhere in the universe.

The revelation of the cooperative work of Gaia and the Hudson River god on behalf of incubating star beings for life elsewhere in the galaxy illustrates yet another layer of the Earth's visionary geography. At one layer, the River-god and its river work with Gaia to embody a theme of galactic consciousness for humanity's psychic consumption; at another level, the River-god's energy body is an incubation retort for birthing cosmic beings who will never live on Earth. This layer is the one that attracts UFO attention, both invisible and seeable.

There is an important nuance to this layering of the Earth's geomancy. The attention that certain species of unfriendly aliens, especially the Grays, put on humans is in relation to a person's obliviousness of the Earth's geomancy and how it maps onto the human body. This means how the galactic *above* and the human *below* both map onto the planet's *in the middle too*. The fundamental principle of visionary geography is that the array of sacred sites and their energy configurations and hierarchical relationships are based on a galactic original and that is also a model of the human energy and consciousness system.

Of course, we are individually and culturally almost completely unaware of this mapping. Our unawareness, it seems, allows the Grays to work right through us, accessing the Earth's sites holographically through their mapping in us. Thus certain ET families can use us as Trojan Horses or dumbwaiters to access geomantic points in the Earth psychically. When they use us as dumbwaiters, they are in our aura and able to manipulate our awareness.[42]

So it pays to be aware of the holographic cosmic map we each bear in us, how it is a miniature living version of the Earth's visionary geography. It may help keep the unfriendly aliens off our backs.

Ultimately, What Is the Relevance of the UFO-ET Sign on the Earth?

Humans and the planet are galactic in origin and process. The UFO phenomenon is the graphic testament to this. Aliens from various star systems have contributed to the creation and evolution of humanity, and they have been implicit in the creation and energy mechanics of the planet. Many ET families have been mandated from the beginning of the planet to have an intimate role in the Earth through its array of geomantic nodes within Earth's energy body.

Table 5-1. Geomantic Features at Selected UFO Hotspots

Site	Features
Frijoles Canyon, New Mexico, U.S.	Dome cap, Mount Olympus, Sipapuni, Three-Star Temple, Lily, Landscape Angel
Devil's Tower, Wyoming, U.S.	Stargate
Hessdalen, Norway	Sipapuni, Dome cap
Mount Shasta, California, U.S.	Dome, 2 stargates, Sipapuni, Mount Olympus, Valhalla, Og Min Cave Heaven, Jewel of Michael, 6 Interdimensional Portals, Palladium, regional Albion chakra, Earth primary chakra, Albion "organ," Epiphany Focus
Balsam Cone, near Waynesville, North Carolina, U.S.	Alien "tent peg," Pleiadian Council of Light subagency, Sipapuni, Dome
San Luis Valley, Colorado, U.S.	3 domes, numerous dome caps, "Black Hole," Prana Distributor
Topanga Canyon, California, U.S.	4 domes, up to 192 dome caps, landscape zodiac, zodiac dome
Hudson River Valley/Pine Bush, New York, U.S.	River-god, Reciprocal Maintenance Resonator

No matter whether the evidence is from abduction reports or experiences, sightings, or glimpses of arcane alien projects within the Earth, this undeniable sign on the Earth tells us this: We live *embedded* in galactic life and affairs. The nagging question, *Are we alone in the universe?* is definitively revealed to be parochial and silly. The question we should be asking is *What are they all doing here?*

They're doing lots. Some activities benefit us and the planet, some benefit only the aliens (abductions), and others seem irrelevant to our concerns.

Some arcane and fairly enigmatic alien energy-breeding projects are under way right under our noses. We gather that some will benefit us one day and others not, while rogue ETs (notably the Grays, but others are involved) occupy themselves with disturbing and spying on these projects as well as presumably running their own breeding experiments, using humans as subjects. Ironically, the Gray-sponsored abductions and forcible encounters with humans—and, it seems, the bulk of the ship sightings (and much of the range of the five Close Encounter classifications)—are but the *sideshow,* almost a distraction from the real events, the ones we should pay close attention to.

These are the revelations of our galactic context (the Earth's visionary geography as a template of the galaxy) and our own galactic essence, of both body and consciousness (the human embeddedness in this cosmic template). Further, we're learning, uncomfortably, that our reality itself is galactic, expanded, foreign to us. Physicality itself seems a strange, fabulous, and sometimes intimidating spacetime theater for consciousness, a much bigger stage than our consensus reality ever allowed us to consider, or imagine. Perhaps the UFO-ET sign on the Earth is itself the unveiling of the much discussed, prophesied, and modeled fourth dimension, the time realm.

People who have undergone near-death experiences often report this experience: It's as if all time—past, present, and future—were laid out before them as a tableau in a vast "now." Another way of conceiving this is through time-lapse photography. Film a plant from when the seed sprouts all the way through to blossoming and seed formation, then speed it up so you watch it in 60 seconds. That's a taste of fourth-dimensional perception: You see something move through time, and you see all of it, beginning to end, as one gesture.

With our first sign, the Marian apparitions, we have the opportunity to birth the Christ Child within us, to generate a new level of cognition, to stick our heads up into the fourth dimension (4D, the fourth layer of Gaia's onion skin) while our body is still rooted in physicality. With our head—our cognition, or budding clairvoyance—in the higher realm of 4D, we start to see a radically new, almost unbelievable world. We look around and realize we are embedded in a sea of stars and activities, in fantastic possibilities, effects preceding causes, mind and matter paradoxes. Our heads popping into the 4D world, we get a preliminary taste of the fantastic scope of awareness that is the Logos, the connective rationality that holds the spacetime cosmos together.

Welcome to the 4D home of the ET and UFO phenomena, land of unrelenting strangeness, but what seems strange to us is business as usual to 4D. UFO witnesses often attest to how the phenomena seemed to irrupt into their reality from another spacetime framework or that they were inducted (and abducted) into a larger, wider frame of spacetime. This is the outskirts of 4D.

In this wider experiential realm, space, time, matter, and light all seem to behave according to different rules from those of our Earth body-based reality. Witnesses often later say it seemed as if spacetime collapsed, that their experiences did not take place in our familiar spacetime framework, and that they became aware of "vast other realities beyond the screen of this one."[43]

Harvard psychiatrist John Mack, M.D., who interviewed 13 abductees for his well-known study, *Abduction,* emphasizes the transformational, consciousness-altering, and spiritual-growth aspects of the abduction experience. Once they remember and come to terms with their shocking experiences, abductees sometimes become aware of their past lives and in fact see themselves as souls who have undergone many cycles of birth and death over long stretches of time, who even may have lived as aliens, who can identify their consciousness transpersonally with various other forms of intelligent life. (Dr. Mack cites one person who identified himself with dinosaurs and ancient reptiles.)

Significantly, "the reliving of abduction material leads abductees to open to other realities beyond space/time," realms that seem to them beyond the veil of ordinary reality or beyond another kind of cognitive barrier that kept them in a perceptual box (consensus reality) defined by the physical world. Many report their new sense of being in multiple times and places simultaneously and of "the discovery of a new and altered sense of their place in the cosmic design."[44]

All this—and it is a heady brew—may still be not quite the point, not quite the main theme. The fourth dimension is a vast arena, so what do we do once we're in here?

We might find a clue in the Cygnus revelations relative to Swannanoa and the mysteries of the Christed Initiation in the

Buddha Body. The Ofanim suggest that, to a large extent, the marvelous phenomena of UFO sightings, ET encounters and communications, and the rest may be a distraction, something that, exciting and fascinating and scary as it seems, may be taking our attention away from the main theme. The "main theme" here would be an agenda put forward by the Supreme Being and the spiritual and angelic hierarchies for humanity's next phase of development, which might be different than we think.

Ironically, for the remark presumably was not meant this way, sometime in the 1960s an editor quipped to UFO researcher Major Donald Keyhoe that the U.S. Air Force was concealing "the biggest story since the birth of Christ."[45] Ultimately, the biggest story since that birth would be the birth of Christ in us.

The Ofanim suggest that the main theme includes transformation and transmutation upon the Earth plane—big, momentous changes in human consciousness, identity, and how we see the world and what is possible. The Christed Initiation in the Buddha Body, that angelically sponsored way of bringing the mysteries and epiphanies of the Christ into present time and in a fresh way free of dogma and institutional control, may be the means for that transformation and transmutation to take place. That means that the presence of various ETs at other levels of development—what seems like an inrush of UFO and ET phenomena in our generation—may be incidental to our own inner molting process whereby we birth a new framework of consciousness. ETs are here to *watch us.*

Perhaps we could see this phenomenon as the coincidental, synchronous blossoming into our awareness of 4D spacetime and the galactic reality, indicators that we are close, that the time is ripe for this transformation. Swiss depth psychologist C. G. Jung suggested something along these lines in 1958, after studying the UFO phenomenon for ten years in terms of psychology.

Humankind's changing psychic situation and the noted flurry of UFO activity after World War II "seem[ed] to coincide in a meaningful manner." The inexplicable aerial ships, provably real, Jung said, were suitable carriers for the projection of human unconscious contents, and the phenomena could be seen as "manifestations of psychic changes . . . in the constellation of psychic dominants, of the archetypes, or 'gods' [precipitating] long-lasting transformations of the collective psyche" at the dawn of the new astrological age of Aquarius.[46]

The UFO experience may be our induction into the fourth dimension, but it is such a vast, multidirectional realm that we need orientation and focus.

It's often said in spiritual training disciplines that on your way to the more sublime realms of awareness, you unavoidably pass through a realm of psychic visions, vistas of strange, enticing spiritual worlds, and all sorts of anomalous encounters with beings, intelligences, and spirits. We could say then that humanity, and the Earth itself, is passing through this troubling intermediate realm of apparitions, astral encounters, and seemingly bizarre revelations of previously unsuspected aspects of reality on our way to something sublime.

I intend no judgment on this intermediate realm of apparitions and visions, nor do I agree with spiritual orthodoxies that such realms should be shunned. The 4D realm is as much a part of reality as anything else and warrants our investigation as an expression of our Supreme Being-given right to know.

We might usefully keep two things in mind, however. First, many beings across the galaxy come here either to observe or to participate in some way in the unfolding of this process. Second, it is prudent to consider the possibility that if the spiritual hierarchies are urging us to put our attention on the main theme, it is quite likely that other forces are interested in distracting our attention from it so as to restrain or slow down the transformation underway on the Earth. "The reason for this," the Ofanim comment, "is the unusual nature of the opportunity existent at this point of time within the whole of creation."

It's amusing: Putting aside the category of abductions by Grays, we have a situation in which numerous star families (ETs in UFOs) buzzing around the Earth are *watching us* undergo an epochal transformation in consciousness. We catch sight of some of these ETs watching us and start *watching them* as if their transient appearance in our reality is the main event, when the truth is they're appearing because we, the main event, are changing ourselves profoundly.

Even when we factor in the category of Gray abductions and look at it with detachment as a singular phenomenon, we find a message in this sign. The reported details of the typical abduction scenario reveal much about the laws of physics and reality that we previously did not suspect and may still disbelieve. But it's still an education to contemplate them: teleportation, demolecularization of the body (transport beams), enforced amnesia, switching off the awareness of witnesses,[47] invisibility, modulating the speed of time, telepathic communication, floating abductees through solid matter and through the air, huge spaceships that can hover soundlessly, then accelerate rapidly, making "impossible" turns.[48]

These feats alone should radically widen our framework for what is possible in the physical world. In fact, maybe the physical world is not what we thought it was, not so limited, heavy, slow, and ruled by mechanical Newtonian concepts. Some physicists today are proposing that humans perceive only a minuscule portion of a "greater reality spectrum," and that our everyday reality, as we know it, may be part of "a shadowy, larger reality" called the multiverse, as in multiple universes. Our standard model of physics, still too much under the influence of Newton, "the current gold standard by which scientists define 'reality'—is just a province within a larger realm called supersymmetry."[49]

A Coda: How the Cepheans Tattooed the Wiltshire Landscape

I will present one last impression of ET activity on the Earth because it provides an intriguing segue into the topic of part 3, crop circles. This ET family involves beings from Cepheus, a constellation pictured as a crowned, seated king. The constellation is located close to Polaris, and in myth, Cepheus was the King of Ethiopia, husband of Cassiopeia (a constellation), and father of Andromeda (also a constellation). The ancients depicted Cepheus as seated in regal splendor, upraised scepter in his left hand, his right hand holding his robes. The Chinese construed this star form as the Inner Throne of the Five Emperors.

The references to Cepheus will become clear in a moment. Here is a clairvoyant impression of the star being whose outer form is

Cepheus: Picture a giant golden version of the Lincoln Memorial, complete with seated Lincoln. The figure here, of course, is King Cepheus. In the space between his knees and shoulders on both sides is something like a hula hoop; looking closer, you see it is energy continuously cycling in that area on both sides and tilted 45 degrees.

Cepheus is depicted as a king because "his" awareness transcends or is senior to the dualistic cycling of energy, represented by the two parallel hoops. The process of the twin cycling is a kind of breathing process: Pictures and images appear on the hoops in one phase, then seem dispersed and dissolved, and over again, in a regular sequence, though your impression is that this cycle may take place over a very long time frame, maybe even astrological ages. The cycling moves through concentration to diffusion and back again, influx, outflux.

Cepheus is king because he embodies, demonstrates, and, for the galaxy, *is* the process of conscious cognition, wakeful, undistorted, pure knowing. In the human body, Cepheus sits behind the bridge of the nose and can act as a "lint filter" to remove foreign energies, thoughts, and activities, which could be visualized as a grayish smog that confounds clear psychic perception. Cepheus sits also inside the planet as an aspect of Gaia's energy fields or auric layers. You could say Cepheus as a star being represents one process among many in Gaia's Higher Self.[50]

Were the Cepheans ever on Earth? Yes. Did they come in ships? No. They didn't need to. They just walked out of thin air and arrived on the planet's surface, specifically in central Wiltshire, England, at the area now marked by the 28.5-acre stone circle called Avebury. Picture hundreds of tall, thin, yellowish light beings, vaguely human in appearance, suddenly appearing in the airspace as if out of another dimension just above Avebury, then fanning out across about 50 miles of landscape, west to today's Glastonbury, east to today's London.

This, of course, was very long ago, probably reckoned in the millions of years. Even conservative archeologists willingly grant that the stones at Avebury must be in the neighborhood of 25 million years old, although they don't propose Avebury was built that long ago.

However, the Ofanim do. The point here is that what I am about to describe the Cepheans as doing probably took place in Avebury's earliest days, not long after it was installed, yet it is now being refreshed, much the way you can refresh a website page by reloading it on your screen.

The Cepheans spread out laterally from Avebury and it is as if they are etching tattoos on the Earth's surface. Seen from above they have created a kind of cat's face of whiskers extending about 25 miles east and west of Avebury with nodes at the whisker terminations, which perhaps are geomantic nodes. You have a series of parallel wavy lines extending east and west, creating a symmetrical image. A reasonable interpretation is to say the Cepheans have stamped Gaia's skin with their energy signature so that it can cycle through her consciousness (and ours).

Now here's where it's relevant in today's time frame. Until very recently the termination nodes on the Cephean whiskers had become variously overgrown, obliterated, paved over, neglected, or forgotten so that the energy cycling had to strain mightily to impart the fruits of its process to the planet, if at all. It is like a motor straining to move a vehicle forward when the brakes are still set.

The proliferation of crop circles, most of which have appeared in Wiltshire over the past three decades, is a way of reawakening this Cephean energy signature dormant in the landscape. The crop circles, though transient, are high-energy inputs meant to jump-start or reload the Cephean cycling, and to an extent, they represent new stampings, new tattoos on Gaia's skin. Of course, this is just one aspect of the enigmatic third sign on the Earth, which we'll now look at in close detail in part 3 to tease out its galactic message.

A Pillar of Fire: Crop Circles—A Language of Light in Albion's Golden Band

6 | *Crop Circles—What Is the Message of These Whorled Patterns in the Grain?*

Unlike Marian apparitions and UFO encounters, crop circles, our third sign on the Earth, are visible to all. You don't have to be in rapture, or psychic, or deeply hypnotized to see them. If you're lucky, you can even walk through one freshly made.

Maturing, supple crops of grain, typically wheat, barley, and rapeseed, are laid gently flat on the ground in complex whorled patterns that can only be seen completely from above, usually several hundred feet, as from a helicopter or airplane. The crops are not damaged, and nearly all the stalks remain unbroken, only gently twisted. Most often, the crop is harvested with little economic loss to the farmer. Crop circles created in living grain are the most prevalent among the formations, but since the late 1990s, circles have also been made in tobacco, flax, peas, potatoes, sweet corn, maize, flowers, rice paddies—even, though rarely, in ice, snow, sand, wild grass, and bracken.

What are the patterns? All kinds of images. Symbols from alchemy, spiritual and metaphysical traditions, animal forms, mathematical forms, abstract patterns resembling insects (called insectograms), and other pictograms. Some formations exemplify principles of geometry such as the Golden Ratio; some comprise fractals; some are solar and lunar glyphs; some seem to represent solar system and galactic relationships; others resemble ancient petroglyph symbols. Many are just breathtakingly beautiful, elegantly executed designs.

Not only is the medium variable, but so is the size. The smallest formations, called grapeshot, are just a foot or so wide, while most circles are several hundred feet in diameter. A 1996 formation at Etchilhampton in Wiltshire was 4,100 feet long, comprised of a chain of circles and pathways; and a 1998 pattern at Alton Barnes, Wiltshire, featuring a seven-petaled mandala, occupied an unbroken, flattened area of six thousand square meters. Among the most complex patterns was the huge motif at Milk Hill, Wiltshire, in 2001, consisting of 409 small circles that created a six-armed design measuring eight hundred feet across.[1]

As with Marian apparitions and UFO encounters, there is evidence that these crop formations appeared on the Earth, though sparingly, before their contemporary advent in the mid-1970s and their acceleration in the 1990s. Just as Marian sightings and UFO phenomena have clearly intensified since around 1980, the incidence and complexity of crop circles increase each summer. Waiting for crop circles in England has become almost a spectator sport and tourist attraction, as visitors are virtually guaranteed a fresh, innovative crop of new circle forms each summer, beginning in early May.

As of 1998, approximately four thousand crop circles had been reported in 70 countries, and the total grows annually. A 2003 estimate said that each year about 250 new formations are reported worldwide. According to one database of 3,200 circles, compiled by the Circles Phenomenon Research International, as of 2002, 1,784 crop formations had been reported in England, 228 in the United States, 135 in Canada, 105 in Germany, 71 in Australia, 62 in the Netherlands, 23 in Hungary, and decreasingly fewer for 49 other countries.[2]

While not all of the world's recent spate of crop circles have appeared in English grain fields, estimates say up to 95 percent of those reported have. Not just anyplace in England either, but specifically in Wiltshire, a county in south-central England, less than 75 miles due west of London, the home of many megalithic monuments, stone circles, henges, and barrows, including Stonehenge and the Avebury stone complex and its neighbor, Silbury Hill.

In fact, the majority of English circles have appeared within a circular area extending in a 40-mile radius from Stonehenge, and in some active summers, up to 15 circles have been reported in that radius in the same day. You could just as accurately draw the center of that circle at nearby Avebury, 30 miles to the north of Stonehenge, a 28.5-acre stone circle, in the vicinity of which a great number of England's crop circles have appeared.

Wiltshire is a rich agricultural landscape that includes the Kennett Valley, the Marlborough Downs, and the Vale of Pewsey, which are areas of rolling chalk hills and gently sloping fields; the region is also "one of the most densely populated ceremonial landscapes in Britain" with megalithic structures "located on hill-top summits everywhere the eye turns."[3]

The coincidence of so many megalithic monuments and the world's concentration of regularly appearing crop circles has led some researchers to "assume some kind of direct connection"[4]—quite reasonably, as I will show.

I mentioned that if you are fortunate, you may be able to walk inside a freshly created crop circle. However, be prepared for strange effects. Numerous physical and psychological anomalies have been reported, including: time-slips or time distortions; peculiar animal reactions; strange sounds; visionary experiences; spontaneously induced altered states; warmth; well-being; giddiness; vertigo; miraculous healing; bouts of artistic creativity; and unpleasant reactions such as nausea, headaches, tiredness, physical pain, and flu symptoms. Negative effects can also include subsequent abnormal menstruation, mental fuzziness, disorientation, and dehydration.

Most reported symptoms were transient, most people experienced only one, and in one study of 187 people who visited crop circles between 1991 and 1993, 48 percent reported no unpleasant reactions at all.[5] One researcher notes that she has physically visited over three hundred crop circles and "felt ill" in only ten percent.[6] Another investigator comments that "many people experienced a sharpened awareness, euphoria, calmness, and joy inside crop circles, with a marked increase in vigor hours after leaving them."[7]

As with the Marian apparitions and UFO phenomena, there are strong, probably orchestrated, efforts to deny the reality of the crop circles. With the Marian appearances, the denial approach, as we've seen, is to refuse official Vatican validation; with UFOs, the approach has been official avoidance of any discussion of the topic, public ridicule, and spurious physical counterexplanations. With crop circles, the denial mechanism has chiefly depended on claims of hoaxing, thus draining crop circles of their extraterrestrial glow and pulling them back down to the mundane human level.

Of course, you cannot deny the physical reality of the crop formations. The strategy is to refute the common assumption that they are not human made.

Starting in the early 1990s, several individuals and groups have come forward claiming they made many of the crop circles themselves. The media, and governments seeking to dismiss the phenomenon, seized on this as a way to make the subject go away. Clearly, crop circles were the clever, inconsequential products of human pranksters who go out in the English fields at night with planks, tape measures, and a lot of pluck. The attribution of circles to hoaxing, of course, opened the door to ridicule and dismissal of the subject and pushed it out to the fringes of credibility, presumably where authorities want it, because the phenomenon is highly numinous and troublingly enigmatic—after all, the predominant theory has been they are ET-made.

No doubt some crop circles have been hoaxes, but evidence is mounting, based primarily on nonduplicatable biological effects on the crops and soil, that a large number of them, if not most, are real and not made by humans.[8]

So *who* is making them? Speculation is copious on this, and it ranges from plasma vortices to extraterrestrials. One of the most intriguing possibilities is based on an actual observed phenomenon generally called a light tube. A few crop circle researchers have reported seeing a variously described "tubular beam," "tube of light," "a brilliant, intense white column or tube of light," or "a translucent glass tube" of variable width (one observer said it was about three hundred feet across as seen from a distance) descend vertically from a cloud to a grain field; after it departed a few minutes later, a new crop formation was revealed there.[9]

The general interpretation of the observers, as incredible as it seems even to them, is that somehow the tubular beam imprints the crop pattern.

"The Circles Are Light Made Manifest"

As with Marian apparitions and UFO encounters, when you understand the *where* of their occurrences you get a valuable insight into the *why*. In fact, the *where* of crop circles—predominantly Wiltshire, England—is possibly the most revelatory of the three signs on the Earth because it unveils a geomantic secret.

Not surprisingly, many people want to know *who* is making these circles if not humans. A smaller number of researchers want to know *how* they're making them. My concern, as mentioned, is the site specificity of the circles—the *where*. Before I go into that, let's consider two observations from the angelic realm (the Ofanim) on the purpose of the phenomenon of crop circles. The first is from 1993:

"At the end of an era there always are signs and portents. The circles and symbols are the interface between the transition from one stage in consciousness and another. The circles are light made manifest. They are a projection from the hierarchical aspect of consciousness. Note a recurring symbol is that of Venus or the alchemical symbols for various elements. These signify this shift."

The shift from one stage of consciousness to the next I addressed in the previous chapter. The Ofanim's comment about the "hierarchical aspect of consciousness" helps us break certain confining categories of subtle experience that we've created as a culture straining to perceive and understand the threshold of the spiritual worlds. ETs or angels? Aliens or superdeveloped technology?

We have created restrictive either/or categories for who or what occupies the next dimension, or even what kind of beings must be there to be capable of affecting our world. It's a reasonable assumption that the whole way of doing reality there—embodying and focusing conscious intent—may be radically different from how we do it where we are.

To frame it in terms of the *hierarchical* aspect frees us from that tension; it is whatever beings, intelligences, or noncorporeal thought-forms occupy the next level of reality; whatever forms they employ to make themselves known or at least detectable by us. "Within the process of change, if your favorite attribute is flying saucers, then you may attribute the circles to those," comment the Ofanim. "If you favor angels, then we come as we are."

Think of it in terms of increasing levels of ontological sophistication.

The Ofanim offered their second statement in 2003: "They are interdimensional messages. It is a communication that comes from the next dimension to be experienced. Crop circles are a basis for a language of light, but it is important to differentiate this from the normal mechanisms of language because crop circles are a language specific to time, place, and feature."

The time, place, and feature they are specific to is what the Ofanim call "the golden band within the body of Albion." This is at the umbilicus of the planet at Avebury and Silbury Hill in Wiltshire and involves complex geomantic arrangements I explain in detail later. Although I introduced in chapter 5 the fact that Earth's belly button is at Avebury, it's a complicated and highly unusual concept to assimilate, so I'll review it again, as it's central to this topic.

The concentration of England's crop circles—in fact, of the world's—around Avebury (and nearby Stonehenge) in Wiltshire is correlated with the high concentration of original geomantic nodes in the landscape, still for the most part marked by megalithic monuments.[10] Basically, all of Wiltshire and its geomantic features comprise a golden band related to the planet's umbilicus, and the geomantic nodes are openings to the next or parallel dimension that access the light frequencies used to create the crop circles.

Crop circles, the Ofanim stress, have ramifications that affect more than the dedicated band of researchers and site visitors, more even than all of humanity, as we shift into a new era, heralded by signs and portents. "They have more to do with the being of Earth, Gaia, and her evolution in conscious cooperation with the potential of consciousness within the human family as an interface between dimensions." It's reciprocal: The crop circles are entraining Gaia, as the landscape angel of Earth, to rise to the next level of galactic cognition, but She needs humanity's participation to be the interface between where our physical reality is now and where it's going.

There are many important ideas in these observations by the Ofanim. Let's go through them one by one in sufficient detail to make the picture clear.

Let's start with the umbilicus. Earlier in the book I talked about the Earth as a living being and as having, as a soul for the planetary consciousness, a landscape angel we know as Gaia. The truth of this situation has certain inevitable consequences. If the Earth is a living, angelically ensouled being, it has an umbilical connection to its mother, just as any biological being has. The Earth has an umbilical cord to both its galactic parents, and that umbilicus exists at only one specific place: Avebury.

One of the many functions of this ancient stone circle is to ground the planet's umbilical connection to its father and mother in the galaxy. As mentioned in chapter 5, the father is Sirius, our galaxy's brightest star, in the constellation Canis Major (the Great Dog), and the mother is Canopus, the rudder of the constellation Argo Navis, our galaxy's second brightest star.

From Sirius comes a gold line of light, from Canopus a silver. They come to the Earth as a double helix, entwining gold and silver lines, and ground at Avebury. Once grounded, each of these lines bisects the planet, traveling around its entire girth like an oroboros, rejoining itself at Avebury. The lines in themselves are not especially broad, varying in width in places and times of the year, but averaging out at between several hundred yards to about one quarter of a mile wide, and passing through many geomantic nodes en route.

That's one aspect of Avebury's umbilical function. A second is that it is the site for Earth's primary dome. Domes, as described in chapter 2, are energy canopies placed over 1,746 preselected sites around the Earth; most of these sites are now either mountains or volcanoes, but when the domes were originally set down on the

Earth, the planet was mostly what we could informally call loose wet clay, still in formation. The domes for the most part summoned up the mountains from out of the flat land.

Each dome represents and presents, holographically, the consciousness of the star being (or great Star-Angel) whose outward form is a high-magnitude star. This sounds rather fantastic, if not implausible, yet it is the case. If you want a visionary encounter with the intelligence whose galactic body we know as the star Arcturus (a high-magnitude star in the constellation Boötes said to be 25 million miles wide), then spend some time meditating at Chaco Canyon in New Mexico. That's where the planetary dome for Arcturus sits, and that's where, if you can allow yourself to believe such a thing, the star god of Arcturus resides.

All 1,746 domes replicate Avebury's umbilical function. Each has an intertwined silver and gold cord attached to its top, which serves as the dome's umbilicus, and each double helix dome cord goes back to its parents at Avebury. That means each dome has a secondary umbilical connection to its galactic source, Sirius and Canopus, and participates in Earth's galactic connections. So the second umbilical function performed at Avebury is to ground the Earth's 1,746 silver and gold cords and to keep them linked to the source.

Now here's a third aspect. Each dome is capable of generating up to 48 subsidiary domes, which are arrayed much like the petals in a ripe sunflower head, that is, in accordance with the Golden Ratio, or phi. Originally, all the Earth's domes were the same size: 33 miles across (they have since shrunk a bit). Within that 33-mile domain, you would find the 48 dome caps arrayed, elegantly and symmetrically, forming a composite flower of light across a 33-mile swath of landscape.

Avebury has a dome with potentially 48 deployed dome caps, and there are 32 more domes in Wiltshire. There could be as many as 1,584 dome caps. Bear in mind, Wiltshire is very small, by U.S. landmass standards, probably not even the size of Delaware, yet it has 33 domes and up to 1,584 dome caps packed into that small space like a tin of caviar.[11] Neighboring Somerset, well packed with megalithic monuments and the home of much ancient Celtic myth (such as King Arthur's Camalate, the Holy Grail, and Avalon), has 22.

Somerset alone has 1.25 percent of the planet's total supply of domes, and Avebury has just under two percent. Very few other planetary regions have this density of domes and dome caps.

Here's why this is important. With domes originally at 33 miles in diameter, most of these half-spheres on the landscape would be overlapping. You have to think of these domes as being "made of" something in between light and matter as we think we know them today. They could easily overlap and still maintain their structural integrity. At 33 miles in diameter, incidentally, the domes would each tower 16.5 miles over the land. The 33 Wiltshire domes, if you could see them from high overhead, would be packed solid; all you could see would be the shimmering, interpenetrating dome canopies, and within them, the many hundreds of smaller dome caps, shimmering but not interpenetrating.[12]

Into this galactically enriched and literally stellar landscape are set the hundreds of various megalithic monuments and the psychically accessible features of Earth's visionary geography—the temples, palaces, meeting halls, and workshops of the gods, as suggested in chapters 1 and 2. The practical effect of this density of domes and dome caps would be an intensification of the normal or resting state of consciousness. It would be uplifted, exalted, elevated to a possibly permanent state of remembrance of cosmic origins and purpose.

Avebury participates in a fourth umbilical aspect. At one level of its organization, the planet's energy body is divided geometrically into 12 equal polygonal areas, each in the shape of a pentagon. The totality of this shape of 12 pentagons is called a dodecahedron ("12 faces"). Each of these polygons, which I call an Albion Plate, comprises a great many geomantic features; in fact, the composition and contents of each Albion Plate replicate almost all the contents of the Earth's array of visionary geography. It's a fractalized system.

One feature that summarizes and contains all the others in a given plate is the anthropomorphic figure I call an Albion. As I noted in chapter 3, the poet William Blake wrote about a giant, ancient human called Albion, and I use the term in that sense: as a colossus of form and consciousness whose body is the full and final expression of all the geomantic parts. Think of an Albion as a container for the entire contents of the collective consciousness and unconsciousness of humanity since "we" first started living here, and all set into a configuration based on the energies and intelligences of eight major stars.

There are 12 Albions, and for a long time in Earth's history, they have all been asleep; in fact, they have never been awake (self-aware) yet. They are scheduled to wake up, first one, then another. The first to awaken will be the Albion overlying the British Isles, France, Spain, and Portugal. This Albion is already stirring in his sleep, tossing fitfully, close to waking up. Appropriately, then, the bulk of the world's crop circles are being imprinted on this Albion's belly, little pinpricks of new cosmic information and programming.

A Swarm of Stars around the Earth's (Black Hole) Belly Button

Here is a fifth umbilical aspect. Functionally, Avebury is "grid central" for the planet. It is, analogically, the planet's master DVD, containing all the original geomantic programming, options, and parameters. Think of Avebury, seemingly a mere 28.5 acres but far bigger on the psychic inside, as a hologram of the entire cosmos as it relates to the geomantic structure of Earth. All features (92 and counting) can be adjusted from here. This is where one can change the mix, research the past settings, access the vast terabytes of compressed data, review growth parameters, star alignments, go back to the original engineering blueprints.

Given the holographic nature of the Earth's visionary geography and Avebury's DVD and umbilical aspects, this site holds another key secret. It is the seat of the planetary hologram for the galactic center, the huge bulge of stars and light at the center of our galaxy as we look down through the Milky Way.

Astronomers agree that from our vantage point on Earth in the Milky Way galaxy, some 28,000 light-years (LY) from "downtown," the center of the galaxy is reached through or is within the constellation called Sagittarius, the centaur-archer. The galaxy itself is about 100,000 LY across with almost one trillion suns. What's at the galactic center? It's a "bizarre place with jets and wisps of very energetic matter, with imploding stars and exploding shells of hot gas," and a dark, enigmatic entity with a mass or gravitational field of almost three million suns that sucks in all light around it. Known as Sagittarius A, this dark enclosed region of space with unbelievably strong gravity is called a black hole.[13]

One reason astronomers infer the presence of a black hole at the galactic center is because the amount of visible matter is not sufficient to account for the tremendous gravitational pull registered there that holds a great mass of stars captive within its field. In fact, visible matter accounts for only one percent. Thus a tremendous mass of dark matter (not physically detectable) must be doing it. Dark matter in this case means a black hole. But it's not just an "ordinary" black hole with an intense gravity field. Astronomers call it a supermassive one. Its size is estimated to be about the size of the orbit of Mars in our solar system.[14]

In its vicinity, though at a safe distance, is a copious cluster of stars—ten million stars swarming within a single light-year of the galactic nucleus. To get a visual idea of their density, picture ten million cherries packed into a space only one-half mile in diameter. Seen from a distance, such as from outside the galaxy, this concentration of stars and its collective magnitude is the "central bloated hub of stars" typical of this type of galaxy.[15]

Translated into Earth terms and our planet's visionary geography, these ten million "cherries" or suns packed around the galactic center are equivalent to the 55 domes (for stars) and up to 2,640 dome caps (also for stars, mostly) packed around the holographic galactic center at Avebury. Similar to the gravitational effects at the galactic center attributed to dark matter, Avebury's master dome holds all the Earth's star domes in its organizing, umbilical field.

This raises an intriguing question: Does Avebury have a black hole?

The fascinating (and for researchers, valuable) fact of the galactic hologram upon the Earth is that you can look at the planetary expression to gain insight into the galactic. After all: As above, so below, and in the middle too.

Some years ago I had the opportunity to spend a week meditating at Avebury at dawn, midday, and dusk around the time of the summer solstice. This was at the invitation of my mentors, the Ofanim, as they wanted to show me something. I also spent time on the Ridgeway nearby, an ancient walking track that crosses some 40 miles of English countryside with numerous extant and vanished megalithic structures strung along its spine like pearls.[16] It turns out that Avebury and the Ridgeway are intimately connected, energetically.

Here's how: As I've noted, one of the 92 features of the Earth's visionary geography is the Tree of Life. This is an experiential, walkable, straight-line array of 30 to 40 sequential spheres of light or dimensions of existence. Imagine a model of reality that has ten parts arranged in a hierarchy from root to crown; now postulate that this same ten-aspected model exists in two more dimensions.[17] You climb this ladder of lights, up from the bottom or down from the top. Biblically, this was called Jacob's Ladder.

Judaism's esoteric tradition called Qabala maps interlocking realms of reality this way and calls the spheres of light "Sefira." What is acutely relevant here is what is on top of this 40-sphere Tree of Life. Qabalists, based on original mystical perception of these ultra-subtle realms, call it *Ain Sof Awr, Ain Sof,* and *Ain.*[18] Think of these as the nimbus of light above your head in three parts, or, if you were wearing a crown (or if your crown chakra, said to have a thousand petals, were illumined), the heat aura emanation or general luster from it.

From the top of the Tree of Life, usually symbolized as a White Head turned sideways or called, more abstractly, the Vast Countenance, you have first an undifferentiated field of incalculably bright light, the *Ain Sof Awr.* Then you have a single condensed point of absolutely brilliant light in an empty sphere; this is the *Ain Sof.* Then, and finally, you have the *Ain,* a velvet-black nothing.[19]

This may strike you as a bit whimsical, but when the Ofanim first introduced me to the *Ain,* experientially, it looked like a black bowling ball. It is a sphere of black containing nothing, and the potential for everything; it is the universe before the supposed big bang, the gravity well singularity, a black hole.

This is how the Ofanim explained it to me:

"When you know the black sphere, there will be no more questions. It is the memory of all questions. It relates to your purpose, life, and existence, here, now, on a moment-to-moment basis. Knowing the black sphere of stable consciousness will take you beyond all questions, all answers, all concepts, all form, all emptiness, all ideas or notions of self nature, beyond the beyond. The black ball is the ultimate question and within the ultimate question is the ultimate answer. It is beyond space and time, beyond concepts, beyond formlessness."

Just as a black hole's fantastic mass and gravity suck all light into a singularity, slow time to almost a standstill, and allow no light to escape, so is the black bowling ball, or Qabala's *Ain*, an ultimate, self-referential enclosed space.

Back to the Ridgeway. In addition to providing an experience of the Tree of Life in three realms, it provides 40 viewing stations for the Earth's umbilicus at Avebury. I mean these not just as literal observation points, but as spiritual filters through which to behold a highly numinous and ultimately mysterious feature. Avebury is the fortieth sphere of light, or the topmost, as you climb the tree; it is the doorway *out* into the transcendent realm, and the doorway *into* the manifest, the first sphere as you climb down.

In the course of a week's meditation within the stone circle at Avebury, during which I participated (or at least observed) the unfoldment of a complex temple structure of light involving many of the stages of the oft-cited Christed Initiation in the Buddha Body, I saw the black bowling ball there. In fact, I saw it two different ways. First, it seemed that I was going psychically blind, that all the lights had gone out. Everything got gray and dim, then suddenly reemerged as a shiny, black leather sphere. It was the *Ain* atop the Tree. A shining, black negative space of pure potentiality. When I realized Nothing was happening, I felt better: I could still *see*, after all. Then I saw it the second way.

The huge sarsen stones that edged the circle, including the ones that had once been there and were now gone—the Ofanim say there were originally 72—became pure white light. Collectively, the stones became so brilliant, their individual lights merged to form a single massive white mirror of light. If you could see Avebury's 28.5 acres from space, it would be a brilliant white mirror.

Why was *Ain* presented to me in two ways? Because you have a black hole and a white hole. Astrophysicists postulate that at the other end of a black hole is a white hole (picture an hourglass: black hole at the top, white hole at the bottom, gravitational singularity in between). Qabalists would say that on the "other side" of *Ain* (the black hole, "shiny, black leather sphere") is *Ain Sof* (the white hole, the "white mirror"), the diamond point of light squeezed out of the black bowling ball, or the back end of the black hole *(Ain)*.[20]

So does Avebury (and, by extension, the Earth) have a black hole?

Yes. If you want to experience Sagittarius A mystically, the supermassive black hole at the galactic center, visit Avebury, its holographic equivalent on Earth, and find the *Ain,* or black bowling ball. Galactically, what we can potentially experience at Avebury is a supermassive black hole that weighs (has a gravity equivalent to) 2.6 million suns and is no bigger than the orbit of Mars around our Sun.

The Key inside the Golden Honeyed Band of Albion

Now that we have a fair sense of the umbilical aspects of Avebury and Wiltshire for the planet, let's focus on the golden band within Albion. To start with, recall my remarks from the previous chapter regarding the intelligences from the constellation Cepheus (the crowned king) in ancient Wiltshire.

I said that the Cepheans spread out laterally from Avebury as if they were etching tattoos on the Earth's surface. Seen from above, they created a kind of cat's face of whiskers extending about 25 miles east and west of Avebury with nodes at the whisker terminations, perhaps geomantic sites. This made a series of parallel wavy lines extending east and west, creating a symmetrical image.

The extent of the Cephean original imprinting in Wiltshire is the extent of the golden band of Albion. Avebury is the umbilicus for Gaia, the entire planet, and it is the etheric umbilicus for the single planetary expression of Albion. I've mentioned that there are 12 Albions for Earth, but there is a thirteenth, a single, composite one that encompasses and consummates these 12 smaller Albions.

Imaginatively, picture a giant human draped or sprawled on his back upon the Earth; he's so big, though, that his body covers all of the planet, his head nudging his feet. At Albion's belly button rises a double-stranded cord, gold and silver intertwined, rising up and from away from the Earth to terminate at the stars Sirius and Canopus. As though somebody painted a swath of gold across Albion's midriff, there is a golden band from his left to right side, from the top of the left to right pelvis. It includes the belly button and umbilicus.

The golden band is the concentration zone for the crop circle images and intelligences behind them, and for the Mystery revelation they offer, as I'll explain.

More abstractly, you could picture a golden rectangle with a star in the middle. That's Avebury; the golden band is Wiltshire and its geomantic sites.

So what's inside the golden band, and why gold? Gold of course is the symbol of wisdom and the transmutation of base elements (lead) into purity. The gold band, or context for Wiltshire's ceremonial ritual landscape, is like a seed, an energy pack, a broad spectrum catalyst, a data compression zone, a honeycomb. The golden band within Albion is filled with a golden honey.

The biblical phrase "the land of milk and honey" is apt here. In Exodus, for example, the land we now know as Israel was called "a land flowing with milk and honey." Is this meant as an image of agricultural bounty? I think not, not originally or geomantically. It's a picture of the stargate network turned on.

Earlier in the book, I described stargates as fifth-dimensionally placed geomantic devices for actual physical transportation of people and goods from points on Earth to points on planets within constellations or to do with stars. In my previous book, *The Emerald Modem,* I said the stargates exist as a network that could, metaphorically, be understood as a jeweled cloak around the planet. I called it a cosmic Robe of Glory.

The activation and use of the stargates involve the coordinated participation of the Archangel Michael and the Supreme Being. Archangel Michael uses his sword to make the connection between the individual stargate and the Throne of the Supreme Being. When this connection is made, it seems as if a golden-yellow light of a high, subtle quality rains or flows down upon the stargate, seen as an effulgent globular beacon in the landscape. This rain of golden-yellow light upon the white globe has the consistency of honey.

To live in a land flowing with milk and honey is to participate in the stargate network under the auspices of the Archangel Michael and the Supreme Being. The *land* is the fifth dimension where the stargates on Earth are found; the *flowing* is the rain of golden-yellow light from Above when the stargate is turned on; the *milk* is the brightness of the stargate; and the *honey* is the golden-yellow rain from Above. Spiritually and physically you are connected with the galaxy and capable of bodily moving across vast spatial distances in an eyeblink.

Not only was Israel once known as the Land of Milk and Honey, but so was England. In the Welsh *Triads,* an ancient repository of Welsh lore, the British Isles had three antique names: the second, presumably in sequence, was the Island of Honey. I take this as a coded reference to the activated stargate system. Why honey? Because it's sweet and an almost perfect food, so it works well as a symbol for the sweetness of divine consciousness perpetually flowing down upon the Earth as nourishment for all sentient life—the honey of God's attention.

To return to Wiltshire with this insight, we have the Earth's umbilicus at Avebury and the copious array of geomantic nodes around it (the Cephean "whiskers"), including stargates embedded like milk drops in this golden, honeyed nutriment.

The Ofanim characterized crop circles as expressing a language of light. To get even an elementary understanding of this, we have to conceive of crop circles differently, more fluidly, more extradimensionally, as, to start with, having a volumetric dimension. We see the images pressed flat upon the grain. That's essentially a two-dimensional expression. Researchers and mystics report that the images are stamped on the grain fields from tubes of light descending from above. That's at least three dimensional, and probably four dimensional (4D).

We'll have to use our imagination here to picture it: Each crop circle image must first be inflated like a balloon to reveal its volumetric aspect; and then it must be set spinning and morphing to reveal its four-dimensional, or time, aspect.[21] Next we need to picture the golden rectangle filled with divine "honey." Inside it, like fireflies on a summer's night, is a constant succession of bright images blinking on then off; each is a new crop circle being imprinted upon the Land of Milk and Honey. Many hundreds of crop circles have appeared in Wiltshire in only the last two or three (well-documented) decades, so we are seeing a time tableau of all these images within the golden rectangle or band.

Picture this golden rectangle as a fabulous palimpsest of sequential 4D images. Crop circles physically last only as long as the grain fields remain unharvested and, of course, they never survive the winters. Yet their 4D imprint remains as an etherically palpable residue in the honeyed rectangle. Try to picture the many hundreds of crop circles in Wiltshire since the 1970s as having a residual imprint within this honeyed golden rectangle—it's like a multimedia light show of symbols, faces, and designs; an open box of letters from a foreign language; an encryption set for humanity.

Here is a clairvoyant impression of the crop circles that may help: The 33 domes and 1,584 dome caps of Wiltshire are vortices drawing the crop circles to them. They are the contact or rivet points for the "dust devils" or smaller vortices that create the crop circles, presumably the tubes of light seen in spinning mode. What we physically see as the two-dimensional symbol imprint on living grain in another level of reality resembles a rotating spirit head within the dust devil vortex. Picture a classic depiction of a god from any of the world's myths; make a stone carving of it; turn this into light; then start it spinning so that instead of one head with one fixed expression, it seems there are dozens of heads, each protean, with varying expressions. This is what I mean by a rotating spirit head.

The rotating spirit head is like the soul of each crop circle image. Just as mystics can see the celestial intelligence or being whose outer body is a star in our galaxy, so are the crop circle image and its 4D original the outer form of the rotating spirit head, which we could usefully think of as the animating, formative intelligence behind the various images and their multidimensional reality.

The rotating spirit heads make imprints on the landscape within the honeyed golden band of Albion. Each time they set down, the expression is different—here a planetary orbital array, here a Golden mean sunflower, there a geometrically precise mandala, in a seemingly nonrepeating visual vocabulary. It's like a cosmic alphabet with thousands of letters in light and fire. Seen over time and across the golden rectangle of Wiltshire, the images blink on and off, constantly, like a stadium of gods one at a time kissing Gaia, leaving lipstick.

We have been witnessing crop circles in Wiltshire for only the last 30 years or so, but the rotating spirit heads have been imprinting their images on the skin of Wiltshire since the time of the Cepheans and the installation of the Earth's umbilicus at Avebury, and, for that matter, the construction of the stone circle. Prior to the advent of grain fields in Wiltshire and the imminence of the upgrade in consciousness we are undergoing, the spirit forms of the crop circles imprinted themselves in the ethers of the region, as if talking privately to Gaia out of human hearing. But now the conversation is public, and we're welcome to listen.

Even though it seems, and it probably is the case, that the crop circles are being imprinted on the landscape from above, when you take this time tableau perspective on Wiltshire, it's as if you're observing a box of buzzing bees. Each time a bee nudges the golden glassed surface of the rectangular box, it leaves an impression, and we call these crop circles. Similarly, it's as if we are looking through the transparent lid into a box of fabulous cosmic letters, the elements of the language of light the Ofanim spoke of, the original, the once and future *codes* for physical reality, consciousness, and the Earth's visionary geography.

Here is a fun possibility for interpreting the totality of crop circles: We know that for every physically observable sacred site, there is also an inner, psychically accessed feature—some type of light temple or spiritual space. In some cases, as with features archeologists call hill forts and the Ofanim call light corrective centers (ditches surrounding flat, empty grassy areas and often remembered in local folklore as "castles"), there are more abstract, geometric inner light forms, such as the five regular polyhedra called the Platonic Solids.

Let's say one remove even from this inner light temple aspect is a coding system, an alphabet of forms, symbols, images, and shapes. We might even think of this as an encryption system, though secrecy was not the intent. Let's say there are several thousand different units in this encryption system, and, metaphorically, let's say the entire system is like a very thick deck of Tarot cards. On each card, there is one image, one code, one letter in the alphabet. Up until now, the spiritual hierarchies who run and superintend our Earth have been playing with the cards close to their chests—like skilled poker players perhaps.

But now, in a generous act of revelation, they have laid all the cards *face up* on the table (primarily Wiltshire's golden band of crop circles) for us to see. Here are all the encodings used in the Earth's classic grid system withheld from our collective cognition until now. Now these encodings, the whole deck, the "genes" that express our reality at all its levels, sounds and colors, are being flashed like cue cards within Wiltshire's golden rectangle.[22]

It's as if the spiritual hierarchies are saying, "Here's how we built your reality and maintain it. We used these. Have a look."

It's a box of letters, an angelic communication matrix in 6D, the original light pattern library for our reality. All of Wiltshire and its 30 years of crop circle images seen as a single entity, as this golden rectangle or golden band within Albion, shift your perception to a more subtle level. The thousands of light letters or pictures (the 4D originals of the flattened crop circle images) are like faces in a vast celestial chorus cheering on the Mystery drama and its central actor. That actor is a sign on the outside of the box, etched on Wiltshire's skin.

On the outside of the golden box, there is a single sign or letter. It is like a papermaker's watermark, subtly visible on the skin of Earth's visionary geography. It looks like the digit 1 and also like the Hebrew letter *Waw* (also spelled *Vau* or *Vav*), whose number equivalent is 6. This is the number coding for the Ofanim, their essential and minimal manifestation signature, *6*, and it's both a number or quantity and a sound, *Waw*. The digit 1 or Hebrew letter *Waw* (written, it looks like a 1) expressing 6 is to the left of Avebury (running north-south), which, on the box, appears as a big 0. In Hebrew, that's the letter *Sammekh*, 60. Together, it reads 10, a number of completion. Or it reads *Waw* 6 and *Sammekh* 60, which totals 66.[23]

Think of this, the 10 or 66, as the text within the text, the meta-message.

You have the Milk and the Honey in the angelic land of Wiltshire. The Milk is the angelic radiance of the Ofanim's 1 or *Waw;*

the Honey is the divine sweetness, or nectar, within Albion's golden rectangle of Wiltshire.

Inside the box, you find the universe of letters in the language of light, the genes and chromosomes, the syntax and grammar for a new synaptic network, a preverbal basis of cognition, a picture syntax written in the sixth dimension. You're inside the mind and consciousness and synapses of the angels. It's like you just went into the black monolith in *2001: A Space Odyssey*. It's indeed full of stars, and all the stars are letters in this picture language of light. It's a space packed with pictures written in light and fire, and you lack the familiar human perceptual framework and analytical boundaries to read it. You have to raise your cognition to a level beyond or before verbal language.

Outside again, viewing the box from a little distance, you sense what the Mystery is, what the intended outcome to this celestial drama is. Put the key in the lock. Put the 1 in the 0; put the Ofanim's key (6) in the lock (or 0) of Avebury.

The sign of the *Waw* on the golden rectangle, to the west of Avebury (not the stone circle, but the 16.5-mile radius of its original dome), is the key to the consummation of the whole enterprise, the decoding Rosetta Stone. The *Waw* overlies six geomantic nodes in Wiltshire, ones rich in crop circle activity, but some not yet geomantically charged.

On a pragmatic level, you would have to find the correct sites, meditate there, participate in the 4D aspects of the crop circles, then "bring" this encoded information, as it were, now stamped on your aura, to Avebury, as the key. You would also have to do this in cooperation and conjunction with the Ofanim. It is their key and, paradoxically, they are the key as well, for *Waw* is their signature.

The intent is for the six sites to be visited and the visitor's aura stamped with the geomantic information or crop circle image, like steps in a code; or maybe you have an encounter with the rotating spirit head or "god" resident at each site. Then you imprint these six signatures within the Avebury stone circle, forming the *Waw* key again there.

The arrangement is this: If you can decode the language of light by seeing the crop circles in their intended multidimensional aspects, then you can use the key to "open" Avebury to enable it to release its bounty. Decoding the language is like discovering the combination to a safe; in this case, the digits and their correct order are found in the crop circle images and at the sites within the span of the digit 1 or Hebrew letter *Waw* that runs north-south slightly to the west of Avebury and still within Wiltshire. That means there are six crop circle sites within the shadow cast by the digit 1 or *Waw* over western Wiltshire; these six sites each contain one unit of the sixfold key. The lock is at Avebury.

You put the key in the lock and everything will turn inside out; Heaven, all the contents and intelligences of the galaxy, will tumble out of Avebury, disgorged, a cornucopia of secrets, mysteries, and revelations delivered at last.

More specifically, when you put the key in the lock at Avebury, you release the thousands of rotating spirit heads buzzing in the box like bees. The box opens, the Wiltshire crop circle zone releases its Mystery revelation like a rush of spores or seeds, or like swarming bees that will pollinate the Earth, its geomantic sites, and human awareness with this next dimensional consciousness.

In other words, the entire crop circle phenomenon has a teleology, a goal. But you have to look at the phenomena as a singular event and at least in 4D. It's schooling us in the basics of a new basis for communication across the threshold.

Who would use such a language, devoid of letters and syntax as we know them? Recently, I asked the Ofanim how they communicate with other angels as distinct from communicating with us humans using a word-based language. "Everything is light vibrating in different frequencies. Every letter, thought, and sound is a light frequency resonance. We communicate in light frequencies in a pure form."

This works in both directions: *before* every letter, thought, or sound in our cognitive domain is a light frequency, a vibratory signature, a picture in light. With the proliferation of crop circles, we're seeing this written outside us for the purposes of our study and mastery. The dialogue in light awaits us. . . .

7 | How to Get Your Head above the Clouds in Three Steps–A Conclusion

So what do the three signs on the Earth taken together add up to?

Let's first have a fresh look at the Christ. Let's put aside for the moment all theology, ideology, dogma, preconceptions, and belief, and just *look*, psychically, at some aspects of what the Christ did while resident on the Earth. Granted, this will be but one of many possible views.

Picture a man with a huge golden head, bright as a sun, radiating rays of golden light in all directions. It's as if he's standing with his head above the clouds, but they're not actually clouds. It's the density of three-dimensional consensus reality. His head rises above it, not out of disdain or superiority, but because his light is so bright it parts and then dissolves the clouds, changing planetary reality.

Golden streams of light, like a strong rain, continually shower down around the Christ from higher up (not up in the atmosphere, but from the next dimension). He has opened a portal for the shower of divine grace and consciousness to rain down on the physical world. He has parted the thick veil separating our 3D world and the next level of reality, the 4D spiritual worlds. Up there, in the higher 4D realm, are the gods, the deities, the angels, the exalted understanding, the visionary realm, communication based on light forms—things most humans have heard of but never thought they could have.

The fresh, invigorating, illuminating energies stream down from on high through the Christ's crown chakra and cascade down to the ground. They infiltrate the atmosphere, the soil, the five elements of matter, and consciousness. They percolate into the energy fields of every human alive on the planet and feed, lighten, and spiritualize matter everywhere. They introduce matter to a new possibility of lightening.

Put simply, the Christ on Earth did something beneficial to matter and matter-based consciousness. He uplifted it, enabling humans to see further. He made possible our future acquisition of 4D reality.

That future is our now.

So here we are today with our three anomalous signs on the Earth—apparitions of the Virgin Mary, prolific alien encounters, and crop circles. What are they? Why are they here? Seen together as a composite message from above, they are three steps we can mount now to enter 4D reality.

Consider the *fact* of their appearance, not the details or proofs or doubts or explanations, just the sheer fact that each of these signs is a *fact* on the Earth. Let's probe for the message of this fact, or what we might call the meta-message of the three signs.

Step one is the apparitional presence of the Virgin Mary around the Earth. These apparitions are planted in planetary reality as blue pillars of the Divine Mother; the Mother of Christ's presence is now sprouting all over the planet. Earlier in the book, I also referred to Mary's residual presence in terms of a global net of the Mothers as a support network for birthing the Christ Child within.

Grounded in the Earth, the Marian pillars (or the net) rise to the outermost edge of our 3D consensus reality, right up against the threshold of 4D. We climb these Marian pillars by starting the process of birthing the Christ Child within each of us, or, to say it outside Christian terminology, we incubate an expression of the Higher Self. The pillars support, nurture, even encourage us.

The numerous Marian apparition sites, already numinous as geomantic nodes in Earth's original visionary geography, have been freshly charged with spiritual potency. We may use this light—in fact, it is earnestly hoped by those Above that we do—as a catalyst, an inspiration, and a helping hand to plant the seed of new spiritual life within us with its promise of expanded cognition.

Just as the Christ seeded the Earth and matter with golden cosmic light, so the Mother of Christ comes to seed the realm of humanity and matter with a nourishing light that will enable us to copy His example. Whether we acknowledge the apparitions, ignore or deny them, the seeding is happening just the same and our physical reality is under transformation.

Each Marian apparition site invites us to get pregnant with the Christ Child within us, and each promises us the Love from Above to nourish our new spiritual life. Whether we physically visit Marian sites or merely think about them or simply trust that the Earth's visionary geography is now seeded with this marvelous celestial "plant food" for our blossoming, it is given to us.

Step two is the prolific array of alien encounters, whether abductions or epiphanies. This step propels our seeing into the galactic level, across the threshold of 3D and 4D realities. Looking around in 4D, we discover that our galaxy, and the galaxies beyond the Milky Way, teem with life and consciousness, purpose, goals, and evolutionary growth. We see that some of these intelligences exist in wildly different forms and regularly interact with humanity on Earth. Some have been doing so for millennia; some are newly arrived participants or observers or irritants in humanity's evolution into 4D consciousness. You could say one of the first things we see with our new Christ Child eyes is the stunning diversity of intelligences throughout our galaxy.

Recall that in chapter 3 I suggested that the Christ, also known as the Word or Logos, is in part the fourth-dimensional stretched fabric of spacetime. So as an initial extension of consciousness, the

Christ puts us into 4D cognition, and Christ cognition at this entry level of 4D is to behold all the stars (sources of mass) as embedded and held together and known by the Christ spacetime fabric.

As self-aware, intelligent beings, we humans are not alone in the galaxy. We never were and never will be. We are enmeshed in a vast interconnected galactic web of sentient life. This is part of the ineluctable dynamic of creation. We realize with a shock that at some point in our planetary history something must have gone wrong so that the "lights had gone out on Earth."[1] We lost the thread of connection, forgot it ever existed, then denied that it was even possible such a thing could exist—only crazy people would think so.

But now, despite intense efforts worldwide to keep us oblivious to extraterrestrial reality and involvement with the Earth, our planet is being swarmed by ETs. We see, or at least hear of, their activities constantly; so thoroughly does this permeate our culture that even if we sit in a mental state of disbelief, ridicule, or atheism, images of Grays and other aliens help sell cars on TV and appear regularly in cartoons and movies.

Our denial is increasingly hard to maintain seriously. Evidence of 4D reality surrounds us annoyingly like mosquitoes.

Let us not forget the double revelation of the Earth's visionary terrain. First, we learn that the Earth has an esoteric, light-filled underpinning, its galactic body, and that the planet's heritage of sacred sites is a doorway into this. The revelation of the Earth's visionary geography itself is a crucial opening for us.

Then there is the even more marvelous fact that this classic geomythic grid—the Earth's original light template—is being used in our time as a celestial message board principally for three signs. Higher intelligences are writing us these signs—Marian apparitions, alien encounters and activities, and crop circles—on this complex and diverse array of geomantic nodes. It's as if the planet is newly wallpapered with cosmic post-it notes: It's time to read the notes.

With step two, our cognition expands radically. Now it is *our* heads that emerge above the dense, swirling clouds of 3D consensus reality, *our* heads that sparkle with the golden light of wider seeing and freer knowing. Our new reality is not planetary, but *galactic:* we live in a population-rich galaxy. We look down at our familiar human body—our fleshly home on Earth—and suddenly it is not so familiar: Stars and constellations and star deities live right in our midst, in our flesh and bones and energy fields, *in us,* in our awareness.

Space and time seem to work differently in 4D; bodily identification and location are more fluid; experience is richer, paradoxical, multidirectional. What we regard as high strangeness—missing time, screen memories, real dreams, the baffling Oz Factor,[2] and the rest— is an aspect of how reality works at this next level of expression. The Oz Factor equals the new (to us) physical laws of the universe.

In step three, then, we each place our golden head—representing expanded cognition—on top of the blue Marian pillar. Our body, like the pillar, is grounded in planetary physical reality, but our awareness now enjoys the 4D revelations.

Step three is the crop circles, which teach us a new language based on an alphabet of light, the communication form of angels and advanced stellar beings. Our heads, now golden and high above the 3D clouds, emit rays, arrows of light, streamers, that rise like tendrils or antennae seeking an even finer light above. Ancient cultures used to depict their sun gods as having golden heads, with solar rays as a rich mane of golden hair, spiky like arrows in flight. Now on this third step, we are each a sun god, a solar deity with golden hair like arrows. Onto each strand of golden hair—think of this as a metaphor for expanded cognition—rain the letters and syllables and syntax of this new language of light.

The crop circles are teaching us the protocols of communication in our new 4D reality. The many hundreds of crop circle glyphs over the years, taken as a whole, comprise a basic entry-level grammar for this new 4D communication.

Endnotes

Introduction

1. Pronouncements and predictions of "impending drastic change" are part of today's "Apocalyptic spirit," wrote Chet B. Snow, Ph.D., in 1989 in a fascinating book about psychically reading the future. Apocalyptic images of dreadful Earth changes lurk in the human collective subconscious, reinforced over the centuries. These affect us in ways we only vaguely realize, Snow says. "They are, nonetheless, part of the 'mass dream' of the future that we here on Earth are projecting, through our subconscious minds, today." So are we reading the future like a written script or reading our own fearful projections into that future, mistaking them for reality? Chet B. Snow, Ph.D., *Mass Dreams of the Future* (New York: McGraw Hill, 1989): xviii, xix.

2. Rudolf Steiner, *The True Nature of the Second Coming* (London: Rudolf Steiner Press, 1971): 38.

3. Rudolf Steiner, *Initiation, Eternity, and the Passing Moment* (Spring Valley: N.Y.: Anthroposophic Press, 1980): 151.

4. Edith Fiore, Ph.D., *Encounters: A Psychologist Reveals Case Studies of Abductions by Extraterrestrials* (New York: Doubleday, 1989): xvii.

Chapter 1

1. James Lovelock, *Healing Gaia: Practical Medicine for the Planet* (New York: Harmony Books, 1991): 6, 20; *The Ages of Gaia: A Biography of Our Living Earth* (New York: W.W. Norton, 1988).

2. Eclectic, *Theosophist* 46:2, 491, quoted in *Devas and Men: A Compilation of Theosophical Studies on the Angelic Kingdom* (Adyar, India: Theosophical Publishing House, 1977): 87–88.

3. Geoffrey Hodson, *The Kingdom of the Gods* (Adyar, India: Theosophical Publishing House, 1980): 114.

4. Ibid., 58, 113, 114.

5. For this reason, such places are often called numinous, a term that means light-filled and exalted and that derives from *Numen,* an old Roman word to denote a minor deity or nature spirit that makes a location numinous or divine. The classical Romans and the Greeks before them commonly thought certain places such as caves, springs, woods, or mountains were inhabited by spirits, or *numina,* whose presence enlivened a site.

6. Frank Waters, *The Colorado* (New York: Holt, Rinehart and Winston, 1946): xviii.

7. O. H. Krill, "The Krill Report: A Situation Report on Our Acquisition of Advanced Technology and Interaction with Alien Cultures," 1988, at: www.v-j-enterprises.com/krill1.html.

8. See: Richard Leviton, *Looking for Arthur: A Once and Future Travelogue* (Station Hill, N.Y.: Barrytown, 1997); *What's Beyond That Star: A Chronicle of Geomythic Adventure* (Forest Row, UK: Clairview Press, 2002).

Chapter 2

1. David Blackbourn, *Marpingen: Apparitions of the Virgin Mary in a Nineteenth-Century German Village* (New York: Vintage/Random House, 1993): 361.

2. Sandra L. Zimdars-Swartz, *Encountering Mary: From La Salette to Medjugorje* (Princeton, N.J.: Princeton University Press, 1991): 6, 10.

3. "Index of Apparitions of the Blessed Virgin Mary and Selected Other Catholic Apparitions," [no author listed], August 21, 1999, at: http://members.aol.com/UticaCW/Mar-vis.html.

4. Robert Sullivan, "The Mystery of Mary," *Life* (December 1996), 45.

5. Kenneth L. Woodward, "Hail, Mary," *Newsweek* (August 25, 1997), 50.

6. Elain Gale, "Mary's Rising Popularity Goes Beyond Faith," *Los Angeles Times* (December 25, 1998), A41.

7. Jaroslav Pelikan, *Mary Through the Centuries: Her Place in the History of Culture* (New Haven, Conn.: Yale University Press, 1996): 2.

8. Paolo Apolito, *Apparitions of the Madonna at Oliveto Citra: Local Visions and Cosmic Drama,* trans. William A. Christian Jr. (University Park: Pennsylvania State University Press, 1998): 33.

9. Rev. Johann Roten, "The Mary Page/FAQ," The Marian Library/International Marian Research Institute, University of Dayton, Dayton, Ohio, January 15, 1998, at: http://www.udayton.edu/mary/resources/aprgraph.html.

10. J. C. Tierney, "Apparitions of the Past: A Statistical Study," The Marian Library/International Marian Research Institute, University of Dayton, Dayton, Ohio, March 13, 1998, at: http://www.udayton.edu/mary/resources/aprgraph.html.

11. David Blackbourn, *Marpingen: Apparitions of the Virgin Mary in a Nineteenth-Century German Village* (New York: Vintage/Random House, 1993): 327, 328, 343, 344, 352, 357, 364.

12. Rene Laurentin, *The Apparitions of the Blessed Virgin Mary Today* (Dublin: Veritas, 1990): 140.

13. Roy Abraham Varghese, *God-Sent: A History of Accredited Apparitions of Mary* (New York: Crossroad, 2000): 2. Also: Michael S. Durham, *Miracles of Mary: Apparitions, Legends, and Miraculous Works of the Blessed Virgin Mary* (New York: Harper Collins, 1995).

14. William A. Christian Jr., *Visionaries: The Spanish Republic and the Reign of Christ* (Berkeley: University of California Press, 1996): 164.

15. Paolo Apolito, *Apparitions of the Madonna at Oliveto Citra: Local Visions and Cosmic Drama,* trans. William A. Christian Jr. (University Park: Pennsylvania State University Press, 1998): 88.

16. One wonders where Mary is coming from and how she enters our physical world. One of the visionaries in the Marian apparitions between 1931 and 1936 at Ezkioga, Spain (described later in this chapter) said she saw the Virgin as a brightness in the sky that opened up, with her inside it; another said Mary was inside a very bright cloud, brighter than the sun, that suddenly opened up; another said she appeared inside a bright hole in the sky some 12 feet wide, that a great brightness emerged from this hole in the firmament, then Mary inside that. (William A. Christian Jr., *Visionaries: The Spanish Republic and the Reign of Christ* [Berkeley: University of California Press, 1996]: 82, 289.) Physicists speculating on the practical applications of traversable wormholes, based on Einstein's general relativity theory, explain that a person seeing a wormhole opening up in the sky might observe phenomena that (though the author does not link them) I see as similar to the Marian apparition formations just described. A witness reported seeing a faint light appear in the air a few feet above the ground; it grew in intensity and brightness, then became a hole that opened up to three feet wide with a light emanating from within it. Out of this hole, which resembled a three-dimensional tunnel, emerged an alien creature, after which the hole closed up and faded away. The physicist presenting this example did so in the context of saying it illustrated how one might see a traversable wormhole interacting with our physical world. (Eric W. Davis, Ph.D., "Wormhole-Stargates:

Tunneling through the Cosmic Neighborhood," National Institute for Discovery Science, Las Vegas, Nev., July 2001: 13.)

17. "Graces Continue at Conyers, Come in Faith and Pray," 2003, at: www.conyers.org.

18. Paolo Apolito, *Apparitions of the Madonna at Oliveto Citra: Local Visions and Cosmic Drama,* trans. William A. Christian Jr. (University Park: Pennsylvania State University Press, 1998): 29.

19. The original Holy House, built to the Nazareth specifications, and later surrounded by a protective church, was complemented by the Slipper Chapel, one mile away; here pilgrims took off their shoes and walked barefoot to the shrine.

20. A palmer, originally, was a pilgrim returning from the Holy Land bearing a palm branch or leaf; also from the Latin *palmarius,* "pilgrim."

21. Although Lourdes is a Ray Master Sanctuary for Quan Yin, whose presence Bernadette Soubirous psychically translated into the image of the benevolent, compassionate "Lady" of her visions, all four aspects of the Virgin Mary appeared there in Soubirous's 1858 visions and can be experienced there, even today.

22. Mary Purcell, "Our Lady of Silence," in *A Woman Clothed with the Sun: Eight Great Appearances of Our Lady in Modern Times,* ed. John J. Delaney (Garden City, N.Y.: Hanover House/Doubleday, 1960): 132, 133.

23. The Tree of Life enables you to walk through the Four Worlds or fundamental realms of existence. The Second World roughly corresponds to what is otherwise called the astral plane, the rich seedbed of forms, ideas, designs, and tendencies that influence and for the most part help create our physical reality.

24. The Third World corresponds to the realm of archetypes and abstract divine plans for reality; it is a more subtle realm than the Second World and in a sense, its "parents."

25. Construction on the basilica began in 1928 and, in 1931, it was the scene of the dedication of the nation of Portugal to God and the Virgin Mary, before an audience of 300,000. This could be seen as the other "bookmark" to the site's activation as Portugal's Energy Focusing Node. In 1916 (the first "bookmark"), its egregor, or National Guardian Angel, prepared the site for the Marian apparitions; in 1931, the site (with its egregor implicit in the proceedings) was publicly dedicated to the nation as a sanctuary for Mary.

26. Richard L. Thompson, *Alien Identities: Ancient Insights into Modern UFO Phenomena* (San Diego, Calif.: Govardhan Hill, 1993): 287, 317.

27. Thanks to Mark L. Prophet and Elizabeth Clare Prophet for making this identification in *The Masters and Their Retreats,* ed. by Annice Booth (Corwin Springs, MT: Summit University Press, 2003): 456.

28. William A. Christian Jr., *Visionaries: The Spanish Republic and the Reign of Christ* (Berkeley: University of California Press, 1996): 20.

29. Ibid., 99.

30. Antonio Amundarain, quoted in William A. Christian Jr., *Visionaries: The Spanish Republic and the Reign of Christ* (Berkeley: University of California Press, 1996): 305.

31. In the first few years after the apparitions began, local supporters tried to make and mark the hillside a place of Catholic cult; a provisional chapel was erected, sited at a place the Virgin Mary reportedly indicated to several seers, but the Church refused to consecrate it. It lasted nonetheless until the Spanish Civil War, when the landowner tore it down. Had a permanent structure been placed at Ezkioga, it would have further grounded the Marian apparitional energy at that site for the benefit of future generations of pilgrims.

32. Minor does not mean unimportant. The complete Albion has 81 chakras—nine major and 72 minor. Minor chakras on the human body are found, for example, at the armpits, elbows, palms, soles, ankles, knees, inner thighs, kidneys, shoulder blades, and the sides and back of the head. The two feet chakras (soles) for this figure are in Iona, Scotland, and Lindisfarne, England, both islands, on the western and eastern sides of the British Isles, respectively. For a system, whether a physical human or a geomantic Albion, to be fully activated and illuminated, all 81 chakras need to be acknowledged and activated. So Ezkioga's role should be seen, actually, in the context of 80 other geomantically heightened sites throughout these six countries in the Virgo Albion.

33. Statements attributed to the Virgin Mary by Rosa Quattrini, 1965–1969, at: www.nd-des-roses.com/english/history/garden.htm.

34. Despite the remarkable geomantic features of this site and the stated intentions of the Virgin Mary as to the site's development, the official clerical response since the 1960s has been opposition, negativity, and aspersion. In 1965, the local bishop even requested that the Catholic faithful not visit San Damiano, adding that the "supernatural origin" of the apparitions had not been authenticated. Church authorities threatened disciplinary measures for Rosa and other supporters of the San Damiano cause, and spoke of their behavior in terms of disobedience to the Church.

35. This hill was originally known as Mount Sipovac, but following a dream—some say it's but a legend—attributed to Pope Pius XI in which an angel asked him to erect a cross on that peak, the site's name was changed in accordance with the placement of the cross. It became known as Cross Mountain, or Mount Krizevach.

36. Sister Briege McKenna, quoted in Wayne Weible, *The Final Harvest: Medjugorje at the End of the Century* (Brewster, Mass.: Paraclete Press, 1999): 4.

37. According to St. Cyril of Jerusalem (315–386 A.D.), Peter and the brothers James and John witnessed the Transfiguration on Mount Tabor, a rounded hill 1,843 feet tall about five miles from Nazareth in Israel. Jesus'

face shone like the Sun, his garments became of white light, the prophets Moses and Elijah appeared around him, and he was overshadowed by a bright cloud from which presumably the Voice of God spoke and praised His son. When the event was over and they departed the mountain, Jesus asked his disciples not to mention the event. The significance of Jesus Christ showing forth his divine nature while still living as a human, theologians explain as a demonstration of the Messiahship of Christ and as a divine proclamation of his Sonship (Son of God).

38. Wayne Weible, *The Final Harvest: Medjugorje at the End of the Century* (Brewster, Mass.: Paraclete Press, 1999): 96, 270.

39. Prof. Paul M. Zulehner, "Medjugorje eine Mystagogische Lektio," quoted in Father Leonard Ornec, "The Beginnings of Pilgrimages in Medjugorje," 1996, published at: www.medjugorje.org/orec.htm.

40. Alice A. Bailey, *The Rays and the Initiations, Vol. V: A Treatise on the Seven Rays* (New York: Lucis, 1960): 278, 599.

41. Wayne Weible, *The Final Harvest: Medjugorje at the End of the Century* (Brewster, Mass.: Paraclete Press, 1999): 71, 107, 143.

42. Paolo Apolito, *Apparitions of the Madonna at Oliveto Citra: Local Visions and Cosmic Drama,* trans. William A. Christian Jr. (University Park: Pennsylvania State University Press, 1998): 15.

43. Ibid., 51.

44. Ann Marie Hancock, *Wake Up America! Take My Heart, Take My Hand* (Norfolk, Va.: Hampton Roads, 1993): 200.

45. The order derives its name and spiritual commission from a dream by a wealthy Roman matron in August 352 A.D. She dreamed that the Virgin Mary asked to have a church built in her honor in Rome, and that the intended site would be covered in snow one morning. Apparently, Mary also appeared that night in a dream to Pope Liberius and told him the same news. On the morning of August 5, there was snow on Esquiline Hill in Rome, and that's where the church was built by this wealthy Roman family. The Missionary Oblates have been adding features to their site since 1958, most recently the Millennium Spire in 1998. The property now offers nine different devotional sites to visitors of different faiths.

46. Ray Doiron, quoted in Mark Garvey, *Searching for Mary: An Exploration of Marian Apparitions across the U.S.* (New York: Plume/Penguin, 1998): 82.

47. Ray Doiron, *Messages from Our Heavenly Mother to Her Children* (Breese, Ill.: People's Prayer Group, 1995): 2; see: www.apparitions.org/Doiron.html.

48. Eryk Hanut, *The Road to Guadalupe: A Modern Pilgrimage to the Goddess of the Americas* (New York: Jeremy P. Tarcher/Putnam, 2001): 154, 172.

49. Popocatepetl ("Smoking Mountain") is Mexico's second highest volcano and mountain and has erupted 15 times, mostly mild eruptions, since

1519 A.D., when the Spanish began keeping records. Two previous eruptions in 1347 and 1354 were remembered by the Aztecs. Archeologists have identified at least ten ritual sites on both peaks at about 12,000 feet, attesting to the spiritual importance of these volcanoes to Aztec culture. Iztaccihuatl ("White Woman") is Mexico's third tallest volcano-mountain. Aztec myth tells us that long ago Popocatepetl was a warrior who fell in love with Iztaccihuatl, the daughter of a tribal chief. This chief gave Popocatepetl an almost impossible task to achieve before he could marry his daughter; she died of sorrow and unfulfilled waiting, after which Popocatepetl carried her to the top of a nearby mountain and laid her to rest at its summit. The summit ridge then assumed the form of a supine woman. Ever since, Popocatepetl has remained at her side (the two volcanoes are very close together) as if with a lit torch (evidenced by the smoke that issues from the volcano). Mount Tlaloc, southwest of Mexico City, was named after the Aztec god of rain, storm, lightning, and thunder; it was believed to be his residence.

50. Maureen Wallace, "Nuestra Senora la Virgen de Guadalupe: Dark Mother of the Lost and Forsaken," *Journal of Sandplay Therapy* 7:1(1998), 6.

51. Amy Martin, "Winter Pilgrimage to Tepeyac," *Awakened Woman e-magazine* (December 1, 2000), published at: www.awakenedwoman.com/tonantzin.htm.

52. Ron Loeffler, "The Feast of Coatlaxopeuh," [no date given], published by Lazyboy's Rest Stop at: www.sxws.com/charis/mary12.htm.

53. She had other names: Ilmatecuhtli, "the Goddess," depicted as a toad called Tlaltecuhtli, shown swallowing a knife; Itzpapalotl ("Obsidian Butterfly"); Temazcalteci ("Grandmother of the Sweat-bath"); Teteoinnan ("Mother of the Gods").

54. Mary Miller and Karl Taube, *An Illustrated Dictionary of the Gods and Symbols of Ancient Mexico and the Maya* (London: Thames and Hudson, 1993): 64.

55. Erich Neumann, *The Great Mother: An Analysis of the Archetype*, trans. Ralph Mannheim (Princeton, N.J.: Princeton University Press, Bollingen Series XLVII, 1963): 152–153.

56. Frank Waters, *Masked Gods: Navaho and Pueblo Ceremonialism* (Athens, Ohio: Swallow Press/Ohio University Press, 1950): 52.

57. The original goddess, perhaps known as Coatlicue ("Serpent Skirt"), then later as Coatlalopeuh ("She Who Has Dominion Over Serpents"), was split into upper (light) and underworld (dark) aspects. "*Coatlicue*, the Serpent goddess, and her more sinister aspects, *Tlazolteotl* and *Cihuacoatl*, were 'darkened' and disempowered much in the same manner as the Indian Kali." Tonantzin got split off from her three dark valences and became the good mother. Later, the Spaniards and Catholics "desexed Guadalupe, taking *Coatlalopeuh*, the serpent/sexuality, out of her." Finally, Tonantzin

became Guadalupe, "the chaste protective mother" and defender of the Mexicans. Gloria Anzaldua, "Coatlalopeuh, *She Who Has Dominion Over Serpents*," in Ana Castillo (ed), *Goddess of the Americas: Writings on the Virgin of Guadalupe* (New York: Riverhead, 1996): 52–55.

58. Mike Dixon-Kennedy, *Native American Myth and Legend: An A–Z of People and Places* (London: Blandford, 1996): 51, 64, 65.

59. Roros, one of four UNESCO World Heritage Sites in Norway, was a copper mining and smelting settlement from the seventeenth century until the 1980s. Today it is a popular tourist destination, located 222 km from Lillehammer and 340 km from Oslo. Roros is also less than 20 miles from Hessdalen, one of Norway's premier UFO sighting locations, and the focus of much scientific UFO study in earlier decades.

60. Sandra L. Zimdars-Swartz, *Encountering Mary: From La Salette to Medjugorje* (Princeton, N.J.: Princeton University Press, 1991): 246.

61. In 1948, Teresita Castillo, a nun at the Carmelite convent in Lipa, Philippines, experienced 19 apparitions of the Virgin Mary in the convent garden. Some messages, including secrets, were conveyed, and a statue was dedicated as an apparition site. Mary declared herself to be "Our Lady, Mediatrix of All Grace." When the apparitions ended, reprisals took place: Local church officials were fired, evidence destroyed, Castillo left the convent, and the nuns were ordered to keep quiet about the events. This was the case until 1990, when new Marian phenomena were observed at Lipa, and the Church finally decided to investigate the Lipa apparitions of 1949. At Necedah, Wisconsin, a farm wife named Mary Ann Van Hoof began perceiving the Virgin Mary at her farm in November 1949 at a place later called (by her) the "Sacred Spot." The apparitions and messages continued into 1950, attracting thousands of visitors. By 1982, 11 books and a great deal of printed material had been published by "the Queen of the Holy Rosary, Mediatrix of Peace Shrine at Necedah." However, many grew uncomfortable with the dark, apocalyptic, sometimes paranoid or demonic tone of the Marian messages, and gradually people stayed away from it. Regardless of the outer circumstances, at both Lipa and Necedah, a Marian geomantic infusion took place.

62. Rene Laurentin, *The Apparitions of the Blessed Virgin Mary Today* (Dublin, Ireland: Veritas, 1990): 9, 17, 21.

63. Ibid., 19.

64. Richard Leviton, *The Galaxy on Earth: A Traveler's Guide to the Planet's Visionary Geography* (Charlottesville, Va.: Hampton Roads, 2002): 329.

65. St. Louis-Marie Grignion de Montfort, quoted in Sandra L. Zimdars-Swartz, *Encountering Mary: From La Salette to Medjugorje* (Princeton, N.J.: Princeton University Press, 1991): 251.

Chapter 3

1. This term comes from Rudolf Steiner, who wrote prolifically on the

entirety of the Christ experience on Earth, from his birth and baptism to the Mystery of Golgotha and ascension. Steiner regarded this as a pivotal planetary event with lasting repercussions, many of which would take millennia to ground fully.

2. Durga's Egyptian equivalent was Sekhmet (or Sekhet, also called Bastet), the lion-headed goddess with the power of destruction. Wearing a sun-disk over her head, Sekhmet in this form was understood to be a wild, warlike manifestation of the sun, her flames devouring Egypt's enemies. As Bastet, she was the mild eye of Ra, but as Sekhmet, she was the scorching eye. She is also, confusingly, the daughter of Ra (the Sun god) and the wife of Ptah (the creator god), and she's associated with hunting and wild animals. Sekhmet wears the lunar horns and solar disk; in her hands she holds the ankh (symbolic of eternal life), a papyrus staff, a shield, and a basket. She is one of the few Egyptian goddesses who look after the Eye of Horus. Among her epithets are: Goddess of Fire and Heat; Mistress of the Gods; Goddess of War; Goddess of Vengeance; Mighty One of Enchantments.

3. Devi-mahatmya, quoted in David Kinsley, *Tantric Visions of the Divine Feminine: The Ten Mahavidyas* (New Delhi, India: Motilal Banarsidass, 1998): 32.

4. W. J. Wilkins, *Hindu Mythology, Vedic and Puranic* (New Delhi, India: Rupa, 1882, 1975): 299.

5. Jan Knappert, *Indian Mythology: An Encyclopedia of Myth and Legend* (London: Aquarian/Harper Collins, 1991): 133–134.

6. We find a Western equivalent for Kali, though not as fearsome, in the Greek goddess Persephone, part-time wife of Hades, King of the Dead and the Underworld. Persephone (also known as Kore, "The Girl, Virgin, or Maiden") was abducted by Hades and forced to spend one-third of her time in Hades' realm as Queen of the Underworld. The remainder of her time she could live in the Upper World of light with her mother, Demeter, a Titan (a class of primeval creator gods) and goddess of vegetation. Thus Persephone was both a dreadful Underworld death goddess and an Upper World feminine figure of hope and joy. The revelation of her dual aspects, death and regeneration, were the basis for the famous though poorly under-stood Eleusinian Mysteries, practiced at Eleusis, a little north of Athens in Greece. Note the parallelism in the consort pairing: Kali-Shiva, Persephone-Hades. Hades, as Lord of the Dead-Underworld, thus has an evident equiva-lency with Shiva, Destroyer of Illusory Existence.

7. Margaret and James Stutley, *Harper's Dictionary of Hinduism: Its Mythology, Folklore, Philosophy, Literature, and History* (San Francisco: Harper & Row, 1977): 137.

8. David Kinsley, *Tantric Visions of the Divine Feminine: The Ten Mahavidyas* (New Delhi, India: Motilal Banarsidass, 1998): 87.

9. We find the equivalent image in the Egyptian mythic pantheon of the

goddess Isis with her infant son, Horus, on her lap. Isis, the wife and sister of Osiris, the high pharaoh, is associated with sovereignty; her name means throne or seat. Horus is the Egyptian perception of the Christ, and in this system he was given two qualities, each representing an Eye of Horus: Horus the Elder and Horus the Younger. In Western terms, we could say Horus the Elder represents the eternally existent, far-seeing Christ, while Horus the Younger is the one we birth within ourselves as the fruit of an initiation process.

10. David Kinsley, *Tantric Visions of the Divine Feminine: The Ten Mahavidyas* (New Delhi, India: Motilal Banarsidass, 1998): 120, 125.

11. Aphrodite (the Romans called her Venus) was the Greek goddess of erotic love, the giver of beauty and sexual attraction, the one who rouses desire in mortals and gods. With the war god Ares, she birthed Eros, the god of love, although her actual husband was the Olympian Hephaistos, the lame smith god (Ray Master Jesus). Aphrodite is also equivalent to the Egyptian love and fertility goddess, Hathor. Hathor was the goddess of song and dance; she used her sistrum to drive evil from Egypt. The protectoress of women, Hathor was also the patron of sexual love and sensual joy, music, dance, even drunkenness; she was associated with love, sex, and fertility, and the creative and fertile qualities of the natural world, such that she was called "Lady of the Vulva." She was often depicted nursing the adult pharaoh with her breasts, although sometimes she was in her guise as a cow filled with stars or as a goddess with cow's horns. Hathor, as Ray Master No. 3 (Nada), was associated with Ray Master Jesus through Ra and the Christ through Horus; she was the consort and lover to Ra (she is also his daughter and mother) and sometimes the mother of Horus, as her name, literally denotes: *Hwt Hr,* means "House of Horus." You can see through these qualities and permutations the essential ray relationship between the major (scarlet) and minor (pink), necessarily linked, as played out in the other well-known public guises, most notably, as Jesus and Mary Magdalene.

12. Joachim-Ernst Berendt, *Nada Brahma: Music and the Landscape of Consciousness* (Rochester, Vt.: Destiny Books, 1987): 17–18.

13. Iranian mysticism said the Seven *Abdals* originated in the constellation of the Great Bear, Ursa Major, and specifically, in the seven stars of what we call the Big Dipper (the tail and sacrum of the Bear). The Bear secretes "an oil so subtle that it was like a spiritual substance," the Iranian mystics claimed. Also referred to as the Seven Poles or the *Aqtab,* these were seven "masters of initiation and intercessors who are invisibly apportioned to our world," though from cycle to cycle of the world, they change names and order. They are seven apertures through which God shows Himself through the Bear's seven stars. In fact, just as the Bear dominates and sees the totality of the cosmos, the *Abdals* are "the eyes through which the Beyond looks at the world." The Seven *Abdals* surround the Pole (as in Pole Star, Polaris,

in the Little Bear, Ursa Minor) and the "hidden Imam" (probably Zeus-Thor) as the "mysterious and invisible hierarchy" that sustains life on Earth. Henry Corbin, *The Man of Light in Iranian Sufism,* trans. Nancy Pearson (Boulder, Colo.: Shambhala, 1978): 52–53.

14. Alain Danielou, *The Myths and Gods of India* (Rochester, Vt.: Inner Traditions, 1991): 317.

15. In Alice Bailey's five-volume *Treatise of the Seven Rays,* dictated to her by Djwhal Khul, the seven rays transmit their energy through three constellations, each in the circle of the ecliptic. In Bailey's model, for example, the first ray transmits to our Sun and then the Earth through Aries, Leo, and Capricorn; while the fourth ray passes through Taurus, Scorpio, and Sagittarius. Each ray has a quality and effect on consciousness, and each influences and informs every kingdom of nature, from mineral to human. These "seven great Ray-Lives" are "psychological entities and builders of form."(Helen S. Burmeister, *The Seven Rays Made Visual* [Marina del Rey, Calif.: DeVorss, 1986]: 19, 44.) According to the Ofanim, 12 of the Ray Masters are involved with the human passage in consciousness through each of the signs of the zodiac. The completed passage is equal to the expression of the Self, an integrated, balanced Round Table of all the signs, both complementary and antagonistic.

16. Father Umberto Loncar, quoted in Paolo Apolito, *Apparitions of the Madonna at Oliveto Citra: Local Visions and Cosmic Drama,* trans. William A. Christian Jr. (University Park: Pennsylvania State University Press, 1998): 87.

17. The World Mother is described variously in world myths. To the ancient Irish she was Dana, and her followers, Ireland's primal gods, were called Tuatha de Danann, "People or Followers of the Goddess Dana or Ana." Dana, sometimes called Brigit (confusingly, since Ray Master Aphrodite-Nada was known by this name in Celtic cultures) appeared before the Tuatha as tall as the heavens, her mantle sweeping the ground like a purple mist. She was hailed as the Mighty Mother and *Mor Reegu,* the Battle Queen. In an Irish tale called "The Earth Shapers," she terraforms the landscape of Earth with her mantle, described as an unrolling silver flame. Brigit's Mantle prepares and blesses the Earth as a kind of cleansing spiritual fire before its physical features, such as lakes and the plant kingdom, are created. Brigit is the "Flame of Delight" in all the worlds, both physical and spiritual, the Tuatha declare. ("The Earth-Shapers," in *Celtic Wonder-Tales,* retold by Ella Young [New York: Dover, 1995]: 3–11.) "The Divine Mother is thus the life-force made manifest, and this force is 'the Spiritual Principle displayed in a female shape.'" (Jean Chevalier and Alain Gheerbrant, *A Dictionary of Symbols,* trans. John Buchanan-Brown [New York: Penguin, 1996]: 678.) The Divine Mother understood as the life-force made manifest is called Shakti in Hinduism; the Goddess Shakti (usually equated with kundalini) is the consort of Shiva, pure consciousness, and she is divine power

or energy, the female, dynamic principle in contrast to Shiva, the male, passive aspect of creation.

18. Rudolf Steiner, *The Gospel of St. Matthew* (London: Rudolf Steiner Press, 1965): 134, 149, 151, 167.

19. Rudolf Steiner, *The Gospel of St. Luke* (London: Rudolf Steiner Press, 1964): 186, 193, 194.

20. *Mahabharata,* translated and retold by Krishna Dharma (Badger, Calif.: Torchlight, 1999): 556.

21. *Bhagavad-Gita As It Is,* trans. His Divine Grace A. C. Bhaktivedanta Swami Prabhupada (Los Angeles, Calif.: Bhaktivedanta Book Trust, 1986): 562–575.

22. Rudolf Steiner, *The Christ Impulse and the Development of Ego Consciousness* (Spring Valley, N.Y.: Anthroposophic Press, 1976): 110.

23. Rudolf Steiner, *The Reappearance of the Christ in the Etheric* (Spring Valley, N.Y.: Anthroposophic Press, 1983): 39.

24. Rudolf Steiner, *The True Nature of the Second Coming* (London: Rudolf Steiner Press, 1971): 35, 37, 38.

25. *Bhagavad-Gita As It Is,* trans. His Divine Grace A. C. Bhaktivedanta Swami Prabhupada (Los Angeles, Calif.: Bhaktivedanta Book Trust, 1986): 583, 584, 588.

26. It derives from the root *vislr,* which means "to spread in all directions"—to pervade; it may alternatively stem from *vis* (as in *visnati,* "to spread," or *visati,* "to enter") and from *visli* (in *vivesti,* "to surround").

27. Radha is portrayed as a ravishingly beautiful gopi-girl or cow-girl, one of the band of adoring female attendants and devotees to Krishna; she becomes Krishna's lover. Sita, as another guise of this same goddess, comes later in Hindu mythic history as does the *Ramayana;* she is less the lascivious, ecstatic gopi and more the model for Hindu femininity, affectionate, pure, and faithful. As for the Christian tradition, alternative (heretical) opinion (e.g., *Holy Blood, Holy Grail,* by Michael Baigent, Richard Leigh, and Henry Lincoln [New York: Delacorte, 1982]) states that Jesus was Magdalene's lover and together they possibly produced a bloodline. The relevant point is that these two Ray Masters have enjoyed a very long working relationship—a preordained affinity—in their activities, and that Nada, as Ray Master No. 3 (and as a Virgin Mary aspect), has also had deep affinity with the Christ (Vishnu), the deeper, original, fundamental cosmic energy transmitted through Jesus, Rama, and Krishna.

28. The gopis (from *gopi,* "beautiful cowherdess") were herdswomen who often left home, families, children to dally with the intoxicating Krishna on the banks of the Yamuna River or in the forest. Often they performed a circle dance called *lilarasa* as each gopi imagined she held the hand of the divine Krishna, but it's also said that Krishna multiplied himself so as to dance with each gopi, thereby holding all their hands. The gopis were madly in love with Krishna, who drove them into frenzies with his flute-playing; he

once boasted he had 16,000 wives (which I think we can read as meaning core devotees).

29. His worshippers, described as wine-intoxicated, god-crazed women called Maenads (*Mainadai*, "mad-women" or "frenzied women"), Thyiades ("inspired"), Bacchants or Bacchae ("women of Bacchus"), would capture wild beasts, tear them to pieces, and devour them. The Maenads practiced Dionysian frenzy and rites of ecstatic liberation; they sang, danced, whirled, and played wild music in the mountains (such as Mount Cithaeron near Thebes, where Dionysus was born). They wore fawn-skins, carried flaming torches, and *thyrsoi* (*thyrsus*, staves wrapped in grapevines or ivy stems and crowned with pine cones).

30. Jenny March, *Cassell's Dictionary of Classical Mythology* (London: Cassell, 2001): 264.

31. The Greek philosophical concept of Logos says it is the Reason-Speech principle of reality. For the Greek philosopher Heraclitus, for example, the Logos meant the world-principle and world-process, the rationality of the universe, and the rational self-evolution of the universe, which implied a knowability by the human mind and spirit. Heraclitus conceived of the Logos as the universal reason governing and *permeating* the world. For the later Stoics, what they called the "seminal Logos" meant God as the organic organizing cosmic principle. God was said to dwell in the human heart as the Logos, which enabled humans to know the Logos as God. The Greek philosopher Philo described the Logos as the "divine pattern from which the material world is copied, the divine power in the cosmos, the divine purpose or agent in creation, and an intermediary between God and man." (*The Oxford Dictionary of the Christian Church*, 2d ed., ed. F. L. Cross and E. A. Livingstone [New York: Oxford University Press, 1974]: 833.) Philo also said the Logos is the image and first form and representation of God. The concept of Logos also describes a pervasive connectivity among all created things; that connection is rational, that is, it serves a purpose, was intentionally instituted, and can be understood by humans because we have reason. The term also connotes the primal Word by which creation began. In the beginning was the Word (Logos), and the Logos was with God and was God, the Fourth Gospel states. This is similar to the Hindu concept of the primal vibratory mantra called OM or AUM, which underlies all of creation. In biblical times, the Logos was said to be the Second Person of the Trinity (the Son), the Creative Word who became incarnate as a human, Jesus the Christ; the apostle John identified Jesus Christ as the Logos made flesh. "John's Logos is not only God's agent in creation; He is *God*, and becomes incarnate, revealing and redeeming . . . Christ is God's active Word." (Andrew F. Walls, "Logos," in *Baker's Dictionary of Theology*, ed. Everett F. Harrison [Grand Rapids, Mich.: Baker Book House, 1960]: 327–328.)

32. Einstein said the speed of light is a universal constant, flowing the same

in all directions and frames of reference throughout spacetime in the *absence* of gravity, which means, other than at places where mass curves spacetime. Metaphorically, then, the speed of light is the Logos in its Elder Horus form of original flat spacetime—the flat rubber sheet uncurved or deformed by mass (stars).

33. The Ofanim are referring to the well-remarked bifurcation of mental and psychic processes between the left and right brain hemispheres. We could equally put this division in terms of male and female polarities of consciousness, or psychic-intuitive and analytical-rational functions. The intent of "rendering the neural connection" is to rebalance the functions of consciousness which, culturally and individually, have shifted too much to the left brain–analytical aspects in Western culture in recent centuries. Current astronomical events may be supporting this. The rare approach of the planet Mars to the Earth in August 2003 (the closest it's been to Earth in an estimated 60,000 years) and the corresponding two-month period of Mars retrograde in Pisces (a "feminine" water sign) was understood by some interpreters as an opportunity to reconcile the archetypal male and female aspects of the human psyche. In a sense, with Mars retrograde, its normally outward-focused, "male aggressive" force aspects (let's read this here as the analytical brain functions or dominant male authority structure in consciousness) were turned inward and thus temporarily less potent in the world. During this Mars perihelion with Earth, peaking in August 2003, the planet was only 34,646,418 miles away compared to the more typical 225,700,000 miles it was in November 2002.

34. Thanks for this insight go to Lisa French, accomplished clairvoyant teacher and director of the Clairvoyant Center of Hawaii (www.magicisle.com).

35. The body location of the chakras or subtle energy centers is by now fairly well recognized in Western New-Age and spiritual-metaphysical writings, but for review, there are primarily seven, from the groin to the top of the head. They correspond and interact with the major endocrine glands along the spine, and are located as follows: anus, pubic area, solar plexus, heart-chest, throat, brow, top of head. The chakras each enable a certain level of psychic perception and connection with the physical and spiritual worlds, though the brow and crown centers are considered to be the most sophisticated and cognitively reliable.

36. Maurice Nicoll, *The New Man: An Interpretation of Some Parables and Miracles of Christ* (New York: Penguin, 1972): 4–5, 6.

37. Jacob D. Bekenstein, "Information in the Holographic Universe," *Scientific American* 289:2 (August 2003), 58–65.

38. For a listing of 62 landscape zodiac sites around the Earth and their sizes, see my previous book *The Emerald Modem: A User's Guide to the Earth's Interactive Energy Body* (Charlottesville, Va.: Hampton Roads, 2004). The list

does not indicate the Canis Major sites, though I plan to publish maps and information on this in future publications. Those interested could start with the two Christ child birthplaces already known: Wick in England and Bethlehem in Israel.

39. The Ofanim once referred to the Supreme Being in this way, as the No-Hand that held the sword. For a more detailed description of this process, see my book *Looking for Arthur: A Once and Future Travelogue* (Barrytown, N.Y.: Barrytown, 1997): 391–403.

40. For a detailed description of the many aspects of the Emerald, both geomantic and human, see my book *The Emerald Modem: A User's Guide to the Earth's Interactive Energy Body* (Charlottesville, Va.: Hampton Roads, 2004).

41. Every Crown or Palladium site is not necessarily in top working order; some have been compromised by other, conflicting agendas, such as ideological control. Ironically, the Crown of the Ancient of Days at Vatican Hill in Vatican City, Rome, with its epicenter approximately at St. Peter's Basilica, is compromised. Geomantically, the head sits in the center of a labyrinth (one of the Earth's 108), the entire hill topped by a dome cap. But the God-face appears to be grimacing, as if trapped, clamped down. A large number of formidable astral beings keep the geomantic energies under tight control, and another very considerable astral being maintains the integrity (dogmatic parameters) of Catholicism (construed here as a living thought-form). The array of physical Vatican buildings blocks access to the labyrinth and curtails its natural energy circulation. A yellow parabolic net is maintained over the city, secured into the (astral) ground by 24 "tent pegs," which seem derived in some measure from the exertions and sacrifices of saints and martyrs. Despite the outward appearance, actions, and rhetoric of the Catholic Church at Vatican City, and the appellation of this site as being the City of God, in many respects the Church's use of the geomantic features is suppressive, and it is more accurate to say, based on clairvoyant viewing of the overall setup there, that it is the City of the Pope, for that yellow net, acting like a mirror, reflects back, not the Face of God, but the face of the papacy.

42. Ironically, physicists may be most at home with this model of multidimensionality, at least as a theory. The model of superstrings, introduced in the 1960s, postulates ten dimensions to the universe; the six extra space dimensions were compacted into a tiny point or geometrical space, smaller than an atom, at the start of creation, leaving four—space (3) plus time (1). Thus spacetime has nine space and one time dimensions. The strings are extended one-dimensional objects, elementary particles in a state of excitation or stretched tension and appearing (theoretically, since they haven't been seen yet) as tiny strings or loops. Physicists found that for superstring theory to work, there had to be a ten-dimensional universe.

43. Of further interest is the fact that the Maitreya Buddha will be

(already is, cosmically) Ray Master No. 2, usually called Kuthumi, the same Great Bear rishi who earlier in Earth history was John the Baptist.

44. Physicist John Archibald Wheeler explains: "Einstein's field equation can tell us the gravity—that is, the spacetime curvature—in and around a star, a black hole, or any other spherically symmetric center of mass." John Archibald Wheeler, *A Journey into Gravity and Spacetime* (New York: Scientific American Library, 1990): 119.

45. The bulk of the Earth's 92 geomantic features lie in the fourth dimension, though some, like stargates, are in the fifth, and a few are in the sixth and seventh, though none are in the eighth or ninth layers. Each layer requires a finer psychic tuning to perceive or illuminate its embedded hologram from out of the lower dimension.

46. Blake wrote about Albion in his major poems, *The Four Zoas* (1797) and *Jerusalem: The Emanation of the Giant Albion* (1804). For Blake, Albion was the figure of the human collective, the ancient, the original, and perhaps the archetype of the human; though Albion was presented as humanlike, he was clearly a spiritual figure for Blake. For the Ofanim, Albion is a concept that represents the totality of human experience, both conscious and unconscious, the collective psyche over the duration of our incarnation on Earth as collected in a prepared cosmic matrix in archetypal human form. I say "prepared cosmic matrix" because Albion's essence comprises certain stars that significantly contributed to the formation and the maintenance of the planet and its visionary geography. Albion is Adam Kadmon templated for the context of Earth-human life.

47. Metaphysical traditions describe this more abstractly as the Cube of Space. Here the postulated ten dimensions of existence are six surfaces on a cube plus the x, y, z axes of directionality and the point of origin or centerpoint inside it. In this model, our 3D reality is inside the Cube; the higher dimensions, or body of Albion, are the six surfaces of the Cube, each a more rarefied dimension that includes the previous. You access the surfaces of the cube (higher dimensions) by following the z axis (time or fourth-dimensional axis) out to the fifth dimension, or first cubic surface. Astrophysicists use the cube as a coordinate way of plotting relative location for cosmic bodies, such as the Earth and Milky Way in relation to the Local Galaxy Group, a handful of galaxies fairly close to ours. In this approach, the Earth, or Milky Way, is positioned at the center of the cube.

48. Rudolf Steiner, *The Reappearance of the Christ in the Etheric* (Spring Valley, N.Y.: Anthroposophic Press, 1983): 87, 88.

49. Rudolf Steiner, *The True Nature of the Second Coming* (London: Rudolf Steiner Press, 1971): 78, 79.

50. Buddhism says the Buddha (not so much the physically incarnate Buddha, but the cosmic Buddha, or essence) has three bodies or forms: the Buddha Body, Speech, and Mind. Each is successively a more rarefied, sub-

lime state of awareness; contacting and inhabiting each is part of the Christed Initiation alluded to here.

51. I apologize to readers who may find me coy or elusive regarding the specifics of this initiation experience. I would rather not tell you about it, but instead help you experience it firsthand. I do this often in geomantic workshops that involve an outdoor, field trip aspect. Even though it has ten stages (plus a bonus eleventh), it cannot be enumerated or followed like a cookbook recipe. It might not even make much sense to merely hear it described. It will make some sense after you've gone through the ten stages, however.

Chapter 4

1. John F. Schuessler, "Public Opinion Surveys and Unidentified Flying Objects," January 2000, published at: www.swl.net/kentuckymufon/science13.html. All poll data, unless otherwise stated, are from this paper.

2. "The Gallup Poll, March 12, 1987, Only One-Third of Public Deny Existence of UFOs, Extraterrestrial Life," published at: www.textfiles.com/ufo/gallup.ufo.

3. Poll conducted by the Scripps Howard News Service and Ohio University, June 12–26, 1995. *MUFON UFO Journal* 327 (1995), 23.

4. "Gallup Poll: Public Belief in Extraterrestrial Life," CNI News, July 24, 1997, available at: www.purgatory.com/xcommunication/dyn.cfm?page=ufo.

5. John F. Schuessler, "Public Opinion Surveys and Unidentified Flying Objects," Mutual UFO Network, January 2000, pp. 12–13, published at: www.swl.net/kentuckymufon/science13.html.

6. Chris Rutkoswki, "Canadian UFO Poll," Alberta UFO Study Group, October 15, 1997, published at: www.aufosg.com/page9.html.

7. It's not surprising that members of specialized study or demographic groups would have higher than average belief statistics. A poll of 70 attendees at the 1983 MUFON (Mutual UFO Network) symposium at Pasadena, California, revealed that 96 percent believed UFOs are real, that 86 percent believed they are intelligently controlled devices, and that 70 percent contended that UFOs are (or carry) ET visitors. Of those polled, 91 percent were white and 66 percent male. Donald A. Johnson, Ph.D., "A Survey of Ufologists and Their Beliefs in Unexplained Phenomena," [no date], published at: http://archive.anomalies.net/sightings%20A-H/BELIEFS.UFO.

8. During its run in the 1990s, *The X-Files* on the Fox Network portrayed the quest of two FBI agents to uncover the truth about presumed alien intervention in world affairs and the U.S. government's (and a shadow organization behind it) complicity in it. The show's pessimistic premise was that a race of aliens (Grays) were planning to take over the world, enslave and eventually exterminate humans, had traded some technology for cooperation, and jointly (with the military arm of the shadow organization) abducted selected civilians for genetic testing and cloning experiments.

Whether, ultimately, there is any truth to the *X-Files* scenario, it certainly presented a plausible theory for alien involvement in Earth affairs and conditioned viewers to the possibility that such intervention had been going on since the 1940s.

9. John F. Schuessler, "Public Opinion Surveys and Unidentified Flying Objects," Mutual UFO Network, January 2000, published at: www.swl.net/kentuckymufon/science13.html.

10. The Roper Organization survey was conducted on behalf of the National Institute for Discovery Science (NIDS) of Las Vegas, Nevada. NIDS conducted their own parallel online survey of 1,847 American adults in 1999 and got similar results. The data presented here in the text presents highlights from both polls. "How Would Humans React If E.T. Landed?" press release, June 7, 1999, at: www.nidsci.org/news/roper/roperpressrelease.html.

11. For more on this, see my previous book *The Emerald Modem: A User's Guide to the Earth's Interactive Energy Body* (Charlottesville, Va.: Hampton Roads, 2004): chapter 8.

12. See: Lyssa Royal, Keith Priest, *The Prism of Lyra: An Exploration of Human Galactic Heritage,* rev. ed. (Scottsdale, Ariz.: Royal Priest Research Press, 1992). The authors propose that the Grays originated in the "womb of Lyra," then spread across the galaxy, including to the star Zeta Reticuli in the constellation Reticulum.

13. The cumulative evidence, based on transcripts of hypnotized abductees, indicates that the Grays for the most part are abusive of human free will and sovereignty, and their actions certainly cloud the field of ET encounters and their intentions. Evidence of benevolent intentions is "at best, ambiguous," concludes UFO researcher David Jacobs. "One thing is certain: Most abductees say the phenomenon has had a devastating effect on their personal lives," putting them in a state of chronic fear, guilt, paranoia, and physical dysfunction. Jacobs cites plausible evidence and reasoning that the push to paint the alien-ET and human encounter phenomenon in a positive light may be a propagandistic spin effort to mold public opinion sponsored by the abducting aliens; even presumed, hypnotically recalled memories of being an alien in a past life may be cognitive implants, some commentators propose. David M. Jacobs, Ph.D., *The Threat: Revealing the Secret Alien Agenda* (New York: Fireside/Simon & Schuster, 1999): 211, 214, 215, 225.

14. See: Angela Thompson Smith, *Diary of an Abduction: A Scientist Probes the Enigma of Her Alien Contact* (Charlottesville, VA: Hampton Roads, 2001). The author recounts 30 years of anomalous extradimensional experiences in which she seemed to have considerable contact with aliens (Grays), including pregnancy and childbirth, bizarre implants and devices, and time discontinuities.

15. The negative version of the DNA involvement has aliens, notably the Grays, forcibly abducting humans for the purposes of using them as brood-

mares in their breeding program by which they seek to create an alien-human hybrid capable, one assumes, of inhabiting the Earth instead of or at least with humans. See: David M. Jacobs, Ph.D., *Secret Life: Firsthand Accounts of UFO Abductions* (New York: Fireside/Simon & Schuster, 1992); *The Threat: Revealing the Secret Alien Agenda* (New York: Fireside/Simon & Schuster, 1999).

16. This suspicion of galactic origins is gaining momentum in the collective psyche. For example, renowned psychic Ruth Montgomery wrote (care of her Guides, whom she channeled) that the Native American tribe of the Cherokees "occupied a planet in the Orion constellation for millennia until some of them agreed to inhabit the reburgeoning earth after the last shift on its axis." Montgomery profiled one Native American in particular, a Cherokee called William Goodlett, and said that he often visited his Orion tribal home in spirit form. Ruth Montgomery, *Aliens Among Us* (New York: Putnam, 1985): 109, 111.

17. James Binney and Michael Merrifield, *Galactic Astronomy* (Princeton, N.J.: Princeton University Press, 1998): 169–172, 437.

18. Dolores Cannon, *The Convoluted Universe,* Book One (Huntsville, Ariz.: Ozark Mountain, 2001): 117–130.

19. Dolores Cannon, *Keepers of the Garden* (Huntsville, Ariz.: Ozark Mountain, 1993).

20. John E. Mack, M.D., *Passport to the Cosmos: Human Transformation and Alien Encounters* (New York: Crown, 1999): 36.

21. One of the primary effects of the UFO phenomenon as a whole may be for those who take it seriously "to fracture their Western scientific view of reality," observes Richard L. Thompson. The UFO phenomenon might be "one way in which the modern materialistic outlook is being gently revised by higher arrangement." Scientists are getting "their comeuppance" by being faced with seemingly unexplainable devices and experiences that defy the known laws of physics. Richard L. Thompson, *Alien Identities: Ancient Insights into Modern UFO Phenomena* (Badger, Calif.: Govardhan Hill, 1993): 404, 414.

22. Ellen Crystall, *Silent Invasion: The Shocking Discoveries of a UFO Researcher* (New York: Paragon House, 1991): xviii.

23. John E. Mack, M.D., *Passport to the Cosmos: Human Transformation and Alien Encounters* (New York: Crown, 1999): 50–55, 222.

24. John Violette proposes that UFO encounters, abductions, psychic phenomena, even near-death experiences take place in an expanded, larger framework of spacetime, in the much hypothesized fourth dimension, in which all events in time are displayed as a present-moment tableau. See: John R. Violette, *Extra Dimensional Universe: Where the Paranormal—UFOs and Abductions, Psychic Phenomenon, the Mystical, and Near-Death Experience—Become Normal* (Bangor, Maine: Book Locker, 2001).

25. Some researchers use the term "zone of strangeness." Abductees

cannot use their voice or move of their own volition; they feel paralyzed, rendered sleepy, or almost unconscious. Natural laws fail to work or work bizarrely. It doesn't seem like a dream, yet *it is* dreamlike. Abductees report moving as if floating in light, passing through membranes, even solid objects, even as if they are about to explode or be torn apart. One abductee recalled under hypnosis that he had the impression there was "some kind of cut in dimensions—that the dimension I was in was coexisting with this, this other dimension." (Raymond E. Fowler, *The Allagash Abductions: Undeniable Evidence of Alien Intervention* [Tigard, Ore.: Wild Flower Press, 1993]: 290, 236.) Based on the anomalous evidence it is possible that the abductee is physically, bodily taken into the fourth dimension (or a reality-energy-time configuration markedly different from our body-based norm), but his experiential body is the astral body (considered by many psychics to be the body of awareness that experiences things later remembered as "dreams"), not the physical self, which would account for the seeming lack of bodily based movement, speech, and volition capabilities, and the dreamlike sense of both observing and participating in the often horrific events. Some abductees report feeling grabbed at the solar plexus, nausea accompanying their movements, a bodily weightlessness, being drawn toward the bedroom ceiling, a snapping sensation at the back of the head that yanks them back into bed. These symptoms are consistent with proprioceptive data reported with astral traveling and the extension of the astral cord from either the solar plexus or back of the head. Consistent with this hypothesis is the data reported by Betty Andreasson Luca; during hypnotherapeutic regression to a 1989 experience, she revealed that she had been physically, bodily transported to a ship and *then* had an out-of-body experience from that point on, being rejoined with her physical body later in her bedroom. (Raymond Fowler, *The Watchers II* [Newberg, Ore.: Wild Flower Press, 1995]: 135.)

26. Budd Hopkins, *Missing Time* (New York: Ballantine, 1988): 12.

27. Budd Hopkins, *Intruders: The Incredible Visitations at Copley Woods* (New York: Random House, 1987): 6, 11.

28. Angela Thompson Smith, Ph.D., *Diary of an Abduction: A Scientist Probes the Enigma of Her Alien Contact* (Charlottesville, Va.: Hampton Roads, 2001): xviii.

29. Ellen Crystall, *Silent Invasion: The Shocking Discoveries of a UFO Researcher* (New York: Paragon House, 1991): 130.

30. Shakuntala Modi, M.D., *Remarkable Healings: A Psychiatrist Discovers Unsuspected Roots of Mental and Physical Illness* (Charlottesville, Va.: Hampton Roads, 1997): 344–348.

31. William J. Baldwin, Ph.D., *Healing Lost Souls: Releasing Unwanted Spirits from Your Energy Body* (Charlottesville, Va.: Hampton Roads, 2003): 104–106.

32. William J. Baldwin, Ph.D., in the course of clinical hypnotherapy of

patients, has discovered a variety of ETs interfering with humans through their energy fields. Some ETs, Baldwin reports, were unaware that their studies were interfering with people; others didn't care. One hypnotized client told Baldwin of a probe at the end of a thin black cord into her solar plexus; it was connected "to a laboratory on a spacecraft" where "an alien scientist" used it to gather information about humans. This alien admitted to having similar probes hooked into three thousand other humans. "Many hundreds of clients have since experienced and described such intrusion with probes, implants, and devices for testing, monitoring, and controlling," writes Baldwin. William J. Baldwin, Ph.D., *CE-VI: Close Encounters of the Possession Kind* (Terra Alta, West Va.: Headline Books, 1999): 21, 22.

33. Alien beams from ships are also operative at certain types of sacred sites. As part of a cooperative effort with the angelic realm at Lincoln Cathedral in Lincoln, England, in 2001, I saw 12 motherships arrayed in a kind of pyramid above and one dimension removed from the cathedral, each emitting rays down into a central portion of the cathedral to suppress a potent geomantic energy present there and to keep humans from interacting with it or even being aware of its presence. See my book *What's Beyond That Star: A Chronicle of Geomythic Adventure* (London: Clairview, 2002): 243–244.

34. You don't have to go to these stations, but they intimidate you into thinking you do. They are little control gates, like an airport inspection station; they erase your information from your sixth chakra. For more information and referrals for qualified psychic healers who can remove these and other alien energy intrusions into the human space, see: www.magicisle.com and www.psychicschool.com.

35. Courtney Brown, Ph.D., a professor at Emory University in Atlanta, Georgia, makes an intriguing, slightly wild-sounding allegation in his book *Cosmic Voyage.* On the basis of what he describes as research "conducted using rigorous and exacting remote-viewing protocols," Dr. Brown asserts that the Grays, millions of years ago, rescued the civilization on Mars from extinction, stored the Martians for a long time in some kind of suspended animation state, unpacked them, genetically altered them, and deposited them in a few places on Earth, somewhere in Latin America (where they passed for native peoples), and in caverns under Santa Fe Baldy, near Santa Fe, New Mexico. Underneath this mountain "is a Martian base that serves as a center for their [Martian] planetary operations." (Courtney Brown, Ph.D., *Cosmic Voyage: True Evidence of Extraterrestrials Visiting Earth* [New York: Onyx/Penguin, 1996]: 112, 115, 116, 323.) Around the same time as Brown's book appeared, Jim Marrs, a respected UFO researcher and conspiracy theorist, wrote that the Grays, Martians, and a third ET group he called the Trancendentals were mostly calling the shots on Earth. Marrs stated that some remote viewers noted as early as 1984 they thought they had

detected "an underground Martian base" in New Mexico. Marrs writes that the Grays placed the Martians in hibernation after the ecological collapse of their planet, but some came to Earth millions of years ago and "went deep underground." Martian space vehicles continuously come to the Earth to visit these subsurface bases; apparently the subterranean Martians "are angry at us right now" because we topside humans "have almost wrecked this world through pollution and deforestation." (An intriguing possible connection, which Marrs does not make, is that perhaps these subterranean Martians are the same as the Hollow Earth people, the ancestors of many Native American tribes who claim they emerged from inside the Earth long ago.) (Jim Marrs, *Alien Agenda: Investigating the Extraterrestrial Presence among Us* [New York: Harper Paperbacks/Harper Collins, 1997]: 483, 485, 486.)

36. As soon as the abduction starts, "nothing is within the realm of normal human experience," writes researcher David Jacobs, Ph.D. "It is an instant descent into the fantastic and bizarre." Often screen memories disguise the true visual reality of the abductors, so that rather than Grays, the abductees think they see wolves, monkeys, owls, deer, angels, or devils, among other possibilities. If they remember anything of the abduction events, usually it is accompanied or packaged in overwhelming fear and anxiety, as bizarre events and seemingly impossible physical movements and actions percolate into daytime awareness. Jacobs speculated in 1992 that as many as 15 million Americans might have had abduction experiences, without conscious recall of them, and he noted that, based on 325 hypnosis sessions with 60 abductees, abductions had taken place in every region of the United States, that in all cases studied, "strange-looking Beings" performed unpleasant medical procedures on the abductees, often after having "switched" them off (rendered them paralyzed or even inert), then made them forget the experience entirely. In 1999, he revised that estimate based on results of a 1991 Roper poll of 5,947 and other data, to 2 percent of the U.S. population, or five million people. The abduction phenomenon, he concluded, "is enormously widespread." David M. Jacobs, Ph.D., *Secret Life: Firsthand Accounts of UFO Abductions* (New York: Fireside/Simon & Schuster, 1992): 24, 49, 50, 306; *The Threat: Revealing the Secret Alien Agenda* (New York: Fireside/Simon & Schuster, 1999): 119, 123.

37. The concept here is that the root chakra, called *Muladhara,* centered in the groin, regulates emotions and conditions of consciousness to do with the element of earth, groundedness, fear, death, and survival. Its reactivity to stimuli is quantified, according to psychics, by a gauge that runs from 0 to 100. Traumatic, life-threatening events will dilate the chakra to 70–90 percent open, leaving one almost delirious with fear, virtually disembodied, and in a state of chronic shock, until it is closed down again to something calmer, like 10–30 percent open. For aliens seeking to cognitively influence humans, or for governments seeking to impose propaganda or

political conditionings on its populace, root chakras cranked wide open are ideal psychic conditions.

38. Several other spots around the Earth had been earmarked—the military term is "painted"—for future equivalent attacks and etheric rips. Each target was painted with a beam emitted by a mothership high above the Earth.

39. The UFO sightings and ET encounters may have a global specificity with respect to the Earth's energy grid. New Zealand airline pilot Bruce Cathie speculated in a series of books in the 1980s that UFO sightings may follow a precise terrestrial grid somehow keyed to what Cathie called the harmonic of light. He worked out a model based on what he called "the mathematics of the world grid." UFOs are actively engaged in a survey of our planet, Cathie says, and their investigations follow the intricate network of crisscrossing energy lines on the Earth, and this network is geometric. By plotting where UFOs had been seen, noting that often they were sighted at 54.43-kilometer intervals along tracklines, Cathie worked out a geometric grid for the entire planet (involving 7.5 minutes of arc for both longitude and latitude) "into which a great number of UFO reports could be fitted." Cathie's speculation was that, for the most part, UFOs seemed to be flying in accordance with a predetermined, geometric energy matrix encompassing the planet, almost as if these were the best or easiest or most appropriate routes to travel (a bit like train tracks). Bruce L. Cathie, *The Energy Grid: Harmonic 695, the Pulse of the Universe*, rev. ed. (Tehachapi, Calif.: America West, 1990): 15, 22–25.

Chapter 5

1. Some of the benign encounters with ETs may be due to the personal history and even preparation of the contactee. Swiss farmer Eduard Meier, between 1975 and 1980, chronicled his numerous conversations with a physical Pleiadian named Semjase, who allegedly allowed him to take hundreds of photographs of her ship. According to Meier, a refreshingly non-New-Age, uneducated Swiss countryman, the Pleiadians had prepared him for his life mission as "truth offerer" since age five, when he had his first UFO sighting. He had telepathic tutelage by two nonphysical beings, and finally Semjase, when Meier was in his forties. The bulk of the Semjase encounters (more than one hundred) took place in a rural area near Zurich, Switzerland. Meier's Pleiadian contact explained that their preference was individual contact and elucidation, rather than mass events; through contact with single humans they could "slowly allow the knowledge of our existence and mission to become known, and to prepare others for our coming." They wanted their presence to be revealed "slowly and without ceremony" so humans would not mistake them for gods whereas, in their view, they were but advanced humans. Gary Kinder, *Light Years: An Investigation into the*

Extraterrestrial Experiences of Eduard Meier (New York: Atlantic Monthly Press, 1987): 56, 104.

2. One researcher, relying on an analysis of 309 documented alien abduction cases, concluded that abductions "appear as opportunistic events, or at least *dark and lonely* conditions seem to favor the experience." He noted that often people get abducted doing ordinary recreational activities, such as camping, hunting, or simply crossing an open field at night. Thomas E. Bullard, *UFO Abductions: The Measure of a Mystery* (Mount Rainier, Md.: The Fund for UFO Research, 1987): 35.

3. How many alien species in total are involved with the Earth? One source (1979) says 70 different races are involved; they derive from different planets, including an occluded aspect of our own planet. The Grays are included among the 70. Raymond E. Fowler, *The Andreasson Affair* (Englewood Cliffs, N.J.: Prentice-Hall, 1979): 145.

4. The Pleiades is a tight star cluster or knot of six or seven bright stars, though some astronomers count nine, and others 11, 13, 14, 16, or 20 as being visible to the naked eye or with only minor optical enhancement. The nine brightest stars of the Pleiades are clustered in a field that is about one degree in diameter or about seven light-years across and 410 light-years from Earth. Modern astronomical photographs show two thousand stars in the general field, but about 250 are likely to be true cluster members. Of the traditional seven, the brightest is Alcyone (Eta Tauri), a thousand times more luminous than our sun and about ten times bigger; the other six include Maia, Taygeta, Celaeno, Merope, Asterope, and Electra.

5. Thanks to Julia Fortado of Hayward, California (see: www. millenni-umminerals.com) for collaborating with me on this and other psychic readings of ETs, including those from Sirius, Canopus, and Orion, later in this chapter. The psychic impressions of these four ET sources is a combination of input from us both.

6. Lest all this emphasis on speech as a generative act seem far-fetched, I draw the reader's attention to Rudolf Steiner's work on eurythmy, an art-dance form he called visible speech and developed in the 1920s. His clair-voyant observation was that as you speak the letters of an alphabet (he used German as his model), a complete air-form version of a human is generated in etheric speech. The image in the air produced by speaking aloud the entire alphabet would be the form of the human etheric body, Steiner said. This form is "a very complicated word . . . The etheric man is the Word which contains within it the entire alphabet." He says that "the entire etheric man as an air-form would be produced by means of the creative larynx . . . a birth continually taking place during the process of speech." He predicted that one day the larynx would replace the genitals as the primary basis for species replication. The description of generating and enlivening an air-form version of the human is also found in Qabala, where sacred speech, based on

correct permutations of the letters of Hebrew, can create all sorts of things, including a Golem, or artificial, soulless human simulacrum. Rudolf Steiner, *Eurythmy as Visible Speech*, trans. Ver and Judy Compton-Burnett (London: Rudolf Steiner Press, 1984): 27, 30.

7. Anasazi is a Navajo term meaning "Old Ones" to denote the original inhabitants of not only Chaco Canyon but much of the Southwest. From our twenty-first-century perspective, the Anasazi are like the Maya: mystical, enigmatic, evidencing a sophisticated religious and social culture, then abandoning their sites and disappearing precipitately. Archeologists postulate that the Anasazi began building their pueblos in the Chaco Canyon area in 1020 A.D., then departed the area, presumably after a severe drought, in 1220 A.D.

8. Castle Rigg stone circle in Keswick in the Lake District of England is another time portal, specifically in an odd rectangular shape deliberately formed by the arrangement of stones in a small section inside the circle. Before the stone circle was created, there was a Pleiadian temple present, though probably only minimally in matter as we are accustomed to it; its visual residue is still discernible to clairvoyant vision. When I first discovered this time portal, I saw various nonhuman beings coming and going from it, as if it were a subway stop; some of these aliens even stopped to interfere with the meditative work I was doing there.

9. There are two Pleiadian lineages in the House of Atreus. In the first Atlas (a Titan, a creator god older than Zeus and the Olympians) married Pleione (a daughter of the primordial ocean, or Oceanus, encircling the cosmos). Their offspring were the Pleiades and Hyades (another star cluster in Taurus). Electra, one of the seven Pleiadian sisters, coupled with Zeus to produce Dardanus, who was the ancestor of the Trojan dynasty. Thus Troy was founded by the Pleiades, through Electra. In the second lineage, Dione is credited with being among the Pleiades sisters; she married Tantalus, and was the ancestor of the Atreus line. Tantalus, a son of Zeus, married the Pleiad Dione and produced Pelops; he married Hippodamia and generated a large family including the two warring brothers, Thyestes and Atreus. Atreus married Merope and generated Menelaus and Agamemnon, and the rest is chronicled in Greek myth, history, and tragedy.

10. A few of the Greek writers, such as Herodotus and Pindar, referred fleetingly to the Hyperboreans who lived in the far north (now understood to be the British Isles, Scandinavia, Greenland, Iceland); they were a marvelous, musical, mystical, and advanced people about whom little was known. The Greek god Apollo, he of the silver bow and lyre, would visit the Hyperboreans regularly and report to the Greeks on their exalted doings.

11. As with Sirius, and other high-magnitude stars, Orion is present on Earth within its visionary geography by way of several features: several domes for its brightest stars; stargates; and representation in 432 landscape zodiacs. I explained in *The Emerald Modem* that Orion, as seen through Hindu astrology

and psychic vision, is known as the Antelope and is associated with Soma, the source of unbroken continuous consciousness, the foundation of awareness of all star beings, and the geomantic feature called the Soma Temple (144 copies on Earth), one of the eight Celestial Cities that surround Mount Meru, the cosmic mountain, as described in Hindu myth.

12. Thus "ETs" from Ursa Major are present in and through your inner heart chakra from birth. But of course this is a somewhat silly way of putting it, now that we see the link between some mandated star families or ETs and the human constitution and consciousness, as well as the Earth. In *The Emerald Modem,* I explain how eight different stars or constellations are associated with the different human chakras and their geomantic expression across the Earth. This is in accordance with the Hermetic axiom "As above, so below," which I've amended to: *As above* (galaxy), *so below* (human), *and in the middle too* (Earth).

13. A possible correlation may exist between Arcturus as Lord of the Dance with his Möbius strip going through groups of stars and modern physics' string theory. This model says the smallest components of the universe are tiny loops that resemble vibrating strings and are about one hundred billion times smaller than a proton. Matter, in this theory, is nothing but the harmonies created by these vibrating strings. A ten-dimensional universe, or hyperspace, is also postulated as the context for the strings. So, is Arcturus's Möbius strip, making its complex movements through the galactic body, the fundamental vibrating strings?

14. J. R. R. Tolkien seems to have sensed some of the sublimity of this. He envisioned elegant wood-based swan ships as seafaring conveyances in the most ancient days of his Middle-earth. He wrote of Alqualondë, the "Haven of the Swans," as the chief city of one of the lineages of Elves. "For that was their city, and the haven of their ships; and those were made in the likeness of swans, with beaks of gold and eyes of gold and jet." J. R. R. Tolkien, *The Silmarillion,* ed. Christopher Tolkien (Boston: Houghton Mifflin, 1977): 61.

15. Richard L. Thompson, *Alien Identities: Ancient Insights into Modern UFO Phenomena* (Badger, Calif.: Govardhan Hill, 1993): 287.

16. In 1948, Walter Russell (1871–1963) and his wife, Lao Russell (1904–1988), acquired the site on the Virginia mountaintop (also known as Afton Mountain). The site then had an Italian Renaissance marble palace and sculpture gardens well maintained since they were built several decades before by a wealthy businessman from Richmond, Virginia.

17. See: Glenn Clark, *The Man Who Tapped the Secrets of the Universe* (Waynesboro, Va.: University of Science and Philosophy, 1946). See also: The University of Science and Philosophy, P.O. Box 520, Waynesboro, VA 22980; tel: 800-882-5683; website: www.philosophy,org.

18. There is some evidence that the overall intent of some types of

abduction experiences is a spiritual initiation. A prime example of this is the extended—in fact, lifetime—sequence of "abductions" or encounters of Betty Andreasson Luca, as chronicled in five books by Raymond Fowler since 1979. Initially, it seemed like a standard abduction by Grays, but as her hypnosis-induced deep memories continued to surface, it became clear there was more to it. According to Luca, the Grays are robotic, remote-viewing factotums for the Elders, a humanlike advanced species of essentially benign intent with respect to humanity and Earth as a whole. The Elders facilitated some exceptional mystical experiences for Luca, including witnessing an astral phoenix, visiting a city and forest of crystal, and walking through the "Great Door" to behold "the One" in a world of light. Luca was told that "many" humans have been taken by Grays, "but only a few have gone to the fullness." I take this to mean either they did not remember the further mystical aspects or never got past the nightmare part of abduction by Grays. Why did Luca? "Because I did not object." Raymond E. Fowler, *The Andreasson Affair* (Englewood Cliffs, N.J.: Prentice-Hall, 1979): 146.

19. Dennett evaluated data from six reported UFO hotspots (Gulf Breeze, Florida; Hudson River Valley, New York; Exeter, New Hampshire; Wytheville, Virginia; Fyffe, Alabama; San Luis Valley, Colorado) to derive ten signs or qualifications for a site being called a "UFO flap area." These included a long history, frequency, and wide array of UFO phenomena, witnesses, publication of reports, investigations, and photographs. The Topanga Canyon sightings of 1992 meet all ten criteria, Dennett states. Preston Dennett, *UFOs over Topanga Canyon: Eyewitness Accounts of the California Sightings* (St. Paul, Minn.: Llewellyn, 1999): 255.

20. Ellen Crystall, *Silent Invasion: The Shocking Discoveries of a UFO Researcher* (New York: Paragon House, 1991): xvi.

21. According to one controversial—some say it is the product of disinformation—compilation of data, UFO sightings seem to follow political boundaries such as state boundary lines in the United States. Every state has from two to ten windows that are areas in which UFOs appear repeatedly year after year, says "The Krill Report," attributed to O. H. Krill (originally released in 1988). There are also major windows, at least two being cited in this source: northwestern Canada down through the Midwest, then up to northeastern Canada; and the Gulf of Mexico, including Texas, Mexico, and some of the Southwest. "The objects will appear in these places and pursue courses confined to sectors with a radius of about 200 miles." The source further states many UFO windows "center directly over areas of magnetic deviation," and UFOs tend to congregate "about the highest hills in these window areas." "The Krill Report, Part 28," 1999, at: www.paranormal.com/compendium/994.htm.

22. The Pennine hills that run like a spine down the center of Northern England and separate Lancashire and Yorkshire have been the site of so

much UFO activity over the decades that this area has been dubbed "UFO Alley." This seems similar in meaning to "ufocals." The Alley specifically centers on a ten-mile strip of land over which "thousands" of UFO sightings have been recorded, along with car stops, time lapses, electrical disturbances, and other "strange things." Jenny Randles, "British Window Areas," [no date given], www.ronaldstory.com.

23. Researcher Greg Long takes a different tack on interpreting the site-specificity data of UFO sightings. He studied the 20-year data from the Yakima Valley in south-central Washington State, where in the vicinity of the Yakima Indian Reservation, at least two hundred documented reports detailed strange occurrences such as orange orbs, close encounters, abductions, subterranean sounds, and other anomalies. Long contends the Yakima data form a self-contained microcosm suitable for study. His explanation is that the phenomena are the result of tectonic strain produced by earthquake faults that run underneath the reservation. In other words, he explains away the reality of UFOs as products of Earth stress in particularly prone areas. Greg Long, *Examining the Earthlight Theory: The Yakima UFO Microcosm* (Chicago, Ill.: J. Allen Hynek Center for UFO Studies, 1990).

24. "UFO Hotspots of the Nation," J. Allen Hynek Center for UFO Studies, Chicago, Ill., published by Burlington UFO Center, Wisconsin, 2004, at: www.burlingtonnews.net.

25. In 2002 alone, 483 sightings were reported throughout Canada, up 250 percent from 1998. From 1989 to 2002, 3,699 cases of UFO sightings were reported. *The 2002 Canadian UFO Survey: An Analysis of UFO Reports in Canada,* compiled by Geoff Dittman and Chris A. Rutkowski, Ufology Research of Manitoba, August 2003, at: www.geocities.com/Area51/Rampart/2653/2002survey.html.

26. William Gammill, *The Gathering: Meetings in Higher Space* (Charlottesville, Va.: Hampton Roads, 2001).

27. The Ofanim explain that Gaia, as the egregor or landscape angel for the entire planet, maintains a fallback position by way of an alternate human evolutionary stream inside the Earth. There, approximately 17,000 humans live in a state of comparable, if not superior, technological development to our life topside, and use the 360 sipapuni throughout the Earth as "ladders" up to the surface, which they visit when appropriate.

28. Gnomes are the elementals who manage the element of earth (solidity, mass, minerals, stones) and sylphs the elementals who manage the air element (motion, wind, air currents). What they look like is somewhat variable among psychics, but generally gnomes look like three-foot-tall, stocky male dwarves, and sylphs something like fairy princesses with swords.

29. For more information, see: www.hessdalen,org; hessdalen.hiof.no; and www.qsi.net/w5www/hessdalenb.html. The Hessdalen spherical light balls typically float close to the ground or at high elevations, may hang

motionless for some time, then suddenly jump or speed across the sky. Sightings and research continue into 2004, with one physicist stating that these "multiform and multicolor lights" cause "a very high release of energy (up to 1 MW)" and show "a very long time-decay (up to 2 hours)," and are "accompanied with sharp electromagnetic perturbations" in their vicinity. Although luminous events (UFO-type appearances or spherical light balls) have been correlated with magnetic disturbances elsewhere in the world, Hessdalen appears to lead the field with the most sightings. Cigar-shaped UFOs have also been seen at Hessdalen. "Astrophysical Methods in the Hessdalen Research," Massimo Teodorani, Ph.D., Italian Committee for Project Hessdalen (ICPH), 2001, at: www.itacomm.net/PH.

30. I say "hill" because there is a viewing/research station on a rise above the Hessdalen Valley, the runway of most of the sightings; it measures about seven miles long by one mile across, running north-south, and has about two hundred inhabitants. Mountains with elevations of about three thousand feet or higher surround it, and two small lakes lie at its south end.

31. In *The Emerald Modem,* I explain how in the original geomantic layout of the Earth, the Garden of Eden was templated in 26 interrelated sites, and that the prime template, the one that activated and held the others in integrity with the original design, was in the Rondane Mountains of Norway. To appreciate this feature, you need to forget the biblical notion of this Garden and its heavy moral overtones. Eden's paradisal aspects are accurate, but they had to do with a harmonious blend of the two poles of human expression—the archetypal male and female as a unified field of consciousness. What makes the Eden template so desirable to other intelligent life forms throughout the galaxy, and beyond, is that in the approximately 18 billion existent galaxies, only six such Eden templates have been made, and one is on Earth with its epicenter in Norway. Further, the Rondane Mountains have not only the primal patterning, but three more of the 26 total extant; this is even more important since 14 templates were lost when the continents of Atlantis and Lemuria sank beneath the seas eons ago. That means four out of 12, or 33 percent of the Edens on Earth, are in the Hessdalen area.

32. "Sometimes a fleet of pure white circular clouds can be seen drifting slowly toward Mount Shasta, and many times one cloud will cap the mountain for long periods of time—which always gives rise to new speculation about spacecraft activity." Emilie A. Frank, *Mt. Shasta, California's Mystic Mountain* (Hilt, Calif.: Photografix Publishing, 1998): 108.

33. Visiting Tibetans have dubbed the area America's Tibet, in reference to its being a barren high plateau framed by mountains; Crestone, which is the home of many churches, shrines, and temples representing most of the world's religions and many of its spiritual cults, is often jokingly called "hippie hill." It's rumored that Wilhelm Reich, M.D., promulgator of

the theory of orgone (prana or chi) and orgone collector boxes, described the San Luis Valley as a chakra or energy center of the Earth. Dimensional portals are said to open and close in the valley, allowing ETs access to our third-dimensional reality. "Indian myths are intertwined with numerous New Age channelers' emphasis on this area as an important world spiritual center in the not-so-distant future." Psychics claim the area has "vortexes of as-yet-undefined energy" that ebb and flow through the valleys' various apertures; native tribes also speak of a sipapuni, or emergence point from the Hollow Earth, as being somewhere in the valley; and the valley is credited with being the birthplace of cattle mutilations, which are generally attributed to or blamed on aliens, presumably seeking animal tissue for DNA. Further, the valley is "one of several holy, revered locations in the Southwest with unusual electromagnetic and gravitational anomalies." Correlations between these data and frequent UFO sightings and Indian reservations or traditional sacred sites have been often noted. Christopher O'Brien, *The Mysterious Valley* (New York: St. Martin's Paperbacks, 1996): 6, 10, 11, 57, 151, 160.

34. For example, one "local" informant in the San Luis Valley told researcher Christopher O'Brien that ten to 12 miles north of Hot Springs and in the Sangre de Cristo Mountains is a secret underground base maintained by the U.S. Air Force. From this base, they send out fighter planes to intercept UFOs. O'Brien remarks that during the eight years he lived in the valley in the 1990s he heard "continual rumors" of underground bases. Rumors circulate that a secret base exists underneath Blanca Peak, on the eastern rim of the valley; the Navajos have a tradition that "flying seed pods" periodically arrived in the valley from elsewhere. (Christopher O'Brien, *Enter the Valley* [New York: St. Martin's Paperbacks, 1999]: 55, 179.) According to researcher Richard Sauder, Ph.D., enough documentation exists (and is publicly available) to prove the existence of several dozen U.S. secret subterranean bases across the country. "What I do know for certain is that there *are* many underground installations here in the United States." What they do is not so certain, though some bases seem to be backup headquarters for various branches of the government; others are more military or surveillance in nature. The construction and use of such underground bases has been going on since the 1950s. (Richard Sauder, Ph.D., *Underground Bases and Tunnels: What Is the Government Trying to Hide?* [Kempton, Ill.: Adventures Unlimited Press, 1995]: 6.)

35. Preston Dennett, *UFOs over Topanga Canyon: Eyewitness Accounts of the California Sightings* (St. Paul, Minn.: Llewellyn, 1999): 249.

36. Ibid., 282, 283, 287.

37. Dr. J. Allen Hynek, Philip J. Imbrogno, and Bob Pratt, *Night Siege: The Hudson Valley UFO Sightings* (New York: Ballantine, 1987): vii, 4, 6, 25, 31, 33.

38. Jane [no last name given], quoted in Dr. J. Allen Hynek, Philip J. Imbrogno, and Bob Pratt, *Night Siege: The Hudson Valley UFO Sightings* (New York: Ballantine, 1987): 161.

39. Dr. J. Allen Hynek, Philip J. Imbrogno, and Bob Pratt, *Night Siege: The Hudson Valley UFO Sightings* (New York: Ballantine, 1987): 13, 189.

40. In the 1990s, the UFO sightings spread a little farther west from the Hudson River into the farming community of Pine Bush. This was then considered the westernmost end of the "UFO Corridor" which stretched laterally across New York State to Montauk, at the eastern tip of Long Island. The Pine Bush sightings (in the Wallkill River valley in Ulster County) exhibited high strangeness with reports of phantom beings, strange animal sightings, mechanical rumblings underground, strange lights over fields, intrusive red mists, white orbs of light, channelings, entity communications, and some abductions. It was later reported that Whitley Strieber's bizarre encounters with the Grays, as reported in his *Communion* (1987) took place in his cabin located near Pine Bush. A geologist named Bruce Cornet, Ph.D., investigated the Pine Bush phenomenon, made popular by *Silent Invasion* (Ellen Crystall, 1991), and renamed the aerial phenomenon TLPs, for Transient Luminescent Phenomena. According to one journalist, Dr. Cornet proposed that the Wallkill River valley was an exact scale replica of Cydonia, the Martian landscape reputed to have the Face on Mars and pyramid, and Dr. Cornet renamed Pine Bush and the Wallkill valley, Cydonia II. In 1999, however, he repudiated his own theories on Cydonia II and retracted his website information on this speculation. Scott C. Carr, "The Rise and Fall of Pine Bush," *Minnesota MUFON Newsletter* 70 (March/April 1998).

41. Blue-green Tiber appeared before Aeneas as "an aged head amid the poplar leaves/a mantle of gray, and shady reeds around him." He says Aeneas's son will in 30 years found the White City (Rome) nearby. Aeneas will find a huge white sow with a newborn litter of 30 white piglets as an indicator of where this new city will be founded. A white sow, pregnant or having delivered piglets, is old geomantic code for a landscape zodiac; surrounding (and including Rome) is a landscape zodiac almost one hundred miles in diameter. Virgil, *The Aeneid of Virgil*, trans. Rolfe Humphries (New York: Charles Scribner's Sons, 1951): 208–209.

42. Thanks for this insight goes to Julia Fortado of Hayward, California.

43. John E. Mack, M.D., *Abduction: Human Encounters with Aliens* (New York: Ballantine, 1994): 17.

44. Ibid., 31, 34, 35.

45. Unnamed editor, quoted in Gary Kinder, *Light Years: An Investigation into the Extraterrestrial Experiences of Eduard Meier* (New York: Atlantic Monthly Press, 1987): 163.

46. C. G. Jung, "UFOs," in *Encountering Jung: On Synchronicity and the*

Paranormal, selected and introduced by Roderick Main (Princeton, N.J.: Princeton University Press, 1997): 152–158.

47. "Switching off" refers to the strange phenomenon when witnesses to an abduction get temporarily paralyzed on the spot, often in midgesture, with their eyes open but seemingly comatose. It's as if the Grays have the ability to stop time, or move faster than our time frame, so they can whisk their abductees away unnoticed by the conscious mind. During hypnotherapy, however, the switched-off witnesses can reclaim their suppressed awareness of the observed abduction.

48. In *The Watchers,* Raymond Fowler presents quoted material from hypnotherapy sessions with multiple abductee Betty Andreasson Luca that suggests some of the alien technology might exist at a "paraphysical" level, somewhere between matter as we know it and light. Luca recalled seeing her abductees (Grays) turn themselves into balls of light and levitate objects and people by way of sparkling lights; that orbs of light were sentient and even observant; and other phenomena that stretched credulity in terms of where we think the boundary is between matter and light. The Grays told Luca part of her mission was to report to humans that this boundary needs rethinking. In 1967, they told her: "They have technology that Man could use . . . It is through the spirit . . . If Man will just study nature itself, he will find many of the answers." In this way, humans will learn that humans are not only made of flesh and blood, but are of the spirit and that this spirit has technological applications. Raymond E. Fowler, *The Watchers: The Secret Design behind UFO Abduction* (New York, Bantam, 1990): 347.

49. Budd Hopkins and Carol Rainey, *Sight Unseen: Science, UFO Invisibility and Transgenic Beings* (New York: Atria, 2003): 49–50.

50. It is worth mentioning that many reports of alien implants (presumably by Grays) are often at the sinus passages at the top of the nose. Psychics report that when a person has too much of this grayish smog, or foreign energy in their energy fields, it can produce a nasally voice, indicating the sinus passages are physically affected by the energy, which goes when the energy is cleared out. In practical terms, when we find the Cepheus cycling within ourselves, we can match with the same process on the planetary level, and help bring ourselves, and to an extent the Earth, into more balance through this fog-dispersing energy.

Chapter 6

1. Andy Thomas, "The Crop Circle Phenomenon—A Beginner's Guide," 2003, at: www.swirlednews.com.

2. Colin Andrews with Stephen Spignesi, *Crop Circles: Signs of Contact* (Franklin Lakes, N.J.: New Page Books, 2003): 76–82.

3. Andrew Collins, *Alien Energy: UFOs, Ritual Landscapes, and the Human Mind* (Memphis, Tenn.: Eagle Wing Books, 1994): 63.

4. Ibid., 63.

5. Ibid., 41.

6. Lucy Pringle, *Crop Circles: The Greatest Mystery of Modern Times* (London: Thorsons/Harper Collins, 1999): 41.

7. Freddy Silva, *Secrets in the Fields: The Science and Mysticism of Crop Circles* (Charlottesville, Va.: Hampton Roads, 2002): 252.

8. Nancy Talbott, director of BLT Research Team of Cambridge, Massachusetts, reported the results of a three-year study (1999–2001) of soil samples taken from crop circles using X-ray diffraction of clay minerals. Her research group found that specific clay minerals, the ones most sensitive to heat (called expandable, including illites and smectites), collected from 69 sampling locations within the crop circle and at 24 control locations 75 to 265 feet away from the circle, exhibited "a subtle but statistically significant increase in degree of crystallization," most notably in the form of mica crystal growth. This crystallization is normally found only in sedimentary rock that has been exposed to massive pressure, of geological scale, usually from lying under tons of rock and being heated from below by the Earth's core for hundreds or thousands of years. This degree of crystallization has never been reported in surface soils, Talbott stated, and anyway, the required geologic weight would have thoroughly crushed the plants, and if the required heat (6,000–8,000°C) had been present, the plants would have burned up. Whatever caused the plant changes also changed the soils under them, and this must be "an energy currently unknown to science." The study also found node-length plant stem increases in the barley stalks (in all 71 samples examined), and other physical anomalies consistent with exposure to microwave radiation. The practical application of this study is that any crop circle exhibiting this type of crystallization clearly could not have been a hoax. The data rules out "direct flattening of the crop circle plants by human beings utilizing planks or boards as an explanation for this event." See: BLT Research Team, "Clay-Mineral Crystallization Case Study: 1999 Edmonton, Alberta, Canada Crop Formation," March 2004, published at: www.bltresearch.com.

9. Freddy Silva, *Secrets in the Fields: The Science and Mysticism of Crop Circles* (Charlottesville, Va.: Hampton Roads, 2002): 138, 139, 140.

10. Archeologists report that there are one thousand barrows (aboveground stone caves) within a ten-mile radius of Stonehenge; these barrows were situated so as to be mostly visible from Stonehenge and clearly to form "a major component of the ritual landscape." Archeologists also state that in the four-county complex called Wessex (which includes Wiltshire) there are still extant four thousand barrows. Sally Exon, Vince Gaffney, Ann Woodward, and Ron Yorston, *Stonehenge Landscapes: Journeys through Real and Imagined Worlds* (Oxford, England: Archaeopress, 2002), 45. Leslie V. Grinsell, *Barrows in England and Wales* (Aylesbury, England: Shire Publications, 1979): 20.

11. While each dome can potentially deploy 48 dome caps, they do not all do so; some domes will have less. The Earth has something in the neighborhood of 83,808 dome caps; no more than this, and most likely slightly fewer. Also, the size of dome caps is variable, ranging from one-half mile to nine miles in diameter.

12. Appropriately, Somerset was once known as the Region of the Summer Stars, and with this geomantic perspective, that poetic name seems very apt. Although the known etymology for Wiltshire is not as geomantically suggestive (the Old English *Wiltunscir* comes from *Wilsaetas*, "sitters, dwellers on the River Wil"), with 33 percent more domes than Somerset, it clearly was a galactically brilliant little piece of acreage. And still is.

13. Fulvio Melia, *The Black Hole at the Center of Our Galaxy* (Princeton, N.J.: Princeton University Press, 2003): vii, viii.

14. To gain a sense of how compacted this galactic central region is, three stars (at least) orbit within 2/100th of a LY of Sagittarius A, traveling at speeds up to 5 million km/hour. The gravity or mass required to keep these three stars on such a tight, fast orbit is about 2.6 million suns. As mentioned in the text, the postulated black hole at the galactic center is about the size of Mars's orbit in our solar system (its median distance from the sun is 141,690,000 miles, so the total expanse of the orbit is 283,380,000 miles), which in a comparable space has only one sun exerting gravity. The "unprecedented" density of dark (to us, invisible) matter at Sagittarius A is more than 100 billion suns/cubic light-year, which can only indicate "a single pointlike object," a gigantic black hole. Fulvio Melia, *The Black Hole at the Center of Our Galaxy* (Princeton, N.J.: Princeton University Press, 2003): 40, 46.

15. Ibid., 6, 35.

16. There are some actual stone structures there such as Wayland's Smithy, a stone chamber, but the Ridgeway consists of mostly many enigmatically named places with nothing physically present other than a grassy field surrounded by one or more ditches, such as Uffington Castle, Liddington Castle, Barbury Castle, and others. According to archeologists, the Ridgeway officially starts at Overton Hill, near Avebury, and proceeds across the top or ridge of land (at a typical elevation of 900 feet), terminating at the Thames River. According to the Ofanim, the Ridgeway starts at the Thames and terminates at Avebury, although you can walk it either way (though with different effects), like climbing up or down a tall tree. The actual original length of the Ridgeway as a geomantic temple is obscured; current estimates range from 40 to 85 miles in length. The Ridgeway as a National (English) Trail today is listed as 85 miles long.

17. Technically, it is more accurate to say each Sefirot equals a dimension of reality, so that, at minimum, you have a model of a ten-dimensional universe in one Tree of Life.

18. These are formally known as the three Veils of Negative Existence. They are "algebraic symbols that enable us to think of that which transcends thought, and which at the same time hide that which they represent; they are the masks of transcendent realities." *Ain* is often translated as Negativity (but not in a moral sense, more of an absence of anything); *Ain Sof* as the Limitless; and *Ain Sof Awr* as the Limitless Light. Dion Fortune, *The Mystical Qabalah* (London: Ernest Benn, 1957): 32–33.

19. "So we must advance away from the Manifest, allowing the god-in-us to point our pathway, Limitless Light being behind us . . . Once we are in the Light we shall be beyond vision. . . . It is the absolute Stillness in the midst of motion . . . the true Peace of AIN. That is the pearl before the swine . . . To reach Spiritual Identity in and with AIN is the Qabalistic Ultimate, like the Buddhist's Nirvana." William G. Gray, *The Ladder of Lights* (York Beach, Maine: Samuel Weiser, 1981): 225–227.

20. There are billions of galaxies in the known universe. Is the inferred black hole at Sagittarius A in the Milky Way galaxy unique? No. Astrophysicists now have evidence suggesting every large, normal galaxy with a disk and central bulge has a supermassive black hole at its center. Supermassive black holes have already been measured in at least 38 galaxies, and in another study of one hundred galaxies, 30 percent produced data suggesting a central black hole. Fulvio Melia, *The Black Hole at the Center of Our Galaxy* (Princeton, N.J.: Princeton University Press, 2003): 174–175.

21. This is consistent with what happens with a landscape zodiac, briefly referred to earlier in the book. A landscape zodiac is a miniature holographic galaxy overlaid on a varying diameter of the landscape. The original (the galaxy above) is like an apple: it has volume. You can't overlay something like this on the landscape and have it be an interactive template for people, for how would you get to the stars at the top of the apple? So the apple is sliced in two, both halves laid out on the landscape, and flattened to essentially two dimensions. This way we can walk, psychically, through the stars and constellations, but without the volumetric reality you'd have if, somehow, you could stride through the starfields of the actual galaxy. However, when you interact with the various constellations in a landscape zodiac, your psychic handshake with the feature inflates it back to its original galactic volumetric aspect. We have to do the same with the flattened crop circles: psychically inflate them, like a balloon, so we interact with their volumetric aspect.

22. A bit of this extradimensional interplay of letter, sound, and color comes through the deep memories of Betty Andreasson and her daughter, Becky, in the multivolume chronicle of their alien abduction experiences. Betty saw her daughter doing this, and Becky herself later remembered doing it (thanks to deep hypnosis): She was at a console (like a futuristic computer) entering letters in an exotic script with colors and sounds. When

you correctly matched the light with the right word, you got tones that then activated something; she wasn't clear what the end result was. Becky said she had to touch the correct circle of light on the console; there were words on the back side. "I touch the light. I touch the language forming in between. The light is strong, different colors are used with the words." Raymond E. Fowler, *The Andreasson Legacy* (New York: Marlowe & Company, 1997): 71–72.

23. This perception is premised on the esoteric Hebrew contention that the 22 letters of their alphabet are sacred not only in a religious sense, but ontologically so. The *Zohar* teaches that the 22 letters are actual fire beings, exalted intelligences that God used to create reality, and still uses to maintain it. The Ofanim, in my experience, tend to confirm this perception. They state: "They [the Hebrew letters] are emanations of the Supreme Being. They are not angels; they are collectively what the Torah [the first five books of the Old Testament] is." The scientist-psychic Itzhak Bentov, in his two books *A Cosmic Book: On the Mechanics of Creation* (Destiny Books, 1988) and *Stalking the Wild Pendulum: On the Mechanics of Consciousness* (Destiny Books, 1988), also confirmed the existence of the Hebrew letters (as well as the 50 letters of Sanskrit) as having actual reality in the spiritual worlds as formative, creative forces. Bentov reported that in one of his visionary incursions into higher reality, he saw the letters of both alphabets as having legitimate structural and creative roles in the universe.

Chapter 7

1. The brilliant writer Philip K. Dick, who often disguised or packaged his profound philosophical insights in the guise of science fiction scenarios, wrote that "The Fall of man . . . represented a falling away from contact with this vast communication network" and its voice, one of whose names was God. Once, "we had been integrated into this network and had been expressions of its identity and will operating through us," but no longer. Philip K. Dick, *Radio Free Albemuth* (New York: Vintage Books, 1998): 112.

2. This term is widely used to indicate the mystical, dreamy nature of alien encounters. It is derived from the title of the book by L. Frank Baum, *The Wizard of Oz*, although Baum did not ever mention aliens as such. The Oz Factor refers to a condition presaging an abduction or alien encounter in which everything seems unaccountably quiet as if switched off, as if all living things in one's vicinity have been turned off, immobilized, stopped in time. All sounds appear to cease during one's encounter with aliens; time seems to stand still; you have the sensation you have left normal physical reality for a dreamlike realm with its own seemingly magical, even quixotic, rules.

Index

About the Author

Richard Leviton is the author of eleven books, including, most recently, *The Emerald Modem: A User's Guide to Earth's Interactive Energy Body* (Hampton Roads, 2004). He regularly conducts workshops and field trips on the subject of myth, sacred sites, and landscape spirituality. He lives in Santa Fe, New Mexico, where he is the director of the Blue Room Consortium, which he describes as a "cosmic mysteries think tank" to do with Earth energies, mapping, and interactions. He may be contacted at blaise@cybermesa.com.

HAMPTON ROADS

PUBLISHING COMPANY, INC.

Thank you for reading *Signs on the Earth*. Hampton Roads is proud to publish a number of Richard Leviton's books on topics such as sacred sites, earth mythology, health, and more. Please take a look at the following selection or visit us anytime on the web: www.hrpub.com.

The Emerald Modem
A User's Guide to Earth's Interactive Energy Body

The Emerald Modem explains that the Earth's numerous sacred sites act as access points—literally modems—where we can plug into the power of Earth's energy grid. Earth-mystery scholar Leviton shows how the world's rich library of cultural mythology, such as Greek and Egyptian, serves as both a guide to these sacred places and a key to unlocking their power.

Paperback • 400 pages • ISBN 1-57174-245-X• $18.95

The Galaxy on Earth
A Traveler's Guide to the Planet's Visionary Geography

Be spirited away to holy sites around the globe with Leviton's travelogue. Visit Machu Picchu, Stonehenge, Athens, and more, and learn what gives these sites their power to transform and even heal.

Paperback • 600 pages
ISBN 1-57174-222-0• $18.95

www.hrpub.com · 1-800-766-8009

The Healthy Living Space
70 Practical Ways to Detoxify the Body and Home

You don't have to be a victim of our toxic world and poisoned environment. *The Healthy Living Space* is loaded with practical, easy, and inexpensive tips for regaining optimal health by detoxifying your body, and maintaining health by detoxifying your home.

Paperback • 656 pages
ISBN 1-57174-209-3• $21.95

Physician
Medicine and the Unsuspected Battle for Human Freedom

As conventional and alternative medicine choices battle for our health-care dollars, Leviton suggests, in impassioned detail, that the real battle being waged is for our souls. Looking from an energetic level, Leviton says that only alternative medicine allows us to evolve spiritually. This is an essential book for making informed health choices.

Paperback • 592 pages
ISBN 1-57174-168-2 4 • $16.95

Hampton Roads Publishing Company

. . . for the evolving human spirit

HAMPTON ROADS PUBLISHING COMPANY publishes books on a variety of subjects, including metaphysics, spirituality, health, visionary fiction, and other related topics.

We also create on-line courses and sponsor an *Applied Learning Series* of author workshops. For a current list of what is available, go to www.hrpub.com, or request the ALS workshop catalog at our toll-free number.

For a copy of our latest trade catalog, call toll-free, 800-766-8009, or send your name and address to:

HAMPTON ROADS PUBLISHING COMPANY, INC.
1125 STONEY RIDGE ROAD • CHARLOTTESVILLE, VA 22902
e-mail: hrpc@hrpub.com • www.hrpub.com